Developmental coaching

Working with the self

University Campus

Barnsley

Telephone: 01226 216 885

Catalogue: **https://webopac.barnsley.ac.uk/**

Class No: ......158. 3 BAC...........

This book is to be returned on or before the last date stamped below. Thank you!

Developmental coaching

Working with the self

Tatiana Bachkirova

 Open University Press

Open University Press
McGraw-Hill Education
McGraw-Hill House
Shoppenhangers Road
Maidenhead
Berkshire
England
SL6 2QL

email: enquiries@openup.co.uk
world wide web: www.openup.co.uk

and Two Penn Plaza, New York, NY 10121-2289, USA

First published 2011

Copyright © Tatiana Bachkirova 2011

A catalogue record of this book is available from the British Library

ISBN-13: 978-0-33-523855-2 (pb)   978-0-33-523856-9 (hb)
ISBN-10: 0335238556 (pb)   0335238564 (hb)
eISBN: 978-0-33-523857-6

Library of Congress Cataloging-in-Publication Data
CIP data has been applied for

Fictitous names of companies, products, people, characters and/or data that
may be used herein (in case studies or in examples) are not intended to
represent any real individual, company, product or event.

Typeset by Aptara Inc., India
Printed in the UK by Bell & Bain Ltd, Glasgow

Mixed Sources
Product group from well-managed
forests and other controlled sources
www.fsc.org Cert no. TT-COC-002769
© 1996 Forest Stewardship Council
FSC

The McGraw·Hill Companies

Dedication

To Daniil, Illya, Alfred and all students
I had a privilege to teach and learn together

Praise for this book

Tatiana Bachkirova has formulated a fresh, innovative theory specifically for the developmental coach. Challenging traditional theories of development, she focuses on the actuality and uniqueness of working with individual coaching clients. This transpersonal approach aims for change not just in the client's head, but in their entire organism: mind, body and soul. Although some may find her more radical conclusions provocative, I found them to be stimulating and thought-provoking.

Her approach to facilitating change is based on three metaphors for the self, to help the coach develop a deeper awareness of the complexity of self, and four types of ego, to address developmental challenges. Bachkirova has written a lucidly argued and groundbreaking exploration of developmental coaching, and the practical implications of her theory will be very useful for experienced coaches. She has produced an example of the type of thoughtful research and enquiry needed to establish a body of knowledge for best-practice coaching.

> *Dr Sunny Stout-Rostron, author of* Business Coaching International: Transforming Individuals and Organizations, *and director of Manthano Institute of Learning (Pty) Ltd.*

A groundbreaking text on the theory and practice of developmental coaching. Fresh, insightful, original and stretching, the book is a pleasure to engage with. If you are a coach looking for something that does not repeat or rephrase what you already know far too well, this book is for you.

> *Dr Ilona Boniwell, Programme Leader, MSc Applied Positive Psychology, University of East London, UK*

Tatiana Bachkirova's outstanding text on the theory, philosophies, and practices of developmental coaching has been long-awaited. This book is a rare beast in the developmental area of coaching - intelligent, articulate and accessible. To date developmental theory in coaching has been notoriously complex and overly-technical. Dr Bachkirova's work combines and extends many existing developmental approaches, making previously opaque frameworks tangible and real. This book has solid value for both novice and experience coaches alike. Essential and enjoyable reading.

> *Anthony Grant, Director of the Coaching Psychology Unit, University of Sydney, Australia*

Contents

Acknowledgement

I am grateful to many authors who wrote on the topics relevant to this book. I am in debt for the work they have already done and for the wide range of articles, chapters, books and research reports with ideas and evidence that helped me to develop this theory. Two of these authors I have to mention specifically for the influence they had on this book. They took great steps in making sense of the complex ideas about the self and related research findings for those who are interested in applying them to everyday life. These two authors are Susan Blackmore and Guy Claxton. I was inspired by their courage and effort to build bridges between first glimpses of understanding that come from science and philosophy with the way we lead our everyday life. Their work inspired me to take my own step of drawing from this fascinating field of knowledge and writing for coaches who help others to enhance their lives.

I want to express my gratitude to Bob Pomfret who produced illustration for this book. He was remarkably patient and understanding even when I was trying to convey some pretty weird ideas and the way they should look. My huge gratitude goes to my colleagues and friends who kindly offered their help in reading and giving comments and suggestions for improving this work. They were constructively critical and at the same time generous and encouraging. Thank you, Judie Gannon, Candida March and Kate Gilbert. My other colleagues and friends Elaine Cox, Peter Jackson and Carmelina Lawton-Smith were the first to hear and discuss with me the main principle and structure of the book. Their questions and suggestions were useful at the first stage of this process. It is important to say that all the students on my module Psychological Perspectives on the Self have been essential in the development of this book because of their great questions and genuine interest in this topic.

I am particularly grateful to Jennie Benedict whom I am very happy to call my friend. She was absolutely invaluable in making the style of this book significantly better than in its first draft. Her support was most important to me at the stages of writing when I could easily be discouraged. I am also grateful to Dr Peter Pritchard for his careful proof-reading at the final stage which made me more confident about the book. Of course, no book could happen without the whole publishing team who were most helpful and professional throughout all stages of this process. And finally my younger son Daniil was very important during this time always reading through my work and believing in me. I have been helped by many other people in many other different ways during this emotional journey. Thank you all. I am really blessed with people in my life.

Introduction

Coaches often say that their coaching is developmental, but when asked what they mean by this, the answers are always very different. Some call their coaching developmental in contrast to remedial. Some say that they work with more than skills and performance in developmental coaching; they see their client as a whole person and search for underlying tendencies and traits to help them reach their goals. Some say that coaching is developmental only if it is informed by special types of theories such as those of Kegan (1982), Torbert et al. (2004) or others. Some say that all coaching is developmental because it brings about all sorts of changes in the client. So what then is developmental coaching?

In this book you will have an opportunity to explore exactly this question. You will be introduced to a new way of conceiving developmental coaching and a new framework for coaching practice. Those of you who are concerned with the lack of theories specific to coaching will find here a theory with concepts and ideas to explore and to debate. Those who wish to enrich their practice will find practical ideas to learn, reflect on and apply immediately to engagements with clients. Those who see *themselves* as a crucial element of a coaching encounter will have an opportunity to explore and enhance their own developmental process. And finally, I hope that you all are likely to become a little bit more developmentally-minded.

To start with I would like to describe how the theory that I tentatively propose in this book came about. I am going to use one of the concepts that will be discussed later in this book: a mini-self. I noticed two particular mini-selves that were always present in my life. The first is 'an inquiring one' that has been fascinated with big and difficult questions about the nature and meaning of life, the nature of us as human beings, consciousness, perception, the nature of self, etc. These questions were not idle, they produced quite strong drives to pursue them: I have read a lot on these subjects, have attended conferences and seminars, and have taken some incredibly difficult classes, for example, in philosophy and neuroscience. My brain sometimes physically hurt and I often found myself utterly confused, trying to make sense of different standpoints relating to some ideas. As there are so many different positions and consequently debates on the topics of self, consciousness or free will, being confused is a justifiable state. Recent findings of neuroscience, however welcome, are not at a stage that can bring sufficient clarity to these debates; they just add more interesting puzzles. In spite of this state of affairs I notice that this semi-permanent confusion does not put my inquiring mini-self off. It is live and active as always.

The second mini-self that has also always been present in my life is a 'practical one' which is never satisfied till at least some solution to an unresolved problem of applied nature is found, however difficult it is. This 'so what' side of mine always tried to extract from any abstract material something useful in real life for myself or for those I was hoping to help, such as my friends, family, clients, and particularly, students. These two mini-selves could happily co-exist and they did until recently. For example, in my teaching I felt it was sufficient to stir up students' thinking with these puzzling questions and then offer some ideas for practice from the different standpoints discussed. This was an approach that I was hoping initially to take in this book, however, fairly soon I began to feel that this was not good enough. Here is my train of thought in relation to this.

The coaching field is famously interdisciplinary. As a result of this we experience it as rather patchy. However, we also enjoy the benefits of this because there are numerous theories in these disciplines that seem relevant to coaching. We can usefully adapt them particularly now, while there are practically no theories that have been developed specifically for coaching. There are some traditions such as Gestalt, solution-focused, existential, etc. that provide great ideas for coaching from the psychotherapeutic field. The approaches they offer are useful, well proven and there are now good text books that help coaches to start from their main assumptions and follow them through to the practical applications (Cox et al. 2010; Palmer and Whybrow 2007; Stober and Grant 2006). If these approaches feel congruent to coaches they can adapt them. If coaches find contradictions in their personal philosophy and the philosophy of these approaches they may find it useful to explore where they stand in relation to such contradictions and how it affects their practice.

However, in relation to the topics I wish to address in this book the gap is too big: neuroscientists, researchers of consciousness and philosophers of mind do not write for coaches. Perhaps these areas of knowledge are not yet at the stage when new ideas and findings can be translated into practice. There are, however, pioneers such as Guy Claxton (1986, 1994) and Susan Blackmore (2003) whose writings already provide very interesting connections between such knowledge and our everyday life. Their inspirational attempts have helped me to take a step further from my previous style. I decided to bite the bullet and try to take this challenge of creating a new approach to coaching. There is a need for a specific theory of developmental coaching and maybe this attempt just has to be made now.

To start with, thinking about the reasons for confusion that exist in relation to the issues of self and free will, I noticed a clash between two different perspectives: a) our 'first-person' subjective experience of living (phenomenological); and b) our 'third person' observation of the natural world (metaphysical). It appears that most of the commentators on the self and consciousness approach this topic from one or the other perspective. Although it is obvious that both are important, the lack of clarity about them in comparing the findings and propositions by different authors creates signifi-cant confusions. I intend to make it explicit in discussion of different sources and in every case that will be explored.

In addition to clarifying different positions on the theoretical issues I hope that the book will help you to see what is more important for you, because we also have these tendencies in relation to the value of information that we receive depending on its source. For example, most coaches say that they are concerned with the agenda of the client and this is the main criterion of the success and failure of coaching. However, this is easy to declare, but difficult to sustain when there is a discrepancy between the client's perception and the organizational needs, expectations and evaluation of progress. Which information about the behaviour of your client has more weight for you: his own or others around him? What information do you consider more evidence based in your professional development: statistically sound results of experiments or rich individual reports based on personal experience? We do have our own tendencies in this division but naming them brings more clarity in understanding ourselves and the issues in question.

What is offered in this book is also, of course, based on the series of assumptions that I will try to make explicit in order to leave them more open for scrutiny. At the same time I aim to provide as much evidence as possible from the theoretically sound ideas and research findings that are accepted in the scientific community. Scientists themselves recognize that at this stage we only have glimpses of insight into these incredible puzzles, but it appears that even such glimpses already challenge our common sense understanding of self and consciousness. I am not dismissing the value of common sense here in comparison to science, but we all know that common sense can happily go around in circles, convincing itself that it is on a voyage of discovery (Claxton 1994). To be fair, science is also prone to self-deception, but at least it is never happy with the status of what is found and its genuine intention is to question and scrutinize every finding. This is something we cannot say about common sense. Science exposes the beliefs about life that are provided by common sense, offering in their place 'not the "truth" (for science can only ever deliver theories) but a more workable myth: a better model of some aspect of life' (Claxton 1994: 10).

So, the tandem of these mini-selves in me is taking the challenge and offering a model for use in coaching, hoping that this myth may be more workable than common sense. It is a work in progress and I am sure that the main contours and the details of this picture will be changing. And if it helps someone to offer another, better, different, more elaborate myth, i.e. approach, to coaching, this will be most gratifying.

The structure and overview of this book

To describe the ideas and practice of developmental coaching as it is formulated in the title of this book – *Developmental Coaching: Working with the Self* – we need to begin with at least four questions:

> What is development?
> What is the self?
> What is the role of coaching?
> What does 'working with the self' mean?

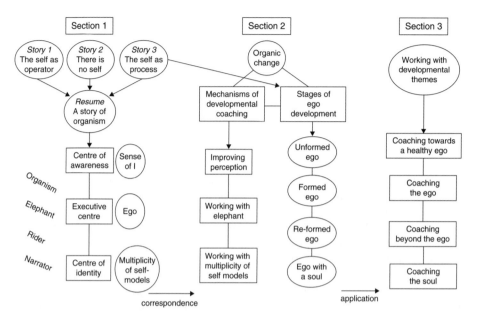

Figure 1   The structure of the book.

The following is a brief overview of my answers to these questions before I engage with them fully in the respective chapters of the book. You can also use Figure 1 to follow the logic and the overall structure of the book.

What is development?

First in the following section of the introduction I will discuss what I mean by development in relation to people. I will suggest that it is a combination of changes in the organism manifested in a sustained increased capacity to engage with and to influence their environment and to look after their internal needs and aspirations. I will present this position on development, comparing it with concepts of learning, education, coaching and change.

What is the self?

As the title of the book suggests, developmental coaching implies working with the self of the individual. Therefore in order to proceed with what coaches may do, it has to be reasonably clear what we mean here by the self. This will be discussed in Part 1, which is the most complex section of the book. What the self is remains an unresolved puzzle in all disciplines of knowledge but I will argue that in spite of the lack of complete understanding, attention to and engagement with this topic is important for coaches. Using pictures, diagrams and metaphors, my intention is to create a model of the self that is reasonably in congruence with what is known so far and reasonably clear for practical purposes. I will describe three different stories about the self that could illustrate how it is currently discussed in different fields of knowledge. The first story will be about the self as an operator of the human organism that may even have life independent from the body. The second story may be called 'there is no self'. It is more congruent with current scientific thinking. The third story is mostly concerned with changes that the self undergoes throughout life. To make sense of all three stories for coaches I will put forward a different story or resumé about the three notions of the self. It will include a description of the workings of the organism that are useful to know about when coaching. With this purpose in mind I will be making a case that includes the following:

- The mind is only a small part of the whole organism.
- The conscious part of the mind is also a very small part in comparison to the unconscious and automatic functioning.
- I will be using an analogy of the *rider* and the *elephant* to illustrate that the role of the conscious mind (rider) in the functioning of the rest of the organism (elephant) is grossly exaggerated.
- It could be said that the organism's engagements with the world are facilitated by numerous mini-selves translating various needs and tasks of the person into actions. Most of them are unconscious.
- I will suggest that something like an executive centre (ego), as a network of mini-selves, allows a person to take ownership of the past, withstand anxiety about the future and build relationships with others without losing the sense of who they are.
- A sign of the developed ego is the capacity of mind/brain to act or refrain from action if necessary in a way that reasonably satisfies the organism as a whole even with the multiplicity of needs and tasks. If this capacity has not developed at some point this may prevent further development of the individual.
- The ego is mostly unconscious, but the rider can learn to predict the behaviour of the organism and could be seen as an advisor to it.
- *Narrator,* a particular linguistic function of the rider, presents various stories of what is happening to the whole organism and creates 'a self' in this process.

What is the role of coaching?

I will be making a case about three types of changes that should take place in the organism in order for it to develop. I will argue that all coaches (not only developmental) can make a difference in the development of their clients if they facilitate such changes. The first of these mechanisms is the improvement in the *quality of perception* both internally and externally. Although we don't see things as they are for all sorts of reasons, this ability can be enhanced, allowing individuals to engage with the environment in a more effective way. As conditioning and self-deception are the obstacles to better perception, the quality of it could be improved by working through both of these obstacles. The second mechanism is a better communication between the elephant (the unconscious, automatic, emotional mind and the body) and the rider. Developmental coaching does not attempt to change the elephant. A shift in the needs of the organism can happen through 'softer' thinking and better work with emotions rather than through an attempt to control the elephant. Third is the change in the way of dealing with the *multiplicity of self-models* – versions of me. It has been said that the self could be seen as a synthesis or as an achievement. This is a task for the narrator and is well suited for coaching. Different theoretical approaches offer useful ways of dealing with this multiplicity and there are useful practical ideas in coaching that can be applied to this task.

What does 'working with the self' mean?

I will illustrate the importance of understanding whether the intended change in coaching is organic. I will also introduce a notion of developmental themes, such as issues of confidence or authenticity, which appear to be changing throughout our lives. I will suggest that there is a pattern in the themes that are brought for coaching that indicates the important role of the ego (executive centre). This pattern indicates that the ego could be unformed, formed or reformed, including another potential stage that I call 'ego with a soul'.

The task of the coach is to engage with whatever theme is presented, using suggestions for working with three main mechanisms of change (improving perception, working with elephant and multiplicity of self-models) in relation to the four stages above. The focus of coaching for these four stages could be named as:

- coaching towards a healthy ego
- coaching the ego
- coaching beyond the ego
- coaching the soul.

In respective chapters we will look at various developmental themes that clients might bring for coaching and discuss the ways of approaching them. Although the list of themes in each stage cannot cover all possibilities, I hope that the presented framework will be used and expanded by coaches, thus enriching our understanding of the developmental process.

Finally, in the conclusions we will discuss specific developmental challenges that coaches themselves would need to consider in the process of becoming developmentally-minded.

Main concepts of development and coaching

To explore developmental coaching in a systematic way it is important to introduce how the term of 'development' is understood in this book. The words 'change', 'learning' and 'development' are probably the most used words in coaching. But what is the difference between 'development' and 'change', for example, or between 'development' and 'learning'?

When we use the word 'development' we obviously mean that there is a change but that this change is in the direction that implies increased capacities for engaging with the external and the internal world and this capacity is sustainable. For example, people can sometimes make significant changes in their lives: change their relationship with their colleagues, change job, change their attitude to a job, etc. But it is quite possible that these changes may not increase their capacities to deal with their environment. On the other hand, we would say that the change is developmental if it leads to increased capacities to deal with and to influence the environment and/or to look after internal needs and aspirations and that these capacities are sustainable.

To draw the line between learning and development is more difficult. I like how Guy Claxton defines learning as 'what you do when you don't know what to do' (1999: 11). Experimenting with new behaviours when the task is new is learning; asking questions to get to know someone is learning; solving an unusual problem is learning. So learning is the process of engagement with the task, often intentional, which may eventually lead to increased capacities. Learning is happening almost on an everyday basis and eventually may result in development. Learning is a process, whereas development is a combination of changes that may come as the result. Development can also happen without learning. As human organisms we develop and our capacities to engage with the world increase. There is substantial evidence for this from developmental psychology. We can also look back at what we were able to do and usually can see a significant difference. Although some physical capacities at some stage may decline with age, psychologically we all have a potential to continue developing throughout life. And learning as a process may lead to development when an increased capacity is sustained over time.

Learning can be self directed and this happens when people encounter a new challenge in any area of their life. It could also be organized when society or organizations offer individuals opportunities for development that they believe are also beneficial for them. Organized learning can take the form of educational provision, training opportunities, etc. Coaching, in turn, is a relatively new form of organized learning that takes into account individual pace and focuses on learning suitable for each person (Table 1).

Let us now focus on the nature of development. Development can happen without the conscious decision of the person to learn and develop. It is an inherited feature of human nature to expand our ability to engage with the world. We have internal predispositions that naturally increase this ability, just as an ability to crawl eventually changes into the ability to walk or our ability to exchange communication with each other leads to an amazing capacity to express ourselves through elaborate speech,

Table 1   Summary of the general subjects discussed

Concept	Description
Development	a combination of changes in the organism manifested in a sustained increased capacity to engage with and influence the environment and to look after internal needs and aspirations
Learning	a process of engagement with unknown situations
Education/training	organized learning
Coaching	individually facilitated learning with a focus on desired changes

poetry, music or art. Our organisms as wholes are able to learn new skills just by engaging with life on an everyday basis and responding to the challenges and demands that life brings. If these increases in abilities are sustainable we can say that these processes are developmental. Sometimes, of course, the process of development may be slow or reach a state of relative stability. A number of factors may be 'to blame': the limitations of natural predispositions, relative stability or adverse effects of the environment, which may include a lack of appropriate support, or there could be various blocks of a psychological nature.

To summarize, the main assumptions about development important for this book could be described as follows:

- Human development is the result of the complex interaction between the individual organism and the world, that could be intensified under certain circumstances.
- Development is manifested in increased capacities on the one hand to respond to external changes and to influence the environment, and on the other hand to look after the internal needs and aspirations of the individual.
- Development happens with or without specific interventions aimed at facilitating it.
- Development happens at a different pace for different individuals but may become static and even reverse in some circumstances.
- There are internal predispositions and external conditions that help a person to become more conducive to development.
- Internal predispositions include capacity for reflexivity in individuals.
- Appropriate support, for example, through coaching, contributes to the acceleration of development.

The book aims to gradually illuminate what developmental coaching is. The following outlines the argument about the nature of developmental coaching leading to practical examples of how it works. Starting from the generic elements of coaching here is a brief description of what will be discussed in detail in Part 2 of the book:

- Coaching is an individualized process of facilitating change in people with the focus on specific targets and/or enriching their lives.
- Various genres of coaching focus on the specific aspects of the individual, e.g. sport coaching is coaching a sportsman; skill coaching is coaching an 'actor' (someone who enacts a skill); performance coaching is coaching a worker; leadership coaching is coaching a leader, etc. They all can have a developmental effect on the individual as a whole. Developmental coaching is explicit in the intention to coach the whole individual even when the goals of coaching are specific.
- Understanding by the coach of how in principle the mind/brain system of the client operates in the functioning of the whole organism is important for developmental coaching.

- Developmental coaching implies a partnership between the coach and the client. Although one of the fundamental assumptions is that the organism as a whole is involved in the coaching process with a significant role for unconscious processes, the coach intends to make all interventions explicit to the conscious part (the rider) of the client.
- Developmental coaching engages with four groups of recurring developmental themes, starting from 'coaching towards a healthy ego' to 'coaching the soul'.
- Working with identified themes, the coach considers relevant interventions that can improve the quality of perception, communication between the elephant and the rider and creativity in dealing with the multiplicity of self-models. The coach is aware that the coaching process and the role of the coach in each of the four groups of developmental themes will differ.
- The implications of the process and potential outcomes of resulting changes are made explicit for all parties involved.

Overview of the literature on developmental coaching

Before describing my own version of developmental coaching in Part 2 I would like to comment on other valuable contributions to understanding this genre of coaching and on what seems to be missing in each of them. Developmental coaching as a term has already been in use for a while, but only recently have some serious attempts been made to formulate exactly what this type of coaching would entail and how it differs from the others (Berman and Bradt 2006; Hawkins and Smith 2006, 2010; Cox and Jackson 2010). In the past, the term 'developmental coaching' has been used for example, in contrast to 'remedial coaching' (Grant and Cavanagh 2004). It was also considered as a choice for people who had reached a plateau in the process of growth. In comparison to 'performance coaching' which focused on organizational outcomes, it was seen as seeking to develop the whole person by building long-term competences rather than reaching specific goals. Sometimes people even talk about developmental coaching using descriptions that are practically indistinguishable from any other type of coaching.

In addition, there has been a distinctive tradition of practical work, including coaching, based on cognitive-developmental theories such as those of Kegan (1982, 1994), Torbert et al. (2004) and Cook-Greuter (1999). We discuss these theories in the third story of the self (Chapter 4) as very important for understanding the self. Interestingly, none of these authors refer to the practical approaches that follow from their theoretical contribution as a form of developmental coaching. Similarly, other authors, who published on the application of these theories (Berger and Fitzgerald 2002; Berger 2006; Laske 2006a), have not often referred to their coaching as developmental, with the exception of Laske. Cavanagh and Grant (2010) though refer to these approaches as a form of developmental coaching, acknowledging at the same time that there are varying definitions of this term, e.g. the most holistic type of coaching. I also see the value of these approaches in understanding developmental coaching. They have much more to offer in comparison to simple algorithms for focusing interventions such as

GROW (Goal, Reality, Options, Willingness) or any other similar model. They offer a theoretical underpinning for practical work with clients. As this is also my intention, we will need to discuss the differences between these approaches and mine at the end of the Chapter 9 when the core of theory will be introduced.

In relation to recent attempts to conceptualize developmental coaching, I would now like to consider the following:

1   Berman and Bradt's (2006) description of developmental coaching as one of the types in their typology of coaching;
2   Hawkins and Smith's (2006, 2010) continuum of types of coaching that includes developmental coaching;
3   Cox and Jackson's (2010) chapter on Developmental coaching in *The Complete Handbook of Coaching*;
4   Some traditional approaches to coaching based on both theories and practices of psychotherapy that could be seen as developmental.

1   Berman and Bradt (2006) describe developmental coaching as one type in their four-category model of executive coaching. Their model defines the differences between the approaches in terms of the goals of the coaching assignment, the scope of work and the type of business scenarios involved. The other three categories are facilitative, executive and restorative coaching. It is interesting that Berman and Bradt have chosen the term 'developmental' to describe a type of coaching which addresses longstanding behaviour problems of executives in both personal and work settings. According to them, 'developmental coaching builds strengths and alleviates deficits in a mission-critical individual who has substantial and longstanding challenges and interpersonal issues' (p. 245). These are people who have substantial difficulties in some aspect of their management style, but for a variety of reasons are able to retain their jobs. They may be highly successful but with serious flaws of character, e.g. poorly controlled anger. Berman and Bradt (2006) apply many theories and techniques developed in more traditional clinical interventions and as such we can certainly see an overlap between this type of coaching and psychotherapy.

Although their typology is reasonably justified by pre-existing models, it is not based on a theory of development. Apart from the obvious organizational need for an individual to change there are no elements that are coherent with the idea of development. 'Building on strengths and alleviating deficits' hardly amounts to a theory-based approach. It also seems unusual to name a form of coaching 'developmental' which is clearly remedial. Although it may serve a developmental purpose for the individuals described, it is not clear why others, without longstanding psychological problems, would not benefit from the use of the theories and techniques implied.

2   Hawkins and Smith (2006, 2010), building on earlier work by Whitherspoon (2000) propose a continuum of types of coaching according to their focus:

- skills coaching
- performance coaching
- developmental coaching
- transformational coaching

'Skills coaching' is focused on the acquisition of useful skills and could usually be offered in training courses for the development of particular competences. 'Performance coaching' is focused on the development of overall applied capabilities in a particular professional role and is based on the skills required. Both these types of coaching are generally offered by the manager as coach or by an internal coach. Developmental coaching, in contrast, is focused on the long-term development of the client as a whole, by helping to increase 'their broader human capacities'. To introduce the difference between developmental and transformational coaching Hawkins and Smith (2010: 242) refer to the stage theory of Torbert et al. (2004). They suggest that developmental coaching 'will tend to focus on increasing capacity within one life stage' in contrast to transformational coaching which 'will be more involved with enabling the coachee to shift levels or "action logics" and thereby make a transition from one level of functioning to a higher one'. They also suggest that in transformational coaching this shift needs to happen right there in the coaching room. It is more likely that both 'developmental coaching' and 'transformational coaching' are practices that are offered by external coaches who would have received a more substantial training.

This explanation allows a useful mapping of various genres of coaching according to the level of complexity involved in addressing the potential goals of the client. I am in agreement with the authors about the role of the first two types of coaching and how developmental coaching differs from them. However, I am not fully convinced that 'transformational coaching' is sufficiently distinct from 'developmental'. It seems to me that the focus on broader human capacities remains the same in both developmental and transformational coaching. Both types aim at producing insight in the client that allows them to see their situation from a different and hopefully wider perspective. It seems that 'transformational coaching' only puts more emphasis on such an insight. I would argue however, that in both types of coaching the insights or shifts may or may not lead to a change in the client's action logic in the long run. One of the main tasks of both types of coaching should be to keep such insight alive for their clients as has been argued by Berger (2006).

I am also concerned about the specific intention of the coach to 'shift the levels'. As has been already discussed (Bachkirova 2010; Bachkirova and Cox 2007a; Berger 2006) along with other potential issues this may create an illusion concerning the simplicity of the developmental process. It suggests the very unlikely event of one side of the mind transforming another part. This may trick us into believing that a qualitative developmental shift could happen through sufficient motivation and effort on the part of the client or worse still – through the magical skills of the coach. I do not want to sound like a complete pessimist – development and transformation do happen, but to call the coaching 'transformational' seems to me too big a promise. 'Developmental' coaching is already a very tall order.

3   *Cox and Jackson (2010)* wrote a whole chapter on developmental coaching, exploring it as a natural progression from skills and performance coaching to a process that aspires to facilitate some progressive and permanent change. Such change in turn may lead to the growth of the whole person providing them with lasting capacities in various areas of their life. These authors justify the value of focusing on individual development in an organizational context by their belief that 'the capacity of the system in which the

client sits (organization, family, society) is itself enhanced by the individual's capacity and so the changes initiated have a secondary developmental capacity beyond the client's immediate situation' (Cox and Jackson 2010: 221).

According to them, the main task of developmental coaching is to ensure 'on-going improvement in the coachee's ability to respond to future events'. These authors put particular emphasis on the need in developmental coaching for the self-determination of the client: 'it is not for the coach to decide that something will be good for the client "in the end" just as it is not for the coach to decide where "the end" is, or if there is such a thing at all' (p. 221). This strongly suggests that their perspective on developmental coaching is very close to the philosophy and theory of the Person-centred tradition, a fact they readily acknowledge. On the one hand it seems logical to identify a core feature of the practical approach and to make a strong link with a particular theory, thus enhancing the approach. On the other hand this solution has limited the account of developmental coaching by these authors. As a genre it could afford to be broader than a particular theoretical perspective and make wider use of others.

At the same time the account of developmental coaching by Cox and Jackson (2010) presents a most coherent and consistent argument on this topic. One of the conclusions that they come to as a result of investigating what is available so far on developmental coaching, is the lack of an overarching theory to guide its practice. This book is, in a way, a response to this challenge.

4 Some traditional approaches to coaching based on theories and practices of psychotherapy that could be seen as developmental. Coaching is now successfully adapting a number of psychotherapeutic traditions. In *The Complete Handbook of Coaching* (Cox et al. 2010), theory-based approaches, such as psychodynamic or Gestalt coaching, are described separately from the types and genres of coaching, such as performance or life coaching. Among the theoretical approaches there are at least seven which have a solid theoretical foundation and are focused on development. Each of them could easily claim to be a theory for developmental coaching. In fact, as the above handbook has been designed to make cross links between theoretical approaches and genres of coaching, the authors of nearly all the theoretical approaches identified their approach as fully compatible with the genre of developmental coaching.

I came up with only two reasons for my intention to further the wisdom that these traditions already contain in exploring an underpinning for developmental coaching. The first one is their more extensive focus on dysfunctionality and problem areas be-cause, of course, they were developed for psychotherapy rather than for coaching. The second reason is their explicit focus on their own particular perspective on development that in many cases excludes the value of the remaining perspectives for coaching.

The description of the above approaches does not mention the integrative coaching or psychological coaching theories which are becoming known in the field. Although they seem to be associated with the relevant fields of knowledge, the apparent lack of a unified and substantiated theory behind them leaves them in a category of many other non-theoretical approaches to coaching.

To summarize some of the characteristic features of developmental coaching as described in the literature:

- It is holistic, addressing the whole person rather than only work-related goals.
- It addresses longstanding behaviour problems.
- It is for those who have reached a plateau in the process of growth.
- It implies working in a different way with people at different stages of development.
- It is helping to increase the broader human capacities of clients.
- The developmental coach is described as a 'thought partner' who assumes a non-directive approach.
- It is a more suitable approach for a better trained external coach rather than for a manager as coach or an internal coach.

Even a brief look at these characteristics reveals that not all of them are compatible. This is not surprising considering the different conceptualizations of developmental coaching and the lack of a unifying theory behind the approach. As a result of this confusion there seems to be little agreement between practitioners on what they do, even if they define their coaching as developmental. Researchers can also be misled and be misleading when they select from this variety only those characteristics that suit their specific purposes. In this way they may claim, for example, that their newly trained managers were delivering developmental coaching in the organizational coaching programme (Leonard-Cross 2010), a proposition that would cause serious objections from others. Although there could be various readings of developmental coaching, an approach that is explicit and non-controversial in terms of the main theoretical propositions and their practical application may be helpful for practitioners and academics alike.

And finally …

For some uniformity throughout the book I call the two members of the coaching partnership 'coach' and 'client', rather than 'coach' and 'coachee'. I will refer to the organization that sponsors coaching or plays an involved role in this process as an 'organization', rather than an 'organizational client'. When it makes more sense to use singular rather plural I will use 'she' referring to a coach, and 'he' referring to a client just for clarity and simplicity, not for any other reason.

I suggest that the book from now can be read in at least two ways. A purely practice-oriented coach may skip the theory and start from the Chapter 5, or even from Part 2 of the book, focusing on the different ways of working with 'the self', addressing different developmental themes of the client's life. Those who prefer engaging with the theoretical underpinning of practice may choose to follow the main argument and the consequent logical structure of the book from the very beginning. There is so much in the coaching field that needs not only to be applied, but explained and understood, that I hope that most of you will choose to do the latter.

PART 1
Three stories about the self: towards a new theory for coaches

1 Introduction to Part 1

I cannot totally grasp all that I am ... the mind is far too narrow to contain itself.

St Augustine

Metaphysics means nothing but an unusually obstinate effort to think clearly.

James, 1890

What is the self? Philosophers, psychologists, neuroscientists, educationalists, therapists and theologians have been asking this question for different reasons and from different angles for a long time. Some of them arrived at a dead end claiming that the self is an ultimate puzzle that will never be resolved, but it seems that the others do not want to give up. Therefore attempts to understand the nature of the self continue.

You, the reader, may ask: what has this puzzle to do with coaching? On the surface it may appear – not much. The nature of self seems too abstract for the concrete tasks of coaching as normally understood. However, if we look at what coaches do, then the gap between self and coaching is not as wide as it seems: coaches attempt to change the way individuals think, feel and act in the contexts of the goals set in coaching. This inevitably influences who they are. Isn't this enough reason to ask yourself, as a coach: what am I intervening *with*?

Coaches often say that they aim to increase the self-awareness of their clients. They often perceive that clients do not know themselves enough. They are right. Research on our general knowledge of ourselves (Dunning 2006; Claxton 2007) confirms that we have no privileged access to our selves. Often people such as supervisors, teachers and trainers know other people better than they know themselves. We are often misguided about what we want: Dunning (2006) gives examples from our dealings with estate agents who are usually better able to predict our choices than we can our own. On the whole, 'the evidence suggests that self-insight is a precious commodity that people believe they possess to a far greater degree than they really do' (2006: 603). To be more specific, Dunning argues that our self-assessment tends to be flawed in one particular dimension: overestimation, which could be quite costly in some particular circumstances. An obvious example is of older drivers who overestimate their declining abilities, or younger and overconfident drivers who believe they can do nearly everything if they have passed the test. In a similar way the outcome of us and our clients being 'strangers to ourselves' is far too evident in coaching: 'In many social and intellectual domains poor performers tend not to know just how badly they perform' (p. 605). The problem is big enough when we tend to deceive ourselves willingly, but the sadder thing is that we are not accurate even when we try to get it right. Is this an issue for coaching? How do you address the discrepancy between personal and external perception of a client's abilities? In what way may you deceive yourself as a coach? Having a better insight into the nature of the self may help us to deal with these issues.

Some coaches might say that intending to understand the issues of the self on such deep levels may be going too far for coaching. They use the analogy of coaching as a car service in contrast to therapy, which is dealing with a serious repair if something went wrong. The theoretical principles according to which the car is constructed may not be so important for someone who just services it, in the same fashion that pilots do not need to know thermodynamics in order to fly the aircraft. This argument might have some pragmatic value particularly when dealing with machines. However, the specialists say that even machines respond in a different way when they are *understood and treated* accordingly. Surely with human beings this observation rings even more true. We know that the way coaches see clients influences what they focus on, the way they build a relationship with them and how they choose their strategies. All of these certainly have an effect on the outcomes of coaching. This is particularly relevant to developmental coaching, where the main focus of coaching is on individuals as 'wholes' rather than their specific skills or performance issues.

I am not arguing that to be a developmental coach one needs to become a psychologist or to learn everything that is currently known about the human psyche. Even if someone has such an intention I would not envy them. The topic of the self does not fit neatly into any category of established psychological knowledge. There is very little about the self that could be called an accepted body of knowledge in all relevant disciplines, such as philosophy and neuroscience. Psychology is no different from them in this respect. There are, however, some perspectives and theories of the self that could already add value to our process of making sense of who we are as human beings and how we change. In this section of the book we will look at what these theories and research can offer for developmental coaching.

No 'correct' way of coaching will be prescribed as the result of this discussion, but, assuming you are a coach, your understanding of why you do what you do will hopefully be advanced and some of your methods enhanced. For example, imagine the same client being coached on the same coaching assignment by two different coaches. Let us call them coach A and coach B. The client is learning to delegate and to share his power. In her approach coach A may emphasize the benefits of the controlled release of pressure to free his time and space for creativity when some tasks are delegated by this client to others. She may also remind the client about his special and important role in developing others and giving them an opportunity to try some new tasks. Coach B on the other hand may be working with the same issue of delegation trying to stir in the client a realization of the futility of an overall control in principle. Both strategies could lead to a desirable outcome of coaching, but possibly, to a different degree for different clients. We will discuss, for example, which of these two may be more developmentally sound, depending on where the client is in his life and what his overall task of development is. The differences in the approaches of these two coaches may depend on the different perspectives on the self that we are going to explore in this section.

First I am going to introduce three different stories about the self that have quite distinct views on the nature and development of the self:

- the first story of the self: the self as an operator;
- the second story: there is no self;
- the third story: the evolving self.

Then I will offer a series of propositions about the self that I would argue make theoretical and pragmatic sense in relation to coaching. I will be using these propositions as stepping stones towards a theory of developmental coaching. The 'what is to be done' aspect of this theory leading to particular recommendations in terms of coaching methods and interventions will be discussed later in Part 2.

I want to clarify from the very beginning my intentions and predicaments in relation to the first three chapters of this section. My purpose in these chapters is to give a background to the decisions that I have made in relation to the notions of self described in the *Résumé*: Chapter 4. This is a more modest task in comparison to giving a fair overview of this enormous, multidisciplinary and very complex field. Although I tried to provide as much support as possible for the main statements and inferences, they are still described in a significantly reduced way and so inevitably simplified and generalized. They certainly do not do justice to the complexity of ideas and experiments that the authors themselves provide in their relevant literature. Therefore I am happy to take any criticism for oversimplification and potential misunderstanding, but hope that my references will be useful for those who are curious enough to search for the original sources. I can strongly recommend as an overview text *Consciousness: An Introduction* by Susan Blackmore (2003), which is an excellent textbook describing in a clear but lively way the state of the field on consciousness and the self. More challenging reading focused specifically on the self but from different perspectives is *Models of the Self* edited by Gallagher and Shear (1999).

2 The first story: the self as an operator

I know that I exist; the question is, what is this 'I' that I know?
Descartes, *Meditations on First Philosophy*

My body is an object all right, but my self jolly well is not!
Farrell, 1996

Before describing this particular story I would like you to think of what is more important to you: what *feels* real or what *is* real? It may sound like an odd question, but in relation to the issues that we are going to discuss here this is important, because the actual existence of the self is the topic of a huge debate. To make some reasonable sense of this debate we need to think of what is real and whether it is different from what feels real. Ideally, you would say, what is real should feel like real to normal people and the other way around: what feels like real should be real. But we have plenty of examples of when what feels real is not: from simple perceptual illusions to the tricks that our feelings play with us when we expect something or are afraid of it or have strong desires. The strange sound in a dark, scary place may be thought of as being made by a dangerous animal. A self-conscious presenter may feel that everyone noticed and laughed at his blunder. We can persuade ourselves that all sorts of things are real only to discover later that they are not. You would say: of course these are the small shortcomings of our human nature, but in principle we are capable of recognizing what is actually real, such as the physical world around us and our existence in it. However, philosophers and scientists are not in agreement even about these broad statements and still debate very different positions on them. Unfortunately, it is far from being clear what is real and how it corresponds to feeling real.

In the light of a potential discrepancy between feeling real and being real you might take a position that, 'never mind what is real: I live in this world in the way it feels and this is good enough for me to know'. In order to deal with other people I would check how it feels to them and what comes as the result of our negotiations we would take as true and real. This is a sensible solution which is absolutely suitable for our everyday life tasks and issues. In contrast, it is also a real feature of human nature *not* to be satisfied with how things just feel to us. It is not only rare philosophers or crazy scientists who are the compulsive diggers for 'truth' – most of us are, too. Those pragmatists and activists, who work all day long to feed, clothe, entertain and move us around in a better and better way, also do. They wouldn't be able to do their job if they didn't care what *is* real and so could be manipulated and improved.

So what we are facing here is two different perspectives: first our 'first-person' subjective experience of living (phenomenological) and the second – our 'third person' observation of the natural world (metaphysical). And as much as we would like to see these perspectives as two different routes to the top of the same mountain of truth this may not be the case. Maybe the mountain is insurmountable and we may be left to stay at its foot and be satisfied with two very different pictures that we can take of it. So let us not forget about these two perspectives when we are going to look at the issue of self and particularly at the first story of the self.

This story of the self gives priority to the first person phenomenological perspective because it starts from how we usually perceive ourselves and think of the selves of others. And only after this does it go on to describe the picture of the world and us in the world from the metaphysical perspective in the way that confirms the actual existence of selves. So what do we feel about the self? It is a sense of the self being

1   a single,
2   continuous thing
3   that is conscious of experiences,
4   has a certain character or personality
5   and is also an agent.

To simplify this position we each perceive our self to be *an operator of a complex machine* (our body), which in turn acts on the environment (Fig. 2.1). This tiny operator sits somewhere in the brain and receives information about how the body is functioning and what is happening in the environment. He/she also has overall strategies and values according to which he/she would prefer to act. First both internal and external information is processed by an operator. Then he/she considers it all, makes decisions and gives command to the body to change the behaviour if necessary. Then he/she may reflect on the processes and results and give commands to the body to make adjustments if necessary.

This is, of course a very simplistic picture because it tries to translate what it feels like into what it may look like to others. So it is already changing phenomenological perspective to a metaphysical one. We all know that when you start describing your internal or even external experience from your unique personal position it is already not the same experience. That is probably one way to explain how a good coach is different from a not so good one. She can understand what the client is struggling to describe from his internal standpoint, which is unique, and by definition, a lonely place. This is one of the problems that philosophers are dealing with and probably that is why understanding consciousness and the self remains 'just about the last surviving mystery' (Dennett 1991: 21). It is a mystery because science and philosophy are not satisfied with the phenomenological perspective. For them to resolve a problem is to resolve it metaphysically: this is their main drive.

Figure 2.1 How would the self look as an operator?

In this pursuit science has made significant progress. With help of amazing tech-nology constantly improving it can explain now a lot about how brains function, how information is processed and enacted. However, it is still not clear, for example, if consciousness makes any difference to all this information-processing or if there is something like a self somewhere among these processes in the brain. As Chalmers put it 'Why doesn't all this information-processing go on "in the dark", free of any inner feel?' (1995: 201–3). Pressing with questions like that, he formulated what is called a hard problem in science: what is the relationship between the physical states of the brain and the conscious experiences that accompany them? The struggle to find an answer to this question continues. Although we are aiming to address a slightly differ-ent struggle: who is the one or what is the thing that is watching these experiences, it would be useful to have a brief review of the situation in relation to the question posed by Chalmers.

The whole story began from the dualism of Descartes (1596–1650) who thought that the mental and the material were separate, but interacting realms. His explanation of this interaction (in the pineal gland!) is now considered to be a wacky idea. Even during his time sceptics argued that the dualism of Descartes condemns us to ignorance about the material world. Berkeley (1685–1753) came up with a 'better' explanation that the material world does not exist at all. His radical idealism meant that the problem of interaction between the mental and the material was solved by eliminating matter altogether. According to Berkeley the material world is only impressions on our senses: 'to be is to be perceived', as he said. Although quite a few famous philosophers were taken with this approach it created a strong counter-reaction within the scientific community. Behaviourism was at the forefront of this reactive movement and has done a good job in promoting experimental studies of human behaviour, replacing introspection. As usual, it went too far in the dismissal of the role and value of our inner world and created another reaction in the scientific community.

So where are we now? Depending on the nature of their explanation of the origin and role of consciousness it is possible (theoretically) to divide philosophers, scientists and various commentators into three main camps: dualists, materialists and mysterians. *Dualists*, as in the past, think that brain activities and subjective experience are separate substances that somehow interact, but they cannot give a reasonable explanation of how this works. *Materialists* believe that brain and mind are the same, but they find it hard to explain how they could be identical when they appear so different. *Mysterians* confess that the understanding of consciousness is a complete mystery and beyond human beings at present or maybe forever (Papineau and Selina 2006).

Coming back now to the first story of the self as an operator, we should be able to observe that this story is more compatible with dualism. Although nothing like a physical operator is found in the brain, according to them there should at least be a special mental substance from which it is made. Materialists, on the other hand, support mostly a second story of the self: there is no self, which we are going to discuss in the next chapter. And as for mysterians (Nagel 1986; Pinker 1997; McGinn 1999), their sad prediction is that we do not have the right concepts to enable us to understand the issue, probably for the same reason 'why monkeys can't do differential calculus' (Papineau and Selina 2006: 108).

There is another interesting way to group different views on the issue of the self. Parfit (1987) described two positions on the self as 'ego' theories and 'bundle' theories. The ego theorists believe that there is (metaphysically) a single continuous self that is a subject of my experiences and which acts as an agent. Bundle theorists say that it only *seems* this way and the self is just a 'bundle of sensation' (Hume 1739): there are experiences but no one to experience them. Needless to say that in Hume's time his proposition was the most outrageous and revolutionary, because even now it has a strong opposition.

Nearly all dualists (Popper and Eccles 1977; MacKay 1987; Gazzaniga 1992) are ego theorists. They believe in the first story of the self as an operator in a similar fashion to Thomas Reid (1710–1796), who argued: 'I am not thought, I am not action, I am not feeling: I am something which thinks and acts and feels'. According to Eccles (1994), for example, the self really does control its brain. There is also a slightly different view in this category that implies that the self exists as a pure subject of experience, an ego-pole which is different from the stream of experiences that are presented to this self. All these experiences are lived through the same self and for this reason it gives structure and unity to this stream of experiences. It must exist, but it is not, itself, something that can be experienced (Gallagher and Zahavi 2008: 200). These two views, however close, are not easy to place under the same umbrella, because we can see that the first one offers a metaphysical solution, but the second is a return to phenomenology.

It is important to notice that there are many more supporters of the ego theory in the world than we could imagine. This theory implies that there is something very special about the self as an operator, much more special than this mechanical picture may suggest. The role of the operator seems so significant in comparison to the body that some schools of thought postulate that in fact the operator may continue to exist when the body has perished. It has the status of a human soul. The operator is so special, powerful and mysterious that according to nearly all main religions it survives the body. The ideas of immortal souls and reincarnating spirits are compatible with this story of the self.

The first story of the self has many features that appeal to our common sense. However, many philosophers and scientists have seriously questioned it. In the literature the actual name of the operator is 'homunculus' and it is used in an ironic way to emphasize the delusion of the proponents of this view. The main critique of it suggests that in terms of brain structures this theory implies that there is one part of the brain which possesses the knowledge needed to interpret the images that the brain formed of the objects. The images are presented to this part (The Operator) and this operator knows what to do with them. The obvious problem with this theory is: if the operator or homunculus was to do all the knowing for each of us, who would be doing its knowing? To be consistent we would have to postulate another even smaller operator inside the previous operator and so on. The chain would be endless, and this essentially disqualifies this solution.

This disqualifying argument was so persuasive for those who studied the self that it created a fear of specifying a knowing self in any way, but particularly cognitively and neuroanatomically. Researchers became more inclined to explore the mechanisms of the brain and their findings gave powerful support to the second story of self which we are going to explore in the next chapter. However, we should not forget that the power of this critique comes from the metaphysical perspective. The first story cannot be easily dismissed from the phenomenological perspective which is still closely related to our personal everyday needs. That is why we are now going to look at the studies in psychology which developed within the boundaries of this story of the self, and which may be useful for coaches.

Psychology about the self

> The states of consciousness are all that psychology needs to do her work with. Metaphysics or theology may prove the Soul to exist: but for psychology the hypothesis of such a substantial principle of unity is superfluous.
>
> William James, 1890

Few would question that people are drawn to psychology in order to know more about themselves. After all, psychology is about us, human beings. It is strange, therefore, that the nature of the self has not been often discussed in psychology. The rare exception is William James (1842–1910) who is, paradoxically, responsible for this limited status of the studies of the self in psychology. His own contribution to the further understanding of consciousness and the self is significant, to say the least. His classic work *Principles of Psychology* (1890) is highly respected even now amongst psychologists and philosophers alike. However, he suggested that psychology needs to concentrate only on the restricted area of this field: studying 'me' rather than 'I'.

James started from what it feels like to be 'me' and put forward a strong case that psychology should not explain away the existence of personal selves. 'The universal conscious fact is not "feelings and thoughts exist", but "I think" and "I feel". No psychology, at any rate, can question the existence of personal selves. The worst a psychology can do is so to interpret the nature of these selves as to rob them of their worth' (James 1890, i: 226). His main concepts for understanding the self that are widely used since are:

- the self as knower, the 'pure ego' or *I*;
- the self as known: empirical *me*, or *Me*, 'an empirical aggregate of the things objectively known' (James 1999: 77).

It is much easier to understand what he means by Me. 'In its widest possible sense, a man's Me is the sum total of all that he can call his, not only his body and his powers, but his clothes and his house, his wife and children, his ancestors and friends, his reputations and works, his lands and horses, and yacht and bank-account' (1999: 69). All of these, he says, together form Me because of the feelings of self-appreciation they arouse and because of the acts they might prompt such as self-seeking or self-estimation.

He describes various aspects (the constituents) of Me such as material, social and spiritual. Body, of course, is the first one within the material aspect, then come clothes and other properties including the wealth and power these can give. The social aspect is about recognition from others. James says that strictly speaking one has 'as many different social selves as there are distinct groups of persons about whose opinion he cares' (p. 70). This multiplicity can lead to discordant splitting in us, or to a harmonious division of labour (1999: 70–1). The spiritual aspects are more difficult to describe as a group, let alone explain why they are called spiritual. He includes here the entire collection of the states of consciousness, all psychic faculties and dispositions, including emotional, intellectual and volitional. This is all that could become a focus of our attention when we think about ourselves as a person.

However, it is *I* or pure ego that is the focus of the first story of the self that we are exploring here. James is clear about this because he asks the question which is right to the point: what is a real knower; is it a stream of passing states or some sort of permanent being? In trying to answer this question he calls it a most puzzling puzzle with which psychology has to deal (James 1890, i: 330). His solution to this is ingenious, but not easy to understand, which is why it is sometimes oversimplified or misunderstood (Harter 1999).

James asks all the relevant questions about the self that we started this story from:

- unity of 'I' in the moment – do all our thoughts and perceptions belong to the same person?
- unity of 'I' over time – am I the same I that I was yesterday?
- agency – is this an 'I' that is responsible for my actions?

He answers 'yes' to all these questions and that is why I think his theory belongs to the first story of self. But at the same time he was aware of the 'conflict' between phenomenology and the metaphysics of the self and offered an original solution. He criticized ego theories for an unsubstantiated proposal of a concrete, simple and spiritual being – a substantial soul. He also was not satisfied with bundle theories which suggested there is no self to be found, because they run too much against our common sense view of ourselves. He thought that there should be a sort of 'owner' of this bundle of experiences. To resolve this puzzle James proposed an interesting solution that 'the thought itself is the thinker and psychology need not look beyond' (1890, i: 401).

According to his theory at any particular moment there is a passing thought which is the only *verifiable* thinker and not in contradiction with the laws of brain processes. This thought remembers previous thoughts and appropriates some of them to itself. So what is holding thoughts together is not a separate ego or spirit, but another special thought that pulls together other thoughts that feel 'warm' and 'mine'. So the unity of experience is provided by the thought itself. His metaphor of a herd and herdsman may help to understand his theory better. The experiences and thoughts are cattle but there is no permanent herdsman, only each thought/cattle appropriates the previous thoughts and passes the ownership of the herd to the next one. If this idea is too weird to take in I hope that the next chapter at least will make it clearer why it is so.

James's theory does make sense to philosophers and scientists nowadays who struggle to understand the actual nature of the self. Although he does not explain how and why the stream of thought is called into existence and how its existence corresponds to brain activities, he suggests a position that can serve as a bridge between these two stories of the self. James also believed that the nature of the self is a domain more suitable for philosophy than psychology. It is difficult to say whether he was right or wrong about this in principle, but the reality shows that psychology has become since then more interested in Me.

The nature of battles about the self and the methods of studying Me was changing while psychology was undergoing some interesting historical changes. It seems that the beginning of psychology was fuelled by a genuine interest in subjectivity and the intention of understanding the internal world of people. The method of study was introspection – just another word for phenomenology as a method, but only of the researcher's own internal and external world. Since then introspection has been found wanting; only psychodynamic theories survived. The great ambition of psychology to become a science meant that a serious shift had to be made to the third person perspective on human beings. In the age of behaviourism, interest in the self as such was put on a back-burner and replaced with things that were clearly observable by the third person, which is behaviour. Then came the cognitive revolution introducing a new model of the human being – someone who learns about the world and acts on it in a way that is similar to a computer. The view of the self was changing along with transitions within psychology: from ego in psychoanalysis serving instinctual forces of dark nature under the stern control of the internalized taboos of society, to the self in behaviourism that is deluded about its freedom but entirely shaped by environment, and then to a completely different view of social and cognitive psychology. Baumeister (1999), for example, describes this self 'as an important and autonomous player who both actively intervenes in the processing of information and is itself a knowledge structure resulting from information processing' (p. 119).

Many interesting studies have been conducted in psychology with the intention of understanding Me (see Baumeister, *The Self in Social Psychology*, 1999 for a comprehensive review). At the same time more psychologists are becoming interested in I and pure ego, particularly in the branches of cognitive and developmental psychology. Unfortunately, an old tension between first person and third person perspectives can still influence these studies and becomes misleading if ignored. For example, developmental psychologist Susan Harter (1999) describes components of the Jamesian I-self as '(1) *self-awareness,* an appreciation for one's internal states, needs, thoughts, and emotions; (2) *self-agency,* the sense of the authorship over one's thoughts and actions; (3) *self-continuity,* the sense that one remains the same person over time; and (4) *self-coherence,* a stable sense of the self as a single, coherent, bounded entity' (p. 6). However correct this description could be phenomenologically, without a blink Harter proceeds to name them as 'I-self capabilities, namely, those cognitive processes that define the knower' (p. 7). You can see how this significant shift has been made unjustifiably from the 'sense' to the 'capability' and so – from first person to the third person description.

In Baumeister (1999) this discrepancy has not been made explicit as well. He describes three active areas of study in contemporary psychology in relation to 'three major human experiences [that] form the basis of selfhood' (p. 2) as:

- reflexive consciousness
- interpersonal being
- executive function

At the same time the majority of the studies in his book, however valuable, are third-person based. What they discuss is certainly more than the sense or experience of the self. In the area of reflexive consciousness he includes the studies of how the self is acquired, stored, transformed and used. In the theme of interpersonal being, the studies aims to understand how the self is involved in interacting with others, self-presentation, self-perception in communication acts, performing to the audience, and so on. In the third group of themes about the executive function of the self, he includes the study of autonomy and volition, self-regulation, decision making and self-defeating behaviour as examples. This is the most controversial area in terms of the first and third person divide and Baumeister agrees that it is less well understood and under-researched. He also admits that all these studies suffer from the conceptual elusiveness of the self, which of course is a typical feature of the first story.

In spite of limited interest in the self as such, there are several other areas of psychology that make an important contribution to our inquiry into the nature of self which may be potentially useful for coaching. Some of these areas are clearly interested in the third person perspective on the self such as studies of personality. Others, studying, for example, dysfunctions of the self have an applied focus in order to develop psychotherapeutic approaches to address these dysfunctions. In these areas of psychology the first person perspective on the self is traditionally more valuable. I will briefly comment on these areas looking at the self as an operator and thinking about their potential use for coaches.

Personality study

It would be valuable to increase our understanding of the various aspects of the self as an operator. For example, we can say that this operator has various attributes that describe a person's character, temperament and cognitive abilities. According to these the operator may find some tasks easy and some tasks difficult to perform; he also has abilities to learn and change some of these attributes. *Personality studies*, for instance, suggest a range of theories and methods that allow identifying and measuring personal traits that are believed to be reasonably stable. Applied psychology in turn suggests ways to use psychometric methods in organizations for recruitment and selection purposes, for creating more compatible teams, for designing tailor-made approaches to individual development. Even if some coaches are not too keen on the use of psychometrics we have to admit that currently organizations are well motivated by the various promises coming from this area of knowledge and expect coaches to be proficient in the use of some methods.

My only caution for coaches is not to forget the chain of thought that led to the creation of psychometric methods in the light of the first story of self. It is an attempt to pinpoint characteristics of something not defined in itself with huge assumptions that these characteristics are reflecting something stable that can be identified by this elusive self; not to mention what is lost or unjustifiably gained through the inevitable translation from the first person perspective to the third. I am not saying that some noticeable tendencies could not be found and taken into consideration, if they only are seen as no more than tendencies. We will return to this topic in other sections of this book.

Developmental psychology

Theories and research findings of *developmental psychology* can help us to see what happens to the self as a young operator. Obviously, young operators are not very skilful yet in doing all the important tasks that we described before and they need a lot of help. It appears that they do not know much about their own attributes. They learn about these from other people, who observe how they act and give their judgments about these acts, often adding their own values in these judgments. These judgments allow young operators to build a self-image of themselves as individuals. A self-image could be helpful for the operator to decide what tasks to get engaged with and what can save him/her from unnecessary disappointments. But this image could be very unhelpful and limiting. Coaches often work with problems that stem from such limiting images in their clients.

In fact developmental psychology has made useful attempts to describe the process through which the self is developed in childhood. Figure 2.2 is created as an adaptation from various sources, but mainly from Hamacheck (1978). It describes how a sense of self initially develops through physical sensations that a baby has of her body, for example feeling pain when biting her own toe; through the realization of what she can do with her body, like reaching for a toy with her own arm but not with her mum's arm; through personal memories that become useful and through cues from others such as hearing her own name and descriptive adjectives (nice, clever, naughty). Imitation of

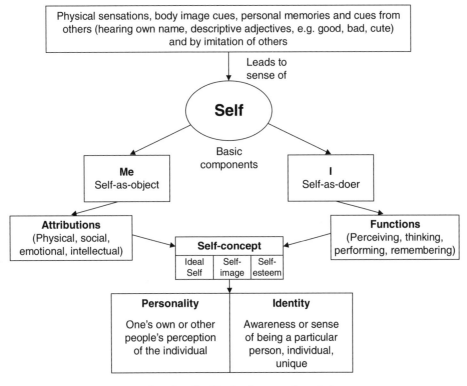

Figure 2.2   Development of self as described in developmental psychology.

others and how they treat a baby and talk about her also play an important role in the development of the sense of a self (Baldwin 1897). Developmental psychologists make use of the Jamesian components of the self as Me and I. They propose that Me could be described by various characteristics that children learn to *attribute* to themselves and I is associated with what they can *do,* such as perceiving, thinking, performing, etc. (Hamacheck 1978).

Claxton (1981, 1994) believes that the development of language plays the most important role in a child's sense of self, a role that could even be described as adverse, if we believe in the value of learning and experimenting with the environment instead of receiving readymade judgements of how the world and the child should be. He gives a very descriptive comparative scenario of the difference that language can make and potential psychological problems that could follow.

> The lioness will belt a cub if it nips her tail, and he will feel hurt for a while and go off and nip somebody else's. He does not go off with the suspicion that he is a bad, dirty little cub, not fit to be seen in the company of nice cubs like Jeremy, and just you wait till your father gets home! He is not made to feel worthless and unloved. He has not suffered a blow to his self-esteem that will

flower, in his adolescence, into schizophrenia. He has just learned that you don't bite your Mum's tail if you know what's good for you.

(Claxton 1991: 38)

The use of language creates conditions in which we carry hurtful labels and harsh predictions throughout our lives. As coaches we often encounter issues that have stemmed from the childhood of our clients. It is not expected that the coach becomes involved directly in dealing with an old trauma but she may find herself regularly stumbling on the consequences of it. It may be useful to remember at least that it is often from the language of the self that these traumas and false beliefs may stem – the self that may not be definable in principle. The least we could do is not to add more dubious definitions but to try to raise some doubts about the old and sticky ones.

Studies of human interaction

From studying the self in interaction other useful things could be observed in the light of the first story. If we see the self as an operator it becomes apparent that sitting there alone in the middle of the brain is not fun. An operator may feel isolated from others and although sometimes there are amazing moments of deep understanding and connection to others through channels that nobody can explain, at the end of the day each operator is essentially alone. It is hard work to understand others or to be understood, let alone feel really close to someone.

There are various studies in psychology that aim to understand an operator in the network of interpersonal relationships with outcomes that allow people to be more effective in self-presentation, to understand others, to build partnership (Holmes 1981; Lewicki 1984; Baumeister 1999). Most of these studies tend to have an implicit view of the self as an operator and not surprisingly they confirm how difficult it is to understand each other and consequently to have an effective interaction. Some practical approaches such as neurolinguistic programming (NLP) for example, maybe in desperation, invent all sorts of tricks to get through to the operator in order to interact with it. As research on the effectiveness of helping interventions shows (Wampold 2001) the relationship with clients seems to be the main factor, but the topic of actually influencing relationships is still as vague as it used to be. Similarly in coaching literature, the coaching relationship is one of the most puzzling and least developed themes so far. So if the first story of the self is true we need all the help we can get to make coaching effective.

Psychotherapeutic theories

The selves as operators may have some problems, of course. Branches of psychology studying abnormal and dysfunctional behaviour and in a milder form, psychological problems of reasonably healthy people, developed some important applied fields such as psychotherapy and counselling. The majority of schools and traditions in these fields consider and work with individuals on the premise that the first person perspective is more important than the third. That is probably why the issue of self in a metaphysical sense was not a central problem for these fields. The well known exception to this is the Freudian theory of the structure of the psyche (id, ego and superego) and there is the less known theory of psychosynthesis by Roberto Assagioli (1993).

As far as other psychotherapeutic approaches are concerned, the weight of their contributions to coaching is based on the first and second person perspective on human to human engagement with clients. As they offer coherent theories and practical approaches it is impossible to overestimate their value for developmental coaching. There are now substantial texts in the coaching literature (Stober and Grant 2006; Palmer and Whybrow 2007; Cox et al. 2010) that successfully translate the ideas and findings of these traditions from the older sister field for coaches. In Part 3 I will comment on some approaches which could be useful at particular developmental stages.

The implications of the first story of self

In short, the first story implies a vision of a little self in the brain, homunculus, or an operator, that is sitting there as if in a theatre, receiving all sort of experiences from within and from outside the body. It analyses them, makes decisions and makes the body act. It is so special that unlike the body it may live forever. However unusual this might sound, this is what common sense in a way dictates. If coaches assume that this vision is true or just don't think about this at all (in this case it is common sense that would take the reins), they would believe in the specialness of this little centre somewhere inside the client's mind. They would try to make a special connection with this special little centre. In communication they would try to get through to it. I will take a risk and suggest that those who believe in the high value of trust as a condition for effective coaching are those who believe in the first story. The logic is simple: you need to make this centre feel good about you or nothing will work.

The focus of coaching may become making this little person in the mind change his mind in order for the whole person to make the changes needed. The task of coaching becomes working with this remarkable thing in our brain that is unique and mysterious. This uniqueness is associated with the inexplicable nature of the operator. It would dominate a coach's view that some characteristics of this adult operator have been written in him for a long time and some never change.

Is there any problem with such view? Not necessarily. Believing in specialness of the operator in the client's mind, being affected by the mystery of his nature, hoping to click with or working hard to establish a perfect connection with this unique centre may also be making your coaching successful. Or you may feel like this for less than mysterious reasons. You may find a scientifically sound explanation to this uniqueness and specialness. It may be the result of various influences of the environment and genetic makeup on the organism, which consequently get attached to this special centre. There is no problem with this view, but there may be a challenge lurking that could offer new and different opportunities not available in this story.

3   The second story: there is no self

We do not deal much in facts when we are contemplating ourselves.

Mark Twain

Yesterday's and today's state of consciousness have no *substantial* identity, for when one is here the other is irrevocably dead and gone.

William James, 1890

The second story of the self is more difficult to take in because it is counter-intuitive. It clashes with common sense about the way we see ourselves as continuous beings who have experiences and are able to be authors of our actions. Some of the positions taken in this story are quite radical, as for example that of Thomas Metzinger (2003) who simply states that 'no such things as selves exist in the world: Nobody ever was or had a self' (p. 1). According to him it is neither necessary nor rational to assume the existence of a self: it is only a theoretical entity, which fulfils no indispensable explanatory function. Biological organisms exist, but an organism is not a self (p. 563). There are many other supporters of this story of the self in scientific circles. For example, Ramachandran and Hirstein (1999) argue that the self as a unitary, enduring thing is an illusion. According to them, at best, the self is a certain function that mediates between motivated-emotional processes and the control of action which 'could give rise to the mythology of a self as an active presence in the brain – a "ghost in the machine"' (pp. 108–9).

One might say that such a radical view is understandable from the current position of 'hard science', but surprisingly, even phenomenology, which is concerned with our internal perspective and our subjectivity, has a very similar view to consider at the very heart of this tradition. According to Sartre (1956) there is no need for a self (ego) as an inhabitant of or possessor of consciousness. If we are absorbed in some activity and living it we do not have any awareness of a self and as long as this living continues the self will not appear. The self emerges only when we reflect on this activity with a distancing attitude, but in this case the self is an object of reflection and not a subject of it. 'My *I*, in effect, is *no more certain for consciousness than the I of other men*. It is only more intimate' (p. 104, original emphasis).

This second story of the self also has a long history, certainly not shorter than the first one. Buddha was the first and probably the most consistent and radical in this tradition. He introduced the notion of no-self according to which 'the idea of self is an imagery, false belief which has no corresponding reality, and it produces harmful thoughts of "me" and "mine", selfish desire, craving, attachment . . . It is the source of all the troubles in the world' (Rahula 1959: 51).

This view of the self is called by Parfit (1987) a 'bundle theory', a name that was inspired by the philosophical theory of David Hume (1711–1776) who introduced the term 'bundle of sensations' in defining the self. He used this term to describe what he managed to observe when he tried to look inside and find *his* own 'self'. Instead he only stumbled 'on some particular perception or other, of heat or cold, light or shade, love or hatred, pain or pleasure'.

> I never can catch myself at any time without a perception, and never can observe anything but the perception . . . [We] are nothing but a bundle or collection of perceptions, which succeed each other with inconceivable rapidity, and are in perpetual flux and movement . . . The mind is a kind of theatre, where several perceptions successively make their appearance; pass, re-pass, glide away, and mingle in an infinite variety of postures and situations.
>
> (Hume 1739: 252–53)

He uses an analogy of a theatre similar to the first story, but with a difference. The self here is not a director of the performance and there is no one in the audience to watch this performance. Another more poetic way to illustrate this theory is offered by Allan Watts: 'I am neither a passive and helpless witness . . . nor an active doer and thinker . . . Inside the skull and the skin as well as outside there is simply the stream flowing along of itself' (Watts 1972: 154).

According to this story there is no self, but only a series of experiences linked together in various ways. 'Bundle theory does not deny that each of us *seems* to be a unified conscious being. It denies that there is any separately existing entity that explains that appearance. There are experiences but there is no one who has them. Actions and decisions happen but not because there is someone who acts and decides' (Blackmore 2003: 98). As Daniel Dennett, a philosopher who strongly argues for a bundle theory nowadays, memorably puts it 'the trouble with brains, it seems, is that when you look in them, you discover that there's nobody home' (1991: 29).

The most serious challenge to the common sense view of the self for many people in the West comes not from Buddhism or philosophy, but from neuroscience that provides evidence to confirm this cheeky statement by Dennett. What they observe in various studies is that the brain consists of millions of interconnected neurons whose activities give rise to behaviours, memories and perceptions. With this evidence not only is there no need for an additional experiencing self; it is clear, they say, that the physical world appears to be causally closed: nothing in the last 100 years of physiological research provides any evidence for separate mental causes. Simply stated, if any special mental forces were lurking in the recesses of intelligent brains, they would surely have been noticed by now for their effects on bits of matter inside the skull (Papineau and Selina 2006).

The consensus from contemporary neuroscience is that neurological processing is for the most part distributed across various brain regions. There is consequently no real unified neurological centre of experience nor is there any real identity across time that could be labelled as self. There is an old joke about Oxford University that might help to see this difficult idea of no-self in a different light.

> An American visitor asks a student to show him the famous and ancient University of Oxford. The student takes him all around the city. He shows him the Bodleian Library and the Sheldonian Theatre, Brasenose College and Christ Church, St Edmund Hall and Lady Margaret Hall, the Department of Experimental Psychology and grand Examination Schools, Magdalen Bridge and students punting on the Cherwell. At the end of his extensive tour the visitor says 'But where's the university?'.
>
> (Ryle 1949, in Blackmore 2003: 113)

Maybe what we see as selves is something like a university that consists of different things but can never be pointed at as a separate entity. But does it make this university an illusion? No, it does not, but we have to remember what the word 'illusion' means: it is not what does not exist; it may be something different from what we see as real.

To see through an illusion of this kind is not easy. Even the fact that the self as a separate entity in the brain cannot be found, is of little help. The status of some religions in the world is a clear illustration for this. Dennett (2005) suggests that it is an unfortunate feature of human nature to rely too much on our intuitions and be unable to abandon them. He says that we should not trust common sense because the theories that are not counter-intuitive are just wrong (pp. 81–4). This is maybe asking too much from us mortals and he agrees that something needs to be explained. After all we would not survive without common sense. So he suggests quite an unusual explanation as to why it feels that selves exist when in fact they don't. He suggests that the self is a centre of narrative gravity, which is real but invisible. When we speak of ourselves (what we did, what we like, what we own), the words come from a single source. This leads us to an assumption that there is an owner, the inner agent in all these stories about us in the world. However, this self-constructed owner is just an abstraction, useful, but an abstraction. These stories are created about me as a main actor in them, thus producing an illusion of me as real. As Dennett describes this: 'Our tales are spun, but for the most part we don't spin them; they spin us. Our human consciousness, and our narrative selfhood, is their product, not their source' (1991: 418).

Interestingly there are similarities between Dennett's position on the self and some contemporary discursive psychologists (e.g. Harre and Gillett 1994) who believe that we are a product of various discourses and selves could be understood by studying such discourses. Bruner (2002) also suggests that selfhood is a part of the public domain, and its shape and nature is guided by cultural models of what selfhood should and should not be (p. 137). The difference though is that Dennett tries to show how physical and evolved brains are constructing such discourses and how the illusion of the self is created.

There is another interesting way of explaining the nature of the self that I found useful during my struggle to understand what the self is. It is *a* fascinating theory of self proposed by Gallen Strawson (1999). The book *Models of the Self* edited by Gallagher and Shear (1999) is mostly based on the debate around his theory. It starts from the consideration of the self in the way it *seems* to us from the phenomenological perspective, however Strawson's view differs from Hume's idea of a stream of consciousness; he sees consciousness with more gaps, disappearances and restarts.

Strawson starts his argument from the description of what needs to be present in order to say that there is such a thing as a self: first, it has to be a single mental thing which is a subject of experiences; secondly, it has to have unity at one moment and over time; and thirdly, it has to have a personality and agency. Then, looking at the self from the metaphysical perspective (what could be said to be truly independent of the subjective perspective) Strawson (1997) concludes that only half of these conditions could be supported with evidence, but agency, personality and most intriguingly, unity over time could not. As a result he offers what he calls 'the Pearl view because it suggests that many mental selves exist, one at a time and one after another, like pearls on a string' (p. 424). And these mental things do not need long-term continuity over time. Each self may last just a few seconds, disappear and a new one appears instead. So the unity of the self is then synchronic (existing for quite a short time) and not diachronic (persisting across time) despite of our common belief. Thus he supports the Buddhists' view that there are no selves that exist persistently. We can also notice some similarities with Jamesian theory of thought, but Strawson unlike James, argues against the agency of the self. He does defend his theory well, but does not explain why we believe in the long-term continuity of the same selves and how these short-lived 'pearls' or mental selves *are* individual physical things: sets of neurons in a state of activation.

To summarize the second story, the self as we normally understand it is a fictional story but a useful one, because it helps us to understand ourselves as persons through our own self-interpretations. It means that one is not a self in the same way one is a living organism. One does not have a self in the same way that one has a heart or a nose (Taylor 1989: 34). The self is constructed in and through narrative self-interpretations. These narratives, however, are not merely a way of gaining insight into the nature of an already pre-existing self. There is no such thing as a pre-existing self, one that just awaits being portrayed in words. To believe in such a pre-linguistically given self is 'quite literally to have been misled by stories' (Gallagher and Zahavi 2008: 201).

It is important to clarify here that although it seems that Buddhists and neuro-scientists are in the same camp in this story, there are some differences that show the Buddhist position to be more consistent in comparison to the scientific reductionist position. If we again use an analogy that is similar to the story about Oxford University, but choose, let's say a car, we could say that a car is a collection of different bits and pieces put together. While they are together we call them a car as a generally understood term, a practical designation. In the same way there are different elements in a person, but there is no identity as a real and permanent thing. The proponents of the first story would say that the self is something *other* than these elements. The reductionistic scientists would say that the self ultimately *is* the sum of the parts or the product of some parts like the brain. Giles (1997) argues that both these positions mean resurrecting the self, so to speak. However, Buddhism's no-self theory 'lets the self lie where it has fallen. This is because the no-self theory is not a theory about the self at all. It is rather a rejection of all such theories as inherently untenable' (Giles 1997: 115).

What are the implications of this view of the self? One might think they would be dramatic if this view is so much against common sense. Apparently not. Some of them will be discussed at the end of this chapter together with the implications of the different position on free will. Others will be gradually developed in the rest of this book, because the view of the self that I propose in Chapter 4 is significantly influenced by this story.

The only one that I would like to mention here is the use of 'self' and 'I' in our everyday language. Accepting the self to be an illusion or 'a condensed version of extracts from the succession of related ideas' (Giles 1997: 144), does not mean that these words are mere sounds and that we cannot use them. They are used in accordance with mutual agreement as a linguistic convention, in the same way that they have been used by Hume or Buddhists for that matter.

Can one change oneself? Issues of free will

> A leaf was riven from a tree:
> 'I mean to fall to earth', said he.
> The west wind, rising, made him veer;
> 'Eastwards', he said, 'I now shall steer'.
>
> The east wind rose with greater force:
> Said he: 'Twere nice to change my course'.
>
> With equal power they contend:
> He said: 'My judgment I suspend'.
> Down died the winds. The leaf, elate
> Cried: 'I've decided to fall straight'.
>
> 'First thoughts are best?' That's not the moral:
> Just choose your own and we'll not quarrel.
> Howe'er your choice may chance to fall
> You'll have no hand in it at all.
>
> Ambrose Bierce, *The Devil's Dictionary*

Part of the false or illusory conception of the self in the second story is the idea that the self is an agent – it can *do* things. Therefore the issue of so called 'free will' is our next topic to explore. As with the debates on the self it divides thinkers into two groups who seriously disagree with each other. It has been said that the problem of free will is the most discussed philosophical problem of all time. It is associated with the most counter-intuitive models of life, time and human nature. On one side in this debate is again common sense: 'I feel as though I am making decisions to act and I act by my own free will' and some sense of being special – not a puppet in the hands of blind nature. On the other side: the way it appears in metaphysics and reflected in various models of time and the laws of nature suggest little room for human freedom.

One such model is a static model of time that differs from our traditional dynamic one which says that time flows from past to present to future. The static model suggests a block universe view of time which is very different from our normal understanding. According to this model time does not flow from past to present then to future, but everything exists simultaneously. It does explain some interesting phenomena, but in turn it has some major challenges. One of them is the direction of time, which, being determined by causation and causality is going one way. We can only perceive the present: we would be overloaded if we could see everything at the same time. This model also raises the issue of fatalism.

There is, however, a difference between fatalism and determinism. Fatalism means that when something happens it happens necessarily, there is no chance for it to be different. Determinism, however, suggests that some states of the universe will change according to the laws of nature into other states of the universe. In this case there is no necessity for this change, because the laws of nature in the middle are an important element. If we learn about these laws then changes can be predicted and influenced. Some even argue that free will and determinism are inherently linked. Rollo May for example, describes it in this way: 'A person moves towards freedom and responsibility in his living as he becomes more conscious of the deterministic experiences in his life . . . Freedom is thus not the opposite of determinism' (1967: 175).

Not everyone though is that optimistic. A typical dilemma is: if the universe runs by deterministic laws then there is no room for free will, everything will happen in-evitably according to these laws. There are two ways in philosophy to continue this debate: non-compatibilitists argue that if the universe is deterministic then free will is just an illusion; compatibilists, though, argue that our desires and action do influence what we do even if these desires are predetermined by human nature, culture or god. Interestingly Claxton (1981) argues that neither is possible to prove. He says that the simple argument that we normally present for the existence of free will is our ability to make a choice when several alternative options are presented. However, to show that this choice was a fact and not just a theory we would have to show that we were at one instant capable of choosing A rather then B 'but this would require turning the clock back to relive that moment again, which we cannot do. So we can never know that it was actually possible for us to have done otherwise than we did' (p. 199).

We are not going to deny though, that from both first and third person viewpoints our behaviour appears to be quite regularly a product of our will. However, the crucial questions to ask: what is behind the will? Is the will itself being systematically caused? According to determinism the answer is yes. According to stochastic determinism there is also a big share of randomness that influences the change. That is probably why 'the brain of a human, or even of a mouse, is a system whose behaviour is unpredictable by any machine constructible in this universe. We are importantly unpredictable save for general tendencies and patterns' (Churchland and Churchland 2005: 62). This means that we should not worry that we are just programmed robots. Although biological, cul-tural and situational factors may constrain and shape the options available to us, we can nevertheless generate autonomous responses within these conditions. To demonstrate this Richard Stevens (2002) offers a useful analogy of a jazz pianist:

> The performance will be influenced by past learning and hearing other musicians play, by genetic and other factors which determine the skill of the pianist. It will also be influenced by the pre-established musical structures which make up the tune being played. And yet a good pianist can produce a pattern of sound which is not only quite individual and unique but at the same it is so personally distinctive that a listening connoisseur could recognize who is playing after but two bars.
>
> (Stevens 2002: 216)

Although we can trace even the distinctiveness of pianist himself to various factors the sense of agency is still justified. Even a scientist (Toates 2002) whose job is to observe how our genetic makeup, upbringing and social influences are embodied in the processes within our nervous system, claims that none of these should undermine our feeling of agency. Of course, the capacity to exercise agency depends upon the integrity of certain brain processes and there are limitations to this ability (Toates 2002: 50), but reasonably healthy people should rightfully feel that they are capable of acting autonomously and rationally and expect others to treat them as such.

This expectation has a big role to play in our perception of agency. Several interesting psychological studies on attribution error show that there is a powerful tendency in humans to explain their behaviour in terms of their own characteristics, rather than in terms of the situation (Lalljee 2002). Other studies, for example, on learned helplessness (Seligman 1975) and the effect of explanatory style (Peterson 1988) suggest that the sense of control is an important part of effective psychological functioning and that ways of making sense of the world, that undermine a person's sense of control, may lead to psychological disturbance. For example, feelings of helplessness are frequently the results of repeated events over which people feel they have no control (Weiner 1992).

In spite of this many other philosophers and scientists (Libet 1985; Wegner 2002; Gregory 2005) insist that free will is an illusion. Before we consider the evidence for their theories it is important to notice, as Blackmore kept reminding us in her book (2003), that 'illusion is not something that does not exist, but something that is not what it seems' (p. 125). She also helps to clarify why the issue of free will is so confusing. The arguments presented before are not touching the most difficult issue. The issue is not about whether human beings are agents – we can safely assume that they are. It is natural for human beings as well as animals to survive 'by having boundaries between themselves and the outside world, and by taking control over certain aspects of their environment. They respond to events, make plans, and act accordingly, at least when they are not restrained or coerced' (p. 125). We also have brains that are designed for generating expectations about the future. They can distinguish between which things are inevitable and which are 'evitable'. Normal brains can discriminate what is possible to avoid with some foreknowledge of what is going to happen. According to Dennett that is what our brains are for (2005: 89). He is quite explicit in his view that the organism as a whole has free will. The problem and the question is, however, what consciousness has to do with this (Blackmore 2003). The word conscious often is lost in these debates, but to make more sense we ought to be discussing it as an issue of *conscious* free will.

To address exactly this question a famous and widely debated study was conducted by Benjamin Libet (1985). He designed a clever experiment to explore the time of appearance of a conscious decision to act. Without describing all the details and variations of this experiment I will comment only on the result that is still considered as controversial. To put it simply he found that consciousness comes too late to be the cause of the action. Further research has not only confirmed his initial findings but can demonstrate not only the lag in timing – it can even predict which hand (left or right) will be used to produce the act, *well before the person consciously intends it.*

> There has been a long controversy as to whether subjectively 'free' decisions are determined by brain activity ahead of time. We found that the outcome of the decision can be encoded in brain activity of prefrontal and parietal cortex up to 10 s before it enters awareness. This display presumably reflects the operation of a network of high-level control areas that begin to prepare an upcoming decision long before it enters awareness.
>
> (Soon et al. 2008: 543)

It appears therefore that conscious free will is after all, not responsible for our actions and decisions. But why is it so difficult to believe that this is the case? Even Libet himself suggests that consciousness may still intervene to veto the unconsciously initiated action, providing a kind of conscious 'free won't'. Claxton (1986) and Wegner (2002) both give similar and interesting explanations to this puzzle. Wegner argues that 'The experience of willing an act arises from interpreting one's thought as the cause of the act' (Wegner and Wheatley 1999: 480; Wegner 2002). An illusion is created in three steps:

1   Our brain sets about planning actions and carrying them out.
2   Although we are ignorant of the underlying mechanisms, we become aware of thinking about the action and call it intention.
3   The action occurs after the intention and so we conclude that it is the intention that caused the action.

Blackmore (2005) put this more simply: in our normal interpretation of events we think that we are going to do something and then we do it, so we think 'Ok, that means that my thoughts caused it'. But what really happens is that, 'there is some sort of brain process that simultaneously causes our awareness of an intention and also the action, and we end up thinking there's a causal relationship where there isn't' (p. 251).

Just recall what often happens when we decide to do something but intentions are unfulfilled or forgotten and something else happens instead: 'I meant to keep my cool but I just couldn't. I'm supposed not to eat pork but I forgot. I'd decided on an early night but somehow here we are in Piccadilly Circus at 4 a.m. with silly hats and a bottle of wine' (Claxton 1994: 59). What is interesting is that these types of evidence of lack of conscious will are usually dismissed. We make them disappear or reinterpret them in tricky ways. We simply don't notice how often we fail to live up to our intentions and get annoyed with those who point this out to us. We can even reinterpret our failure of control as an actual success: 'I changed my mind'.

Even in cases when our actions match our intentions the rationality of that decision is also in doubt. 'How did you draw up your list of considerations? Did you "decide" which ones to look at, or did they occur to you? How long did you take over it? Are you sure that all relevant, and no irrelevant, issues have been considered?... Were there not perhaps some semi- or sub-conscious influences on how you framed the question to yourself? How can you be sure?... Did you decide to trust some authorities and not others? How did you choose when to stop deliberating and come to a conclusion?' (Claxton 1986: 60) suggests that it makes better sense to see the relationship between thought and action as a *hit-and-miss attempt at prediction* rather than control. We may eventually learn to notice our own tendencies to respond to the situations with the resultant thought of what 'I' might do now, but this thought should be seen as a prediction referring to what the *organism* will do (p. 61). He gives an amusing illustration of how we learn and sustain our illusion of control.

> Imagine a person sitting by a stream, idly watching things float past her. After a while she notices a regularity: whenever a cork goes by, a little later a bottle follows. In order to amuse herself our observer invents a game in which she pretends not to notice the corks, and then every-so-often, out of the blue as it were, calls out 'Bottle!' – and sure enough, each time she does so, a bottle floats into view. After a while, she gets so good at the game that she is able to 'see' the cork – the signal – without any conscious recognition at all; so much so that she 'forgets' about the corks and falls prey to her own illusion. Now she is convinced of the executive power of her conscious mind, of its autonomy and author-ity, and begins to identify herself – who she really is – with this illusory sense of control. 'Look! I can *decide* "bottle"'!
>
> (Claxton 1994: 206–7, original emphasis)

Claxton (1986, 1994) makes this picture richer by showing how we come not to be aware that most of our actions are involuntary, routine or unreflective. He argues that of all our conscious experiences it is thought with which we most closely identify, and most central amongst them are thoughts that are involved in the selection and control of action: choosing, deciding, intending. In his usual ironic style Claxton (1994) describes our 'thrill of the chase' in involving ourselves in marginal matters like choosing and buying things in order 'for the Self to experience its pivotal feeling of *autonomy*. In a world where we are daily reminded that at least 99 per cent of things that affect us are beyond our control, it can be reassuring to focus intently on the 1 per cent that is currently represented by the choice of curtains for the spare bedroom' (p. 113).

However illusory and game-like this sounds, Wegner argues for an important func-tion of the mechanism that supports an illusion of conscious free will. He says that all life is a big 'whodunnit' in which we are concerned with which action is done by us and which by others. It is necessary in order for us to take responsibility for our acts and morally judge people who have done good or bad things. 'We trust each other's sense of authorship, and use it as a way of allocating punishment and rewards to people in everyday life' (Wegner 2005: 253). This system may not be perfect, but very important nevertheless and we should probably agree with Wegner.

Summary and some additional thoughts on free will

To summarize, the second story treats conscious will as an illusion. Our actions spring out of innumerable combinations of forces and connections in our brain/mind/organism constantly interacting with environment. More often than not all of these is unavailable for conscious awareness. So decisions are being made, but they are made not by a conscious rational agent, but by underlying processes. The rational self only notices the decisions being made and thinks that *it* is the author of these decisions.

But we do have responsibility for our actions because it is an action of the organism as a whole. Even those who see free will as an illusion believe that it is important for us to live as our common sense suggests, because without belief in free will it would be difficult to function among others and to take responsibility for everyday issues. So ultimately there is no free will but ordinarily there is.

And in the long run we can influence decisions by heightened awareness and reflection. With better awareness more links and neural centres are activated, allowing for better perception of situations and so more adaptive and creative actions of the organism as a whole. Without awareness only those forces and links are activated that have something to do with, probably, the strongest needs, fears, desires of individuals who perceive themselves as completely separate.

Implications of the second story of the self

The first implication of the second story of the self which may sound theoretical or too simple is the confusion between the first and the third person views of the self. Not only scientists or philosophers are prone to mix them up. We also do. If it feels to us that something exists then we may assume that it actually exists with all the consequences of deluding ourselves. Watching this tendency may save us energy and time to say the least. There are enough real issues to face in life in comparison to something as ephemeral as, for example, self-image.

Secondly, this discussion confirmed for me a well known wisdom that action speaks louder than words. It is an action rather than an articulated intent that seems to be a more true description of the person as a whole. What can be said even in principle is only a slim representation of what is actually going on in the organism before and when it acts. That is probably why Claxton implies that 'the particular way in which the act appears ... always says something general about the philosophy of life of the author, as the act itself tells us specifically about his current wishes' (Claxton 1981: 200). This is very similar to Sartre's (1997: 32) reminder that we are 'nothing else but the ensemble of [our] acts and every action betrays its values'.

In relation to free will the picture that has been painted may scare people, but interestingly enough both Claxton and Wegner agree on the immensely positive effect of accepting this view of 'free' will. Wegner (2005) says 'There are a whole lot of things that I don't have to worry about controlling because I know that I'm really just a little window on lovely machinery that's doing lots of things' (p. 255). People could be scared that giving up on control would make them worse off, which is a common elaboration of the belief that control is real, and invested in a part of me that ought to be more moral than the rest. 'The thing that does happen is the reverse. As I relax into myself, I get more and more in touch with my unity, the wholeness and integrity that my *theory* has denied' (Claxton 1986: 69, original emphasis).

And finally, realization of the above complexity in relation to the issues of deeper concern for coaching such as choices, responsibility, development, and so on can influence the coaching approach. Coaches who see the value of such a perspective do not need to doubt the client's story or intentions, but will see them as only one angle on the situation as a whole. This perspective can affect their coach-client relationship as interaction of two organisms, their view on the effort to help and on the magnitude of success/failure of coaching among many others. Much more will be discussed on the implications of these ideas in Chapter 4 and in all four chapters about practical approaches.

4 The third story: the evolving self

Evolution is an ascent towards consciousness.

P. Teilhard de Chardin, The Phenomenon of Man

This story of self is not concerned so much with what sort of thing the self is, what it is made of or what we can say about the structure and elements of it. This story is focused instead on the numerous and detailed observations of various scientists about significant changes in human beings. This story suggests that whether the self is a thing or not a thing, it is not something fixed and unchangeable, but rather, something evolving. 'It is an achievement rather than a given' (Gallagher and Zahavi 2008: 200). It also means that self-knowledge and self-understanding is not something given once and for all, but can be developed with varying degrees of success.

In this chapter we will look at a number of psychological perspectives on the evolving self such as those developed by Kegan (1982, 1994), Loevinger (1987), Graves (1970), Wilber (1979, 2000) and Torbert (1991, 2004). But first I would like to offer a brief story of Steve's working life (Box 4.1) that I hope would help us to make these theories more familiar and real.

BOX 4.1 The story of Steve's work life

Steve came to work for a large organization straight from university with enough knowledge to get the job, ready to learn more and thinking only about how much this work could advance his career and support his lifestyle. Gradually he learned the rules of teamwork, got used to seeing situations from others' point of view, grew to like his team and began to genuinely care for its success. It was particularly noticeable when his team was in competition with others. With his experience growing and showing, he was promoted to lead the team. He began to learn about the work process from the point of view of various teams and came to realize the need for collaboration rather than competition. Then Steve got promoted again and again and had to develop even wider perspectives on the work by thinking about the needs of the whole organization. But with time it came to him that although he could deliver what was needed for the organization, his personality had been somewhat squashed and his values of caring for a wider community were not well aligned

> with the values of this organization. He left this job and took another higher position in a different organization. Gradually he came to a similar realization of a mismatch, linking it this time to the nature of organizations all together. He decided to work for himself, enjoying the freedom to create his own business, and later developing his own team in accordance with his high moral standards. Much later he realized that he was embracing an even wider perspective on life. With this perspective he could work nearly anywhere as long as he could see an opportunity to contribute to the values of humanity and the world.

The story of Steve's work life, though too condensed, is deliberately constructed to show only significant changes that were happening in him as a person and the actions that followed. It does not concentrate much on the phenomenology, but you can guess what sorts of feelings about himself and the world had accompanied every stage of his life. It is unlikely that these changes were about Steve's personality and how he was different from other people. Presumably his MBTI (Myers-Briggs Type Indicator) profile, for example, did not change much throughout this process. But something about his self was changing significantly and it was possible to observe through his choices and actions. These changes in the third story of evolving self are seen as vertical or developmental changes.

This story of the self is based on research studies that suggest that people differ in ways that could not be explained by personality types, learning styles or personal preferences, all of which are usually seen as relatively stable for each individual. This story suggests that people differ not only from other people but also undergo significant changes in themselves, for example, in the way they make meaning of their experiences. The changes in these capacities occur in a logical sequence of stages throughout the life of each person. They influence the depth and complexity of what people can notice and therefore operate on and change. What is important is that this development can be influenced by other people who can provide appropriate support and challenge in a timely way. In order to be able to do this the third story suggests that coaches, for example, need to understand the mechanism of change and learn about how to identify the developmental trajectories of their clients.

As in the two previous stories of self we will begin with a brief history of what has been happening in three major strands of this psychological tradition. The first strand began with intensive research in developmental psychology which focused on changes that could be observed in children. First we should mention, of course, the important work of Jean Piaget (1976) who studied the role of cognitive structures in the development of a child and identified several distinct stages in the way children and young people think. Later his work was extended to include stages, for example, of moral reasoning (Kohlberg 1969), intellectual development (Perry 1970), reflective judgment (King and Kitchener 1994) and 'orders of mind' (Kegan 1982, 1994). The focus of these later studies was mainly on cognitive changes in adults in the way they make sense of the world and themselves in it.

The second strand is ego development, to which, as it is most relevant to the main focus of this book, I will give more attention. The term ego development was introduced by Loevinger (1976), when she discovered a new variable in her highly regarded research. As was shown previously by Sullivan et al. (1957) she found that her research subjects differed in terms of interpersonal maturity or the capacity for interpersonal integration. Loevinger wrote that she was hesitant at first about using the term 'ego' to define this factor. She was concerned that this term is closely associated with the psychoanalytic theory restricted to the first years of a child's life. But she found that no other terms were inclusive enough to describe the phenomena that she had identified. This was also my choice of the term which will be discussed later together with the ideas from Cook-Greuter's (1999) research.

The starting point of Loevinger's research was to develop an objective test of a mother's attitudes towards problems of family life. The results of her initial study were quite puzzling. First of all they did not fit with any existing theory (this is not a huge problem in itself), but they revealed a challenging anomaly. Some groups of women almost unanimously answered the questions one way; other groups almost unanimously answered the same questions in an opposite way. In spite of every effort to identify any other factors that could explain this anomaly the only one the researchers found was *ego development*. A new test was eventually constructed that helped to confirm that a range of differences between groups of women could be explained by the level of ego development. Each person seems to be progressing from one stage to the next as the result of his or her own pattern of interests and social circumstances. Table 4.1 is an example of how specific stages of ego development identified in this study (Loevinger 1987: 226) are manifested in the typical interpersonal mode of the person. We will discuss them later in this chapter in three groups (Table 4.2). Eventually these stages were further extended to include post-autonomous ego development by Cook-Greuter (1999, 2004) and action logics by Torbert (1991, 2004).

The third strand in the history of adult development theories is based on the research conducted by Clare Graves (1970). He studied 'levels of existence' which were later described as 'worldviews' and 'values' by Beck and Cowan (1996). This strand is now known as 'spiral dynamics' and is discussed in their book with a particular focus on the organizational context.

All the studies that are mentioned here are conducted in the tradition of developmental structuralism which looks for patterns that connect specific psychological

Table 4.1 Typical interpersonal modes of the person according to stage of ego-development (Loevinger 1987)

Stages of ego development	Typical interpersonal modes
Impulsive	Egocentric, dependent
Self-protective	Manipulative, wary
Conformist	Cooperative, loyal
Conscientious-conformist	Helpful, self-aware
Conscientious	Intense, responsible
Individualistic	Mutual
Autonomous	Interdependent
Integrated	Cherishing individuality

phenomena. According to this approach, individual characteristics are emergent and coming into being in a predictable and sequential way. This approach usually starts from the first person perspective as it is interested in the experiences, attitudes and personal views of people on these aspects of themselves. However, the ambition of this approach is to find observable differences and patterns in the phenomena studied. Therefore the various questionnaires and tests are designed to identify and measure personal accounts, which means the third person perspective on the first person perspective on the self.

Particularly valuable contributions to the third story of self have been made in my view by Ken Wilber (1979, 2000, 2006). He pulls together many theories and much research relevant to this approach, for example, on emotions (Goleman 1995), needs (Maslow 1954) and spiritual awareness (Fowler 1981) thus illustrating that there are many more aspects or personal qualities in us as human beings that can be observed in developmental stages. His most comprehensive model is also multidimensional. It coordinates numerous theories and explains their value in four main domains of reality: the internal self, the external self, the internal collective and external collective. According to this model development should be explored from all domains and multiple order perspectives.

Observing development according to various stages some interesting patterns are found in all developmental lines. For example:

- Stages take considerable time to develop and cannot be 'skipped', because each is built upon the previous one, and in a particular way. Wilber (2006) calls this 'holarchy', which is similar to the relationship between atoms, molecules, cells and whole organisms. Holarchy simply means that it is not possible to go from atoms to cells 'skipping' molecules.
- With each successive stage the qualities of the previous stage remain as properties of the new stage. Therefore, with each new stage, a person can use anything learned in a previous stage, like a baby who learns to walk does not at the same time forget how to crawl.
- Each developmental line (cognitive, emotional, moral, etc.) is unfolding in the same way but at a different pace for each particular person. This means that someone could be, for example, at the highest stage intellectually, the lowest stage morally and somewhere in the middle interpersonally. Figure 4.1 represents a snapshot in time of how an individual's development might look like if we were able to measure each developmental line.

Looking at this picture it is possible to see why we are so different and why it is unfair to categorize people judging them by only one quality and assuming all others to be similar. However, even the way they are drawn as all vertical may create a temptation to think that there should be one yardstick against which all of them could be measured. Some may think that there should be a line that is more important or more indicative of the overall development. Wilber (2000) though makes a very strong case against any claims that some particular lines can be central in describing development or even that it is possible at all to describe overall development.

Figure 4.1   Level of development in different lines.

> Although substantial empirical evidence demonstrates that each line devel-
> ops through these holarchical stages in an invariant sequence, nonethe-
> less, because all two dozen of them develop relatively independently, overall
> growth and development is a massively complex, overlapping, non-linear
> affair, following no set sequence whatsoever.
>
> (Wilber 1999: 291–2)

However, Wilber himself seems to privilege one particular line: a cognitive one. It is
important to notice though that he defines cognition more broadly than just intellectual capacity. In this wider sense the cognitive line is 'the capacity to take perspectives'.
Therefore cognitive development could even be measured in terms of the number of
others with whom one can identify and the number of perspectives one can take. This
creates a parallel between cognitive development and consciousness as such, if we see
consciousness as 'the degree of openness or emptiness', a 'space' in which all lines
arise. In this case 'the more phenomena in that line that can arise in consciousness, the
higher the level in that line' (Wilber 2006: 68). His integral approach to understanding
humankind is an example of how considering the whole range of perspectives is developmental in itself. In Steve's story the expansion of perspectives is probably the main
feature of the changes that happened in him in relation to his working life.

Another point of curiosity may be about how each line is divided into sections:
how stages are identified. The authors of each developmental line have, of course, their
own logic on this. The number of stages usually varies from three to fourteen. Wilber
(2006), however, suggests that it is not important 'how you slice and dice development'.

For reasons of simplicity he often illustrates as the most typical pattern the logic of Kohlberg's (1969) levels of moral reasoning. According to this theory, development starts from the *'pre-conventional level'*, which describes a narrow perspective of a person only focusing on his own needs: he is on his own with the world often against him. On the second *'conventional'* level a person's world expands to include those who are close to him. The *'post-conventional'* level expands his perspectives further to include maybe the whole world as he perceives it.

Another simplifying meta-perspective is offered by McCauley et al. (2006). They also suggest three large categories: dependent, independent and inter-independent. *Dependent* adults can coordinate their needs with the needs of others but depend on them for their approval and orientation. *Independent* adults understand themselves better and can rely on their own values and orientations in making decisions and taking actions. *Inter-independent* adults are more flexible in terms of their identity influenced by various life-contingencies and they are concerned with their own and other people's ongoing development. If you look back now on the story of Steve's working life these three levels can be clearly recognized, but there seems to be even more there that could be noticed.

Stages of development

It is not an easy task to describe the actual developmental stages. One simple problem is that there are so many interesting theories with different conceptualizations of stages and nearly all of them are relevant to coaching. Therefore it is difficult to decide which to choose and which to exclude. Another problem is that although they aim to elicit particular features of the individual, quite a few of them overlap significantly even if they claim to emphasize only their particular feature. This is not surprising – all our characteristics are interdependent and are in complex multiple relationships to the others. In some cases the authors of the theories choose to focus on more cumulative characteristics, such as ego development (Loevinger 1987) or levels of existences (Graves 1970), which makes them difficult to compare. Some theories attempt to cover the whole life-span of the individual (e.g. Kegan 1982), while others (e.g. Torbert 1991) focus on the development of adults only. Some of the latter stop earlier, but others extend their stages to the higher 'post-autonomous (e.g. Cook-Greuter 1999) or spiritual realms of development (e.g. Wilber 2000). To give a fair representation of these approaches the options are to choose one theory and to stay reasonably faithful to the main idea of it or to pull some of them together according to the criteria relevant for their particular inquiry. I choose the latter approach which I believe to be suitable for this book and I will explain my rationale for this decision.

First of all I will deliberately reduce the number of discussed stages (broad successive orders) to three (Table 4.2) and not only for the reason of simplicity. According to various statistical data these three stages seem to be the most characteristic for the majority of adults. For example, according to different sources only less than 3 per cent of the adult population reach the stages that follows these three (Torbert 1991; Beck and Cowan 1996; Wilber 2000). Therefore it is much more likely that coaches will be working with clients from these three large groups.

Table 4.2 A cumulative description of the three stages in adult development

Stages	Unformed ego	Formed ego	Reformed ego
Cognitive style (based mostly on Kegan)	Socialized mind *Ability for abstract thinking and self-reflection*	Self-authoring mind *Can see multiplicity and patterns; critical and analytical*	Self-transforming mind *Systems view; tolerance of ambiguity; change from linear logic to holistic understanding*
Interpersonal style (Loevinger and Cook-Greuter)	Dependent Conformist/self-conscious *Need for belonging; socially expected behaviour in relationships; peacemakers/keepers*	Independent Conscientious/ individualist *Separate but responsible for their own choices; communication and individual differences are valued*	Inter-independent Autonomous/ Integrated *Take responsibility for relationship; respect autonomy of others; tolerance of conflicts; non-hostile humour*
Conscious pre-occupations (Graves)	Multiplistic *Social acceptance, reputation, moral 'shoulds and oughts'*	Relativistic/Individualistic *Achievement of personal goals according to inner standards.*	Systemic/integrated *Individuality; self-fulfilment; immediate present; understanding conflicting needs*
Character development (Loevinger, Cook-Greuter and Kolhberg)	Rule-bound *'Inappropriate' feelings are denied or repressed. Rules of important others are internalized and obeyed.*	Conscientious *Self-reliant, conscientious; follow self-evaluated rules; judge themselves and critical of others*	Self-regulated *Behaviour is an expression of own moral principles. Concerned with conflicting roles, duties, value systems.*

I have chosen changes in the *ego* as a defining category in the description of developmental theories, in agreement with Loevinger (1987) who believes that ego is the 'master trait' that subsumes other developmental aspects. I refer the stages of ego development as unformed ego, formed ego and reformed ego. These stages correspond to the developmental framework that I am proposing in Chapter 7 and so will be useful as building blocks for this framework.

The stages are described in four major aspects of the individual: cognitive style, interpersonal style, conscious preoccupations and character development as most descriptive according to Loevinger (1976). The main input for each of these aspects is drawn from the theories of Kegan (1982), Graves (1970), Wade (1996), Torbert (1991) Cook-Greuter (1999) and Wilber (2000).

Cognitive style

Cognitive style represents the level of cognitive development manifested in conceptual complexity, abstract reasoning and tolerance of ambiguity (Loevinger 1976). The whole range of research (Kolhberg 1969; Sullivan et al. 1970; King and Kitchener 1994;

Commons et al. 1982; Manners and Durkin 2001; Commons 2007) found significant correlation between ego development and the above manifestations of cognitive development. As a particular example we will use Kegan's theory of orders of mind (1982, 1994). One of the valuable elements of this theory is that Kegan not only describes the developmental stages but proposes a mechanism of change from one to another by the shift from subject to object. It is a useful element for coaches who aim to influence the way individuals make meaning.

In Kegan's theory things that are a Subject can prompt us to action but cannot be observed or reflected on. We cannot stand back and take a look at them because they are part of us. Things that are an Object, on the other hand are 'those elements of our knowing or organizing that we can reflect on, handle, look at, be responsible for, relate to each other, take control of, internalize, assimilate, or otherwise operate upon' (Kegan 1994: 32). Drath (1990) gives a good description of the role of both saying that to be a Subject is to 'see with' rather than to 'see through'. He also gives a good example of 'cultural blindness':

> We see with our culture-bound norms and expectations, accept them as given, and cannot examine them for what they are – that is, we cannot see through them. Our cultural heritage is something we are, not something we have. The culture holds us; we are embedded in it and cannot rise above it. A cognitive-developmental shift, however, is possible when we become aware of culturally determined differences and the distance they create from others. Such understanding could make cultural influences an Object, opening up new ways of seeing ourselves and of relating to others.
>
> (1990: 486)

It becomes clear that the more individuals can take as Object, the more complex their worldview becomes, because they can examine and act upon more things. Therefore their conceptual complexity, abstract reasoning and tolerance of ambiguity are increasing. Some authors describe the mechanism of the shift from Subject to Object as an essential element of coaching, helping the client to build *psychological muscle* in order to hold something out from him as an Object (Berger and Fitzgerald 2002: 31). Here is an example of such a mechanism at work in the coaching process.

> In his new role of head of department a client received feedback suggesting that his way of one-to-one communication with people made some of his staff uncomfortable. He asked his coach to help him to respond to this feedback which he found puzzling. They explored this feedback together with the coach's own observations of his interactions with her and others. It appeared that the coachee's style involved unusually long pauses that people perceived as withdrawals. These apparently made those colleagues who were more self-conscious than others feel insecure. The client was not aware of this. His style was so much a part of who he was that he could not reflect on the effect of it on other people. As the result of coaching, his style from being Subject has

gradually changed into Object leading to the client's increased ability to notice it and modify it when necessary.

(Bachkirova 2010: 140)

Kegan and Lahey (2009) describe the cognitive complexity of adults changing from a 'Socialized' mind to 'Self-authoring' mind and then to 'Self-transforming' mind. At the earliest 'Socialized mind' stage people are shaped by the expectations and perspectives of other people in their personal and social environment. For example, in terms of the informational flow at work 'what I think to send will be strongly influenced by what I believe others want to hear' (Kegan and Lahey 2009: 17). They can also be highly sensitive towards the form of communication and can be influenced by the imagined subtext of the messages rather than their intended meaning. They are interested in concrete, visible aspects of experience and tend to use clichés to describe it, not seeing these as such (Cook-Greuter 1999).

During the 'Self-authoring mind' stage people enjoy the freedom of making their own judgments using their own criteria. They can step back from the social environment, evaluate it and make choices as to their role and actions. They tend to be aligned with their own belief system, their ideology or personal code; they can take a stand, set limits and create and regulate boundaries. In terms of working with others 'consciously or unconsciously I have a direction, an agenda, a stance, a strategy, an analysis of what is needed, a prior context from which my communication arises' (Kegan and Lahey 2009: 19). This may create filters to what information might come through to this person as their priority is in receiving information that has been sought. It allows a great focus and determination but could be a recipe for disaster if their plans are flawed (Berger and Fitzgerald 2002; Berger 2006; Kegan and Lahey 2009).

In the 'Self-transforming mind' stage people can stand back from their ideology or personal authority. They can see that one system, including their own is always partial; they can tolerate contradictions and conflicts and are more comfortable with multiple perspectives on issues. The logic changes from linear to holistic understanding. They may still have filters to information, but are not fused with them and at work therefore generate an atmosphere where the diversity of views is welcome (Kegan and Lahey 2009: 20).

Interpersonal style

This style represents the attitude towards interpersonal relationships, the understanding of others and the preferred type of relationship. According to developmental theories each successive stage represents a broader and more complex understanding of the self, others and the self in relation to others manifested in the better conceptualization of emotions, empathy and interpersonal style. A range of research studies confirms this proposition (Loevinger 1976; Carlozzi et al. 1983; Labouvie-Vief et al. 1989; Lane et al. 1990; Cook-Greuter 1999).

Individuals operating from the *dependent stage* are aware of other peoples' needs and can demonstrate empathy. They can subordinate their own needs to other people. However, their sense of self is derived from their connection with others. They need to be accepted and approved of and may find it difficult to make decisions when there are many important stakeholders involved in a situation. They are led by the need to belong and invest in keeping a pleasant atmosphere in their groups. They see relationships in terms of expected behaviours (loyalty, trust, being friendly, etc.) rather than in terms of deep feelings and motives (Cook-Greuter 1999).

Independent stage people can take responsibility for themselves and for tasks that concern others. They care about good communication: can express themselves spontaneously and encourage others to do so. They are capable of true empathy and can build meaningful relationships, but may invest too much in their own views and standpoint. Conflicts are seen as potentially useful if they lead to clarification and better solutions.

Those people who operate from the *inter-independent stage* are less invested in their own self-system and can integrate contradictory aspects of their interaction with other people. They can see similarities where others may see differences and therefore respect uniqueness and the development of others. McCauley et al. (2006) called this stage inter-independent to emphasize the view of the self as mutually independent and to avoid the confusion of this concept with the common understanding of interdependent, which is mutual dependence (p. 638).

Conscious preoccupations

This simply means what the person is mainly concerned with. The names for the three categories are borrowed from Graves (1970). This aspect of the developmental structure implies that *multiplistic stage* people are concerned with social acceptance and reputation: they deeply care about what other people think of them. Group norms are of high importance: 'shoulds' and 'oughts' are the focus of attention together with the sense of shame and embarrassment if they are not fulfilled.

Two other groups, *relativistic* and *individualistic,* describe people who care about the achievement of their personal goals according to their inner standards. They think about their ideals and values and try to figure out their own and other people motives and reason for behaviour. They start enjoying 'being' and 'feeling' in addition to 'doing' and become 'now' oriented. They are fascinated by the various voices within and try to find a 'true' self.

Systemic and *integrated stage* people are well tuned to psychological well-being and aim for self-fulfilment and development of others. They tend to search for the overarching meaning in their life, looking to come to terms with conflicting needs and existential issues such as freedom, authenticity and the meaning of death.

Character development

This aspect incorporates impulse control and types of moral concerns affecting individual behaviour. It may be manifested in internalized self-control, respect for the rights and individuality of others and internalized moral principles. It may also be associated with emotional self-regulation. There is substantial empirical support for developmental stages in these respects (Loevinger 1976; Kohlberg 1969; Manners and Durkin 2001).

At the *rule-bound stage* the rules are simple and strongly attached to the group they belong to. These rules are mainly internalized and obeyed. Behaviour is moral to avoid disapproval of others and failing their duty. They feel shame if their actions produce undesired results. 'Inappropriate' feelings are denied or repressed. Others with different views are morally condemned.

Conscientious stage people have fully internalized societal standards and matched them to their own standards. They are motivated to behave morally to maintain self-respect and respect of the community. They are self-regulated in relation to their own 'shoulds' which include their goals and ideals. Guilt is a central emotion if they feel that they do not live up to their own standards. They are also very critical of others.

The behaviour of *self-regulated stage* people is an expression of their own moral principles. They are aware of the often conflicting roles, duties and principles in different contexts, but can own these conflicts, orchestrate amongst them and stay reasonably balanced. They are guided by the universal ethical principles which include respect for their own and other people's individuality and autonomy.

Evaluation of the third story

I hope you can see from this cumulative description of various aspects of the person that the third story provides an important angle on the self. This story has strong support from research based on both first and third person perspectives, including long-term longitudinal studies (e.g. Kohlberg 1969). These significant and predictable changes in the nature of the self suggest the importance of including a time line in order to understand it further.

At the same time as with any theory the third story of the self has some potential blind spots and issues to consider. To start with we have to say that both the developmental theories and the measurements of development in each of them are intertwined. This means that the theory provides a framework that is very appealing and persuasive, but the glasses to examine this framework are provided in one package. You have to put them on in order to explore it, which already restricts independence of judgment. The measurement instruments, however, are very labour intensive. For example, the subject-object interview (SOI) developed by Lahey and associates (1988) is used for the assessment of 21 gradations within Kegan's orders of mind. It requires 60–90 minutes of recorded interview and a highly skilled scoring of the transcript. There is also the Washington University Sentence Completion Test used to measure Loevinger's (1976) stages, which has been updated by Cook-Greuter and Torbert et al. (2004) as the Leadership Development Profile (LDP). The assessment with these instruments could only be done through some relevant organizations. This of course has an implication for coaches in terms of their ability to judge the value of these theories and to apply them properly in practice.

To make the first of these tasks easier there is a reasonable body of research that confirms the conceptual soundness of the theories. The organizations mentioned above are also constantly working on improving inter-rater reliability among their trained scorers. The research, however, also highlights some aspects of this story that remain problematic. For example, the research studies that have been done usually use small samples, mostly from cohorts of college students in the same cultural setting. They are often concentrated on a restricted range of orders/stages therefore late stages are researched much less the earlier ones. There are still not enough longitudinal studies of the whole spectrum of stages, which is a shame because it is only in this way that the sequentiality of orders can be confirmed. Some authors also questioned several specific aspects that can potentially interfere with or even undermine the quality of measurement. These aspects are verbal fluency, educational and social background and traditional levels of intelligence (Manners and Durkin 2001; McCauley et al. 2006).

Among some other concerns, I would like to highlight the lack of research on the link between developmental stages and the level of functioning of individuals in particular contexts such as in organizations. An exception to this is research of the Torbert's group (2004). There are also serious reservations as to the prediction of progressive sequence in development. Although several longitudinal studies provide support for sequentiality of stages, they also challenge the theorized irreversibility, for example, of ego development (Kohlberg 1981; Adams and Fitch 1982; Redmore 1983; Bursik 1990; Westenberg and Gjerde 1999; Manners and Durkin 2001). Adams and Fitch (1982) in the study of change in identity over a year found in a moderate sized sample that 61 per cent of students remained stable, 22 per cent progressed, but 17 per cent regressed. The question remains as to when and why people experience stage regressions.

Implications of the third story

One of the important implications of the third story of self is the actual fact of the possibility of change in the self, which is a crucial piece of information for developmental coaches who are in the business of influencing such changes. This story also gives an indication as to the direction of progress. There seems to be strong evidence for gradual emancipation from instinctual responses, then from conformity to societal standards, then from excessive individuality towards a different mode of being where meanings are created from the widest perspective.

Coaches and clients will benefit from understanding their individual differences. It may not sound new: the same was advocated by the personality studies. However, this story describes vertical rather than horizontal changes. For example, indecisiveness in the behaviour of the client seen with the use of both lenses may lead to different coaching strategies and different interventions. In his earlier writings Wilber (1979) suggested that some psychotherapeutic approaches are better suited than others when working with people at different developmental stages. This logic may be similarly applied to coaching approaches. According to Kegan the quality of the helping process also depends on the presence of those 'who can see, recognize, and understand who the person is and who he or she is becoming . . . Support is not alone an affective matter, but a matter of "knowing"; a matter of shape, as well as intensity' (1982: 260).

And finally, developmental theories emphasize the importance of the personal growth of practitioners themselves (Bachkirova and Cox 2007). It is the coach as a person, rather than the application of particular techniques or methods, that makes a difference in coaching practice. Therefore, coaches have to be aware of their own stages of development in order to reflect on their own role in the coaching process and the dynamics of the coaching relationship. With each new stage they reach they become more capable of taking a number of perspectives on situations and of understanding more people (Bachkirova and Cox 2007). They are, thereby, able to articulate, influence and change more critical situations in the coaching process.

5 A résumé of the three stories of the self with new propositions for coaches

> Self has turned out to mean so many things, to mean them so ambiguously, and to be so wavering in its application, that we do not feel encouraged
>
> F. H. Bradley, *Appearance and Reality*

We can see from all three stories that to reach some reasonable understanding of the self is not an easy task. In spite of some courageous attempts to create theories that meaningfully link both phenomenological and metaphysical perspectives (James 1890; Strawson 1999, 2009; Velmans 2000), philosophers and scientists who have strong attachments to their viewpoint continue to debate, dismissing those who are in the other camp. The strongest voices at the moment come from neuro-sceptics who argue that it would be a fallacy to accept the literal properties of the self from the content of phenomenal self-experience. And these convictions have strong support from recent studies, for example, change blindness (see Chapter 8). However, the 'other side' very reasonably argues that it is unclear why the reality of the self should be determined on the basis of whether it mirrors exactly some sub-personal mechanisms or some external entities.

> If we were to wholeheartedly endorse such a restrictive metaphysical principle, we would declare most of the world we live in and know and care about, illusory. For someone to declare everything peculiar to human life fictitious simply because it cannot be grasped by a certain mode of scientific comprehension, not only reveals one's prior commitment to a naïve scientism, according to which (natural) science is the sole arbiter of what there is, one also self-defeatingly (no pun intended) runs the risk of undermining the very scientific realism that one champions.
>
> (Gallagher and Zahavi 2008: 213)

As we can see, both perspectives present very compelling arguments suggesting that an 'either or' standpoint probably needs to be replaced by a 'both' standpoint. Struggling with this I came to the conclusion that the problem is that there is more than one legitimate notion of self. It seems inevitable that the self could be seen differently from both perspectives: phenomenological (subjective; from the first person) and metaphysical ('objective', or more precisely – inter-subjective; from the third person). Both perspectives are important for understanding the phenomenon of the self. As a result this chapter will be addressing at least three notions of the self and the relationship they have with a common sense understanding of the self that we normally rely on in coaching.

From the phenomenological perspective we will be looking at the self as an experiential dimension postulating a simple 'I' as the most basic pre-reflective sense of self. Then from the clearly metaphysical perspective we will look at the properties and areas of the brain that are associated with the actions of the organism as a whole. We will postulate that there is a neurological network that we will call an executive centre (ego) responsible for the coherent behaviour and normal functioning of the individual in the world. Finally, we will address the notion of self as a narrative construction. We will discuss an aspect of human nature (narrator) that should explain the view of the self as we consciously and linguistically conceive. This should be consistent with phenomenology of our experience, but also make sense from the metaphysical perspective. Overall a case will be made on the basis of current findings in various studies that the three main elements for understanding the self are:

- sense of *I* as a pre-reflective self-consciousness;
- *ego* as an executive centre;
- *self-models* constructed by a *narrator* (conscious and reflective linguistic function of the mind/brain).

I as a pre-reflective sense of self

> Everyone is presented to himself in a particular and primitive way in which he is presented to no one else.
>
> Frege, *The Thought: A Logical Enquiry*

What I will be calling *I* here is an experiential dimension or a basic pre-reflective sense of self which provides a sense of experiences being 'mine'. According to Gallagher and Zahavi (2008) it entails 'a primitive form of self-referentiality or for-me-ness' (p. 50), without which the person most likely would not be able to function. It is also postulated that even animals have this sense. Claxton (1994) describes *I* as a vantage point with respect to the external world. It 'can be seen as a kind of address, a reference point in space, which the brain-mind has to take account of in computing the strength and direction of a pounce or swerve' (p. 81).

The experience being mine does not mean contrasting it with others (Husserl 2001); it simply means the first-personal givenness of experience: what I am experiencing now is presented to me, rather than to somebody else. 'It is like a source of light which, in addition to illuminating whatever other things fall within its scope, renders itself visible as well' (Frankfurt 1988: 162).

Pre-reflective self-consciousness is not the same as self-knowledge, identity or reflection (Sartre 1956; Shoemaker 1968; Brook 1994; Gallagher and Zahavi 2008). It is immediate and dynamic. In relation to self-knowledge, if someone is having an experience they automatically stand in an intimate epistemic relation to the experience, a relation more primitive than knowledge. We may call it 'acquaintance' (Chalmers 1996: 197). In relation to identity, pre-reflective self-consciousness is not static as self-identity is – it is a dynamic and temporal self-differentiation. It could be seen as a pole of identity rather than identity as such. Pre-reflective self-consciousness is also different from reflection. Reflection, by returning to past experiences and investigating them, may help to overcome the fragmentation of self-sense, which is provided pre-reflectively. But it is never the same as the actual experience at that point of time. Reflection may allow the richness of understanding of the experience with the use of a wider perspective and relevant images and linguistic ideas from memory, but there always remains a difference between the lived and the understood.

Damasio (2000: 187–9) makes a clear case for the value of this sense, which he calls pre-linguistic consciousness. According to him, it produces a nonverbal point of consciousness that is barely explicit, half hinted, but that creates the beginning of the knowing mind and the beginning of self-sense undisturbed by the fabricated verbal narratives of the brain that may not necessarily accord with the truth. The examples of split-brain research give amazing evidence of how the left hemisphere generates stories about the events observed by the right hemisphere, stories sometimes reasonable and sometimes not. Damasio believes that telling stories, in the sense of registering what happens in the form of images, is probably a brain obsession which began relatively early in terms of evolution.

To enhance our understanding of the sense of *I* we can use Damasio's (2000: 194) idea of core consciousness. Although he describes it in a third person perspective it may help to elicit the sense of I as an effect of 'a neural and mental pattern which brings together, in about the same instant, the pattern for the object, the pattern for the organism, and the pattern for the relationship between the two'. Although the individual will experience only an object in this instant all these patterns are present: 'you are the music while the music lasts'. It does not last long: with our well developed linguistic capacity the language interpretation starts pretty quickly and experience becomes more complicated by naming/labelling and possibly misinterpretations. Nevertheless, the ability of the organism as a whole to sense a direct pre-reflective contact with the environment and others is still there and worth striving for however difficult it might be.

It is important to see that *I*, as this sense of self, is not an isolated, worldless self, nor is this *I* located in the head. It means an experiential interaction of the whole organism with the world, a self-experience of a world-immersed agent. Although it may appear as a minimalist notion, so basic that it can hardly distinguish us from other animals (Claxton 1994), it is simply essential. Some have argued that no organism can survive or act without being able to distinguish between self and non-self (Dennett 1991: 414).

In terms of differentiating these notions of *I* and the notion of the narrator, that we are going to discuss later in this chapter, it is important to notice that the experiential pre-reflective *I* is a precondition for the linguistic self-models created by the narrator. Several authors argue for the existence of this primitive, pre-conceptual self from very early childhood (Gibson 1986; Neisser 1988; Rochat 2001; Gallagher 2005). They describe it as an embodied or ecological self that starts with the exploration of their own bodies. It manifests itself as an integrated sense of where I am spatially in relation to the immediate environment, and what I am capable of doing in any particular situation.

Our primitive, pre-conceptual selves do not make us unique. A description of my experiential self will not differ significantly from a description of your experiential self. However, the narrative self-models will be significantly different. I will be defining myself through my personal history, my moral and intellectual convictions, my relationships with others and most importantly – through my actions.

This pre-reflective *I*, being unfocused and unarticulated, serves the pre-conscious registration of stimuli, non-intentional passive tuning to changing situations and automated responsiveness. With language and other social capacities our engagements with the world become immensely more complex, however this first feature should not be forgotten by coaches. It is crucial that influencing and relationship, the most significant themes of coaching, need to be looked at with this notion of self in mind and we will discuss later how developmental coaches may benefit from this.

Thinking about the organism from the third person perspective

> Language cuts the world up, though the world itself is seamless and systemic.
> Guy Claxton, 1994

Now, when we turn to the third person perspective it feels a little bit more justified to use diagrams to describe the relationship between different elements of human nature. Let us begin with the broadest view, assuming that human beings are complex, open, adaptive, dynamic systems. These systems include physical brains and bodies. These bodies and brains are aspects of wider physical and social systems. This so far depicts a non-controversial side of the story. It becomes more complex when we turn to the mind and so we need to proceed slowly. I will be describing all other proposed elements of the self in this story illustrating them graphically and populating the original Figure 5.1 with each of the new concepts. Figure 5.5 will include all elements necessary to describe this story. We will need these concepts to discuss in the next section of the book what the tasks of developmental coaching are, and why.

Taking a human being as a unit of analysis we start with the relationship between the body and the mind. The mind is only a small part of the whole organism, much smaller than indicated by the proportions in Figure 5.1. By mind we mean all psychological states and processes that may or may not be conscious.

Rider and elephant relationship

The conscious mind is much smaller in comparison to unconscious and automatic functioning. Only a tiny, rather special, fraction of brain states have conscious concomitants. I will be using the analogy of the *rider* and the *elephant* to illustrate that the role of the conscious mind, as a rider in the functioning of the whole organism is grossly exaggerated. I borrowed this metaphor from Haidt (2006), but use one of these two terms slightly differently: the elephant is not only the unconscious mind but the

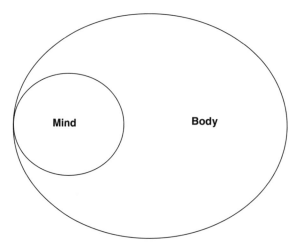

Figure 5.1   Relationship between the mind and the body.

whole organism minus the conscious mind. The job of the rider is to think, interpret and make meaning of experiences using language and imagination, but it is the elephant – the rest of the organism – that engages with the environment and acts (see Figure 5.2).

The rider (our conscious mind) usually operates as if it is in charge of the whole organism. We feel a sense of agency and control. Accepting that it is natural and probably inevitable for human beings to feel this way, I suggest, nevertheless a different proposition and add more evidence to it in addition to what has already been discussed in Chapter 3 of the second story of the self.

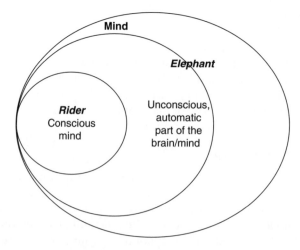

Figure 5.2   Relationship between conscious and unconscious parts of the mind.

A long time ago Freud indicated that the proportion of conscious to unconscious in our psyche is very unequal. He believed that for the most part we do not know why we act the way we do. Even ego according to Freud is not entirely conscious. Although the task of the ego is to check 'reality' and to coordinate between the demands of id and superego, ego itself is just a consequence of deep psychological conflict between the conscious and unconscious. This was a significant insight into human nature that produced useful approaches to the treatment of serious psychological problems and to deeper understanding of ourselves in our everyday relationships and conflicts. One of the positive outcomes of the Freudian legacy is that nobody now can afford to ignore the role of unconscious both in psychotherapy and in coaching (Lee 2010). However, the negative outcome is somewhat pathologizing of the unconscious: 'Instead of being an intrinsic, valuable, even vital, ingredient of psyche, the unconscious became seen as both a contentious hypothesis, and a source of disruption and disorder, associated with mad and violent storms that could threaten the civilization of mind and society' (Claxton 1994: 157). This probably contributed to the long period of unfair value balance in western societies glorifying rationality and neglecting the unconscious together with emotions. Thankfully since Freud we have learned much more about the role of the unconscious and its balance with the conscious. It is well accepted now that what goes on in the nervous system is unconscious and our conscious experiences depend upon unconscious processing – even thinking could go on without consciousness (Blackmore 2003). There are well-researched cases that demonstrate for example that some brain-damaged patients can perform complex sensory-motor skills without any awareness that they are performing them. This suggests that consciousness may serve only a monitoring role and is not necessarily involved in individual motor acts (Toates 2002: 82). Some amazing examples demonstrate what people can do when consciousness is absent altogether.

> A sleep-walker, for example, may carry out elaborate actions and even hold a simple conversation without waking up. Stranger things still can happen after brain injury. A person with damage to the visual cortex may lack all visual sensation, be consciously quite blind, and none the less be capable of 'guessing' what he would be seeing if he could see. I have met such a case: a young man who maintained that he could see nothing at all to the left of his nose, and yet could drive a car through busy traffic without knowing how he did it.
>
> (Humphrey 2002: 67)

At the same time we can say, yes, these are interesting examples, but they do not reflect how normal people function. In reality we feel that we process the information consciously and it certainly contributes to our actions. This is true to some extent, some information is processed consciously, but even this fact, paradoxically, can put the power of the conscious under another big question mark. In terms of the amount of information that can be held at a point in time, conscious processing of information is much more focused and therefore limited, in comparison to unconscious processing. Some investigators (e.g. Baars 1988) claim that we can only hold one item at a time in conscious awareness. A new item will displace the old. However, if we observe not even the most extreme activities but a simple act of driving or cooking we can notice how many different functions are performed at the same time. This is very characteristic of unconscious processing when many separate parallel operations can be carried out (Toates 2002: 82). It seems that if we only relied on conscious processing of information not much would be done.

There are even more radical views on the limited role of consciousness in comparison to the whole body. Some of them suggest that perhaps intelligence does not reside in consciousness, but it is the body and the whole organism that are the holders of intelligence. The research in neurobiology that gives interesting information towards such a proposition was conducted by Pert (1997). She claimed that the immune system is very much 'brain-like' when she identified molecules from the peptide family that communicate between neural and immune systems. She proposes that white blood cells, for example, could be seen as bits of brain 'floating around the body'. Certain chemicals that can only be found throughout the nervous system also were found in both the endocrine system and the immune system. Apparently they are also located in certain parts of the body, such as the heart or the lining of the gut, giving a different meaning to the metaphorical expression of 'gut feeling'. The implication of these findings is that mind might not be local, but distributed around the body, the body might be the unconscious mind (Pert 1997).

How did it happen then that in our ordinary perception of things the rider takes all the credit that it does not deserve? This is how Claxton summarizes his analysis of the role of consciousness in the evolutionary process:

> Originally associated with a marvellous mechanism for spotting and responding to basic emergencies, it has become, through an interlocking series of evolutionary accidents and coincidences, primarily a mechanism for constructing dubious stories whose purpose is to defend a superfluous and inaccurate sense of self.
>
> (Claxton 1994: 150)

He gives a comprehensive description of these accidents and coincidences in a very convincing way. Other thinkers also pointed to these unfortunate turns in human evolution when the conscious mind took centre stage (Krishnamurti and Bohm 1985). Haidt (2006) speculates about other influences during this process on the basis of reasonably recent history. In comparison to previous history, he suggests that twentieth-century technology gave people more control over their physical world mainly through rational thinking. Social sciences were proposing the idea that people are rational agents who set goals and pursue them by using information and available resources. These views and values weakened the reputation of the unconscious probably more than the Freudian legacy of the dark side of the psyche.

However, it is gradually becoming obvious that the power of the rider is not as large as we might like to see it. For example our modern theories about rational choice and information processing do not adequately explain the weakness of the will. It is obvious that people continue to do what they know is not good for them. Even if they try to exercise self-control the controlling processes are costly and cause what is called ego depletion (Baumeister et al. 1999). Coaches themselves can give millions of examples of how well-intended plans of clients just do not get materialized or many unintended behaviours keep happening. So if it is not a rider that is in charge of the organism, who is? The next proposition of ego and mini-selves should move us closer to answering this question.

Ego and mini-selves

As we said at the beginning of this chapter there are at least three legitimate notions of self that have to be present at the same time in order to make sense. The sense of *I* was the first and the ego is the second. Although I am using this term after Freud you will see that the nature of the ego that I propose is quite different from his. The main feature of this notion of the self is its role in action. I will be making a case that the organism's engagements with the world are facilitated by numerous 'mini-selves' that seem to be translating various needs and functions of the person into actions. Most of them are unconscious. I am going to call this network of mini-selves an executive centre or 'ego' (see Figure 5.3).

Studies in neuroscience suggest that there are various points of activation in the mind/brain which correspond to the involvement of the whole organism in performing various life tasks. If we look in a simplified way at what happens from the very sensation of the internal need or external stimulus to the activation of certain areas of mind/brain, then to the performed action and given feedback to mind/brain, we can say that this cycle represents, to some extent, our traditional view of the role of the self. This view of self typically implies that the self, somewhere in the middle of this cycle, is responsible for all actions, which we now know is not the case. If however we apply the term

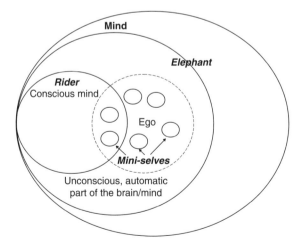

Figure 5.3   Relationship between ego and mini-selves.

mini-self to each particular pattern of activation in each particular experiential cycle then this term could be justified. So we will use this term 'a mini-self' for a combination of brain/mind states and processes that are involved in the whole organism's engagement with a certain task. To be slightly more precise, mini-self is a particular pattern of links between different areas of the brain that become activated or inhibited when the organism is involved in an act. These patterns may involve not only sensory stimuli, but memory, cognition, interpretation of meaning, and so on. They may allow for adaptation to the internal state of the organism and external conditions (physical and social). Action also may not necessary be a physical act. It could be manifested in speech or even in restraining from action.

An example of strong support for this picture of mind/brain work, well supported by empirical research, comes from the neuroscientist Gazzaniga (1985) who studied the split brain – the brain where the *corpus callosum* (the bridge between the two sides of the brain) is cut for surgical reasons.

> I think this notion of linear, unified conscious experience is dead wrong. In contrast, I argue that the human brain has a modular-type organization. By modularity I mean that the brain is organized into relatively independent functioning units that work in parallel. The mind is not an indivisible whole, operating in a single way to solve all problems. Rather, there are many specific and identifiably different units of the mind dealing with all the information they are exposed to. The vast and rich information impinging on our brains is broken up into parts, and many systems start at once to work on it. These modular activities frequently operate apart from our conscious verbal selves.
>
> (Gazzaniga 1985: 4)

To describe the mechanism of mini-selves working in the mind/brain we could also use an interesting visual image suggested by Claxton (1994). He describes the brain as a discotheque of octopuses: some of them are awake, some are asleep most of the time. Those who are awake can tickle others to make them awake. When some of them receive impulses from outside through their mingling and dancing they transfer this to others who stimulate the action of the organism. But none of these octopuses is the king. When they are mingling, each to various degrees of involvement, the organism can perform many different functions. A group of octopuses would be a mini-self.

So in the involvement of the whole organism with various tasks we could say that various mini-selves become formed in each particular moment of time and reappear consistently in the long run. For example it could be a mini-self that serves the organism when it is thirsty or mini-self that is responsible for driving. Some mini-selves are responsible of a single action and are comparatively simple, but some could be more complex, for example, the one that operates when I am in the company of certain people, the one that works when I am critical of myself, and so on. Some are very complex and reflect a particular type of behaviour or even a manifestation of personality traits of the individual. That is why some theories of sub-personalities (Rowan 2009) and multiple personalities can be seen to be in agreement with this part of the theory.

Sometimes we can be aware of two or more different mini-selves fighting each other at the same moment.

> I am often confronted by the necessity of standing by one of my empirical selves and relinquishing the rest. Not that I would not, if I could be both handsome and fat and well dressed, and a great athlete, and make a million a year, be a wit, *a bon-vivant*, and lady-killer, as well as a philosopher; a philanthropist, statesmen, warrior, and African explorer, as well as a 'ton-poet' and saint. But the thing is simply impossible. The millionaire's work would run counter the saint's; the *bon-vivant* and the philanthropist would trip each other up.
>
> (James 1999: 73)

On the one hand we can say that all of these mini-selves are unconscious because we cannot be aware of the working of the brain that corresponds to our engagement with the world. But we may be quite familiar with the manifestation of the whole cycle and recognize the emotional/cognitive and behavioural patterns associated with it. We can say: yes, I recognize this mini-self.

Some studies that involve therapeutic hypnosis provide interesting evidence of quite different personalities revealed under hypnosis, which Watkins (1993) calls ego-states. They could be as large as being able to include, for example, various behaviours and experiences activated in one's occupation. Or they could be as small as representing behaviours and feelings that were elicited in school at the age of 6. Studies of multiple personality disorder (MPD) also provide interesting evidence. But even apart from findings from clinical psychology we can see that the idea that we all have multiple personalities is quite plausible if we use a simple definition of personality as a coherent and characteristic way of seeing, thinking, feeling and behaving. In early childhood, when we do not have an agenda of being consistent, a small shift of emotion or attention can transform one 'coherent and characteristic way' into another as if by magic:

> Hence when five-year-old Mandy puts on Mum's high-heels and strides down the hallway 'being' a supermodel there is little or no connection in her head with the tomboy Mandy who fought her brother for possession of the rocking horse the day before; or the studious Mandy who spent all morning trying to learn her alphabet.
>
> (Carter 2008: 27)

In adulthood the famous psychological studies by Milgram (1963) and Zimbardo (1991) show how personalities as defined above can dramatically change to match a different situation and what is required from them. In Milgram's experiment various individuals from the most caring professions were administering a significant level of electric shock to other individuals when this was demanded of them by an authority figure. Similarly in the Zimbardo's prison experiment normal students revealed 'emerged' coherent personalities of an apparently sadistic nature. Both experiments suggest that human behaviour is much more under the control of situational forces than most of us

Figure 5.4   The image of the working of mini-selves.

recognize and want to acknowledge. This is not such a controversial idea: we recognize that we have different sides to our self which are influenced by circumstances. However beneath these sides we tend to believe in the authentic or true self. The point of this chapter is that there is no authentic self – only these different sides or what we call here mini-selves. 'Every new situation gives a shake to the kaleidoscope of my personality' (Claxton 1994: 124).

To summarize: each mini-self is responsible for its own engagement with the world. They can work in parallel as different configurations of the patterns of neural activation. This is only possible because most of this activity is unconscious. Many different mini-selves serve the person at the same time. Now when we have an idea of mini-selves we can introduce the overarching term 'ego' meaning a combination or network of mini-selves. Ego is not something distinct and tangible. It is a cumulative result of the working of mini-selves, which is manifested in functions and abilities of the whole organism in action. It is a neurological network through which the needs and desires of the organism are translated into action or as Damasio (2000: 23) suggests – 'a collection of brain devices whose main job is the automated management of the organism's life'. To continue the image of machinery, Figure 5.4 illustrates how our mini-selves do their job in the overall mechanism of the ego.

We cannot say that the entire ego is unconscious. It makes use of our memory, thinking and reflective processes. Our conscious abilities are important for the ego in helping to deal with life tasks by becoming more efficient in predicting the behaviour of the whole organism in various circumstances. It allows for a more efficient functioning of the organism and the emotional contentment that comes from the sense of mastery when dealing with one's environment.

The big question remaining is what connects all the work of the mini-selves; how is this miracle of unification achieved? We have already discussed that it cannot be a supervisory Self which emerges from nowhere and takes control. Humphrey (2000) explains this unification by the power which is inherent in all mini-selves for, literally, their own 'self-organization' (p. 36).

> I may indeed be made up of many separate sub-selves, but these selves have come to belong together as the one Self that I am because they are engaged in one and the same enterprise: the enterprise of steering me – body and soul – through the physical and social world. Within this larger enterprise each of my selves may indeed be doing its own thing: providing me with sensory information, with intelligence, with past knowledge, goals, judgements, initiatives, and so on. But the point – the wonderful point – is that each self doing its own thing shares a final common path with all the other selves doing their own things. And it is for this reason that these selves are all *mine*, and for this reason that their experiences are all *my experiences*. In short, my selves have become co-conscious through collaboration.
>
> (Humphrey 2000: 35–6, original emphasis)

This type of collaboration that Humphrey alludes to is in effect a description of the ego that can be developed to various degrees in each individual at different stages of their life. According to its level of coherency and maturity the ego can be unformed, formed or reformed in a similar pattern as we described in Chapter 4. It is interesting that in some cognitive-developmental theories the way the ego is described is comparable with my definition. For example, this is how Cook-Greuter (1999) describes ego as a process: 'the function of ego as a process is to organize, synthesize and integrate experiences from both internal and external sources and to mediate among them' (Cook-Greuter 1999: 39). Although, in my vision of ego I do not attach such importance to cognition as most cognitive-developmental authors do, I agree with them on the crucial role of a well-developed ego as a prerequisite for further development. Even those who aim for a spiritual route, (which often implies a quite different and ill-defined notion of ego), have to be aware of the warning from nearly all thinkers in this field that 'You have to be some-body before you can be no-body' (Engler 1986: 17). In my view of ego as an executive centre which satisfies the need of the whole organism to function, there is no need even to try to eliminate it. This ego is not responsible for obstacles to spiritual development. What is will be discussed next.

And finally how would we know that ego, in the sense that we use here, is developed? The most simple sign of it would be the capacity of mind/brain to act or refrain from action if necessary in a way that reasonably satisfies the organism as a whole with its multiplicity of needs and tasks. As the result of this developed capacity a person is normally able to take ownership of the past, withstand anxiety about the future and build relationships with others without losing the sense of who they are. One of the first tasks for developmental coaches will be to develop a sense of the state of the client's ego from the goals and issues they want to deal with.

Narrator and *self-models*

> Just as I can spin a hypothetical story to account for your funny little ways, so am I able to theorize about myself.
>
> Claxton, 1994

In the second story of the self the traditional assumptions implying that the self is a pure identity pole or a real thing in the mind, were consistently criticized. Gallagher and Zahavi said that the information-processing systems of the mind/brain simply 'caught up in a naïve-realistic self-misunderstanding' (2008: 199). But who or what can we hold responsible for this misunderstanding? In order to find the 'perpetrator' we have to introduce the third notion of self. According to it the self is a narrative or model or story told by the *Narrator*. Although the self cannot be found amongst the fluctuating clusters of different functions and states of the mind/brain it can be conceived of as a centre of narrative gravity (Dennett 1991). Therefore, you will not find a self in Figure 5.5 because with this third notion the self is a theory/model/story continually constructed and reconstructed by the narrator – it is like various versions of '*me*'. The narrator is also not a physical or mental substance – it is a linguistic function of the conscious mind that operates when the person attends to himself or herself. And

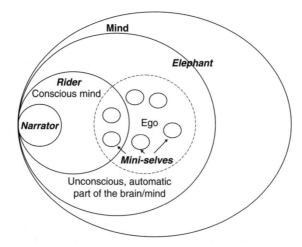

Figure 5.5   Relationship between ego, narrator and mini-selves.

again Gazzaniga (1985) is convinced about the existence of such a role to account for the data he gathered in his research on the split brain.

> According to my model, the brain is constructed in modular fashion in which particular modules would be free to respond to the literalness of environmental contingencies, yet a brain system built in a modular way would also need a single interpreter to explain the various behaviours emitted over time by the modules, enabling a human to construct a unified theory of self, an activity most of us have carried out. It turns out the brain is organized in precisely such a fashion.
>
> (Gazzaniga 1985: 195)

The narrator works to present a good story about the role of self in relation to what is happening to the whole organism. The story is created by looking outwards at the behaviour and how others react to us. 'My character reveals itself in the style with which I pursue my goals and go about my business' (Claxton 1994: 90). It may also include feelings and experiences associated with various mini-selves in action. By making use of external observations, familiarity with some mini-selves, information from memory and imagination the narrator weaves all of this into a story that with any luck may capture to some extent the live organism in its complexity and engagements with the world.

The stories created by the narrator are not the work of a historian – our conscious mind (rider with narrator) does not have access to the real causes of behaviour; 'it is more like a work of historical fiction that makes plenty of references to real events and connects them by dramatizations and interpretations that might or might not be true to the spirit of what happened' (Haidt 2006: 143).

One of the main and most fundamental stories is a theory of self as a coherent (uniting the various experiences in one), separate, continuous unit which has various attributes. When the narrator is awake one of its main jobs is to sustain this story. It is interesting that sometimes we can even capture the moment when the narrator's working shift begins:

> When I used to wake up in the middle of the night not knowing where I was, I could not even be sure at first who I was; I had only the most rudimentary sense of existence, such as may lurk and flicker in the depths of an animal's consciousness...But then...out of a blurred glimpse of oil-lamps, of shirts with turned down collars, [I] would gradually piece together the original components of my ego.
>
> (Proust 1981: 5)

This notion of self is specifically human because it is based on the use of language. Sometime in evolution, language offered us new avenues for meeting the ever more complex demands of living in society. Language came to be used when we needed to make our experiences relatively coherent and integrated over longer time periods. With language we extended our biological boundaries to encompass a life of meaningful experiences. And it is language by means of which experiences, behaviours and associated mini-selves are combined into language-based conglomerations of character that we use to describe ourselves. According to Dennett we cannot prevent ourselves from 'inventing' our selves in communication with others (1991: 418).

The role of others in one's character should not be underestimated. When I interpret myself in terms of a life story, I might be both the narrator and the main character, but I am not the sole author. 'The beginning of my own story has always already been made for me by others and the way the story unfolds is only in part determined by my own choices and decisions' (Gallagher and Zahavi 2008: 201). The values, ideals and goals that constitute the models of self are conditioned by the community of which one is part. So in this sense one cannot be a self on one's own, but only together with others, as part of a linguistic community. In turn, the story being created not only shapes one's own self, but provides a framework for understanding others.

In psychological literature this story of self used to be discussed under the name of self-concept which Baumiester (1999) calls 'the time-worn notion'. This term has been replaced with a new one – 'self-schemata' (Markus 1999) – a cognitive generalization about the self which is derived from past experience and which organizes the processing of self-related information. The new word is different from self-concept because individuals can have multiple and even conflicting self-schemas, which resonates with the description of self-models or stories by the narrator as presented here. Individuals with articulated schemas apparently demonstrate a better ability to process information about themselves in this domain, predict their behaviour and resist 'counter-schematic' information about themselves (Markus 1999). It appears then that the effort that coaches put in, in helping clients to know their self-schemas, is fairly justified.

There wouldn't be much of a problem with the functioning of the narrator and its stories of the self if we were satisfied with the fact of the variety and multiplicity of these stories. But the ambition of the narrator is to create an overarching self and it invests too much in sustaining its significance over time. For example, when our actions seem not to fit with the expectations of this self the narrator works very hard to build a plausible account of what happened, ignoring some details and exaggerating others at the expense of a real account. This self-created system may become so important that all the survival resources of the whole mind/brain/body system could become mobilized and dedicated to it (Martin 1998). 'The trivial can take precedence over the biologically fundamental. People can kill, even kill themselves, in order to avoid embarrassment, or to gain a material advantage that they do not really need' (Claxton 1994: 108).

There are two levels of confusion created by the narrator. The first and most important one is between an agent/an organism/an individual revealed in action and the self-story put together by the narrator. Claxton describes this as the most fundamental problem which would be very important for coaches to understand.

> ...science, from one end, and mystical experience, from the other, give us descriptions of the 'actor' that are quite unlike the 'character' that I experience and remember myself to be. For the true actor is (like the people inside the pantomime cow) in practice unknown to us, and in principle unknowable – whereas I think I know the 'character' rather well. And the true actor is a

system that included much of what I think of as 'Me', but is much wider and deeper. The 'character' is individual, while the actor is ecological. Who we are is fundamentally misrepresented by the Narrator.

(Claxton 1994: 118)

This level of confusion is well illustrated by the cognitive dissonance theory that suggests that if we have a belief about what we do but we are confronted by the fact that we do something different instead, we feel very uncomfortable and need to find a way to release the tension caused by it. So we might engage in all sorts of self-justifications. Gazzaniga (1985) provides a reasonable explanation for this phenomenon.

What has never been clear in dissonance theory, however, is why the organism engages in the behaviour that is at odds with a belief in the first place. Why do all the conflicts develop? Enter the answer from our review of brain research. I suggest it is because our brains are organized in terms of independent modules, each capable of action, of carrying out activities that test and retest the beliefs that are being maintained by our dominant left brain's language and cognitive systems. The conflict is produced by a mental module eliciting a behaviour, a module that can function independently from the dominant, language-based system of the left half-brain.

(Gazzaniga 1985: 139)

The second level of confusion is in the relationship between the models of the self and a conglomerate of these. If we were satisfied with an idea of a community of selves, as changing models that take the stage in changing situations, it would be less problematic. A careful observation of inconsistencies in our self-presentation would support this as a sensible attitude. But we seem to be aiming for more than that. We want to support an image of one unified and consistent self over time that provides integrity and identity. The narrator cannot relax, it keeps working on the synthesis of stories making up a self and so essentially misrepresenting it (Fingarette 2000).

Finally let us emphasize that there is no significant correspondence between mini-selves (as constituting ego) and various self-models created by the narrator. It would be great if there was, and probably gradually the narrator may become more observant and wise in creating stories that reflect much more closely the engagements of the whole organism with the world. But meanwhile the confusion remains and although it is tempting to think about both the rider and the narrator as *the self* and the centre of agency and control, their role is no more than advisors to the organism as a whole. The sooner we realize this the sooner we can begin educating our narrator in everyday life and in coaching.

Summary

To summarize this section for use in developmental coaching and for avoiding confusion with the concept of self, let us agree on the following:

- There is no self in the sense of a homunculus in the brain – it is a fiction.
- There are at least three notions of self that reflect the way that the organism works: a pre-reflective sense of self; an executive centre or ego, as a network of mini-selves; and self-models or versions of me, created by the narrator.
- The notion of ego is particularly important for developmental coaches, because 1) it is associated with action; and 2) it is the stage of ego development (unformed, formed and reformed) that may indicate the need of working in a different way with each particular client.
- And finally, it is impossible to eliminate the use of the word 'self' from our vocabulary. You will see it in the book sometimes in a pure linguistic sense, like talking about our*selves*. When it is necessary to be precise I will use one of the three notions discussed in this chapter or another meaning attached specifically to it in the subtitle of the book: working with the self. We are going to discuss this in the next section.

PART 2
A theory and framework for developmental coaching

6 Introduction to Part 2

In relation to the title of this book so far we have addressed two questions: 'what is development?' and 'what is the self?' This was necessary to be explicit about my view on human nature and the role of self in it before the approach to coaching that is built on this view is introduced. This should make it clear why and how I have made many decisions about the nature and practice of developmental coaching. In this section we can now discuss two further questions that were posed in the Introduction:

- What is the role of coaching in development?
- What does 'working with the self' mean?

As my main intention is to develop a practical approach that is underpinned by theory, I would like to start by describing what I believe should be present in a fully fledged theory-based approach to coaching. Ideally all essential elements from Table 6.1 have to be present and explicitly described, from the main theoretical assumptions to practical interventions.

Table 6.1 Essential elements of a theory-based approach to coaching as represented in the book

Number	Essential elements of a theory-based approach to coaching	Where addressed in the book
1	Main concepts and assumptions about human nature congruent with the proposed theory	Introduction and Part 1 Particularly Chapter 5
2	Conditions for change and development to occur	Chapter 7
3	Obstacles to development	Chapter 7
4	Mechanism of change and development	Chapter 8
5	Developmental process/framework	Chapter 9
6	Tasks and goals of coaching	In each chapter of Part 3
7	Essential processes and dynamics involved	In each chapter of Part 3
8	Role of the coach and relationship with a client	In each chapter of Part 3
9	Methods and techniques for facilitation of change and development	In each chapter of Part 3
10	Advantages and limitations of the approach	Chapters 7, 9 and Conclusions

As far as the first requirement from the list in Table 6.1 is concerned, in the Introduction I have described in brief the main concepts involved in the description of the theory. Then the whole of Part 1 was devoted to the main concepts and assumptions about human nature with Chapter 5 specifying my position. We will start this part with the summary of the main points again in order to be clear how the steps that we took towards understanding the self in Part 1 can serve as a foundation for the theory of developmental coaching. The next chapter of this part will be about the nature of change and how change may lead to development. The obstacles preventing those changes will be addressed there at the same time. In Chapter 8 we will discuss the mechanisms of development, and these will be closely connected to the ways of working with the obstacles to development. The developmental process will be discussed in the Chapter 9 in the light of the new developmental framework consisting of four stages. The elements 6 to 9 of the theory-based approach will be explored in Part 3 in separate chapters according to each of the four stages of ego development. My thoughts on evaluation of the approach are described in Chapters 7, 9 and 15.

7 The main principles of developmental coaching

Man's mind is designed to select the best compromise between what he wants to do and what he can do.

Claxton, 1981

In the introduction we discussed how development is understood in this book. It is seen as a combination of changes in the organism manifested in a sustained, increased capacity of the client to engage with and to influence their environment and to look after their internal needs and aspirations. These changes may happen spontaneously, as a result of the engagement of the organism with the environment. However, we are working in a field that is interested in helping individuals to change what and when they wish. We are therefore looking to identify internal predispositions in the client which could affect the pace of development. But more than anything else we are interested in finding out which external conditions such as appropriate support and challenge can help a person to become more conducive to development and which tools are appropriate to use in this process.

Any kind of coaching can play a role in this process, if we define coaching in the most general sense as 'an individualized process of facilitating change in people with the focus on specific targets and/or enriching their lives'. It could be coaching as a *conversation* – an interactive process that unfolds in time and simply describes what happens between two people who are engaged in such a conversation. In this meaning coaching can be seen as widespread in practically any setting and between all sorts of people. We can say that parents, tutors, friends, colleagues and managers may be coaching on a regular basis if in their own way they help another person to process whatever is important for them. Coaching in this sense is a conversation in which a topic of importance for one person becomes a focus of attention for both. Another use of the word 'coaching' is 'a service or practice', offered by a professional with some guarantee of quality ensured by his/her relevant competencies (knowledge of the process, necessary skills for facilitating it, professional attitude to relationship, etc.). An important element of coaching in this meaning is that the parties have an implicit and explicit contract that sets a context, conditions, responsibilities and an initial focus of work (Bachkirova and Kauffman 2009).

In the second meaning of 'coaching as a professional practice' there are various genres of coaching that may focus on some specific aspects of the individual. For example, sport coaching implies that the person is coached as a sportsperson. If we think about skills coaching we have in mind that aspect of the person that is involved in using this particular skill, like an 'actor', who enacts a skill. When we think about performance coaching it is a worker, the professional side of a person that is being coached. In leadership coaching we coach a leader or in executive coaching we coach an executive. All these processes can have a developmental effect on the individual as a whole. But only in developmental coaching are we explicit from the very beginning that our intention is to coach the whole individual even when the goals of coaching are specific. We aim to develop wider human capacities that may have an effect on all areas of that person's life.

It is important for developmental coaching that the coach understands how elements of the client's self operate in the functioning of their whole organism. That is why, in Part 1, we discussed in detail the following three notions of self that help us separate, and at the same time, emphasize, three different modes of who we are and the way we change. These three notions are:

- *Pre-reflective sense of self,* which is the most basic notion of self that emphasizes our first-person pre-linguistic sense of being separate from our environment and active in it, simply because of being a living organism. It could be called 'a centre of awareness'.
- *Executive centre or ego, as a network of mini-selves,* is probably the most important notion of self for coaching, because it is through the multiplicity of mini-selves that we engage in numerous experiential cycles and can function in the world. This network of mini-selves is designed to start from certain opportunities and motivations and to activate sophisticated and flexible patterns of response. Therefore, the ego, functioning mainly subconsciously, is responsible for satisfying our needs by acting in a straightforward way when these needs are unambiguous. However, when there is greater ambiguity, complexity or greater leisure the mini-selves may involve conscious layers of information from memory, perception or beliefs. When more conscious elements become involved in various mini-selves we may develop a habit of delaying a final evaluation and spend more time looking for subtler layers of significance so becoming more conscious. We may become aware of drives and instincts represented in some mini-selves being involved in conflicts between themselves or with the conscious rider. We call this network 'an executive centre', not in a sense that it is the main one, but in a sense that it is involved in executing actions.
- *Self-models or various versions of 'me', created by the narrator,* are conscious stories or theories of self that we think we are. These stories are put together because of our ability to use language. They may correspond to actual mini-selves, or perhaps not at all. A combination or potential synthesis of these self-models can be called 'a centre of identity'.

I call these aspects or notions of self 'centres' only for reasons of uniformity and simplicity. Only the first of these centres may feel like a centre from the phenomenological perspective. Neither the executive centre, nor the centre of identity, does in fact resemble a centre in the sense of the epicentre of a storm. If this were the case we would be tempted to see the self in its old meaning of a homunculus. A 'centre' that I want you to have in mind is probably more close to the meaning of centre as in 'shopping centre' where a lot of things are happening but there is no one command centre from which the activity is regulated or just being influenced. Unfortunately, neither science nor philosophy can explain yet the intricacies in the operations of all three centres. My intention therefore is to describe the self through metaphors that at least do not contradict the current findings of science and the most plausible, in my view, theories of philosophers. I am aware though that these metaphors are not in agreement with common sense, but this is a step that I believe needs to be taken sooner or later.

The challenges of developmental coaching

The task of the developmental coach is to be aware of the complexity of the self and to engage with all three centres in order to facilitate change in the client. However, this task is associated with big challenges (Table 7.1). The first challenge may start from the very beginning: if the client wants to change, where does this intention come from? It might be a reflection of a genuine need of the organism as a whole that was picked up by the rider and well formulated by the narrator in a new story of the self that wants to change. Or this could be a misguided and filtered perception based on cultural expectations which again is simply translated by the narrator into a plausible story. The coaching process will inevitably be affected by the source of these intentions. Quite often coaches do not even ask this question: the client presents the goal to work on and they go ahead engaging with it as, for example, the GROW model suggests. It has been argued however that these first goals often become redundant in the course of coaching (Clutterbuck 2009). Developmental coaches, I would argue, need to take time and effort to find out how this goal/intention is grounded in the elephant. They may also need to explore what self-models are associated with this goal and what other self-models may hinder the process.

Another challenge could be even bigger. Although not all coaching is behavioural there is an unspoken expectation that the results of coaching should not only be felt but also be visible for the client and for the sponsoring organization. These results should be reflected in new behaviours and actions. With this expectation in mind it seems that

Table 7.1 Potential ways of addressing the challenges of developmental coaching

Challenge in developmental coaching	Alternatives in terms of addressing the challenges
The origin of the intention for change	Elephant or rider
The method of influencing	Under the radar of consciousness or openly
Relationship with organizational agendas	Individual-focused or organization-focused
The source of change	Effort for development/self-improvement or self-acceptance/authenticity

the executive centre should be the main focus of coaching. But if the executive centre is mainly unconscious how does the coach get through to it? If for example, we focus mainly on the elephant which holds the main power, will this coaching then be just a manipulation? Or should we all learn hypnosis to bypass the rider? This may be a quick and efficient route to address some specific goals of clients and there are types of coaching that make use of the interventions designed to bypass the rider, for example NLP coaching.

It is unlikely though that many developmental coaches would be in favour of such an approach. There are some simple and less simple explanations for this. From the point of view of the client, we know that hypnosis has existed and helped people for many decades, however the sense of wariness in many is still present: it is not easy to allow someone 'to mess with your mind' even if you know that they are qualified and trustworthy specialists. It also does not give you much understanding and/or many tools to use when you are on your own to deal with other, or future life challenges. Even the specialists themselves have little understanding of the process. Although some simple techniques seem to produce good results, nobody knows why and how. Also the humanistic philosophy of many coaches does not sit well with the specialist's power position that this approach implies, even when permission for such interventions is granted (Welman and Bachkirova 2010).

The other reason why working under the radar of the rider would be objectionable for developmental coaches is the belief in the self-determination of the client (Cox and Jackson 2010). Some of them would also insist, as person-centred philosophy suggests, that clients themselves have the capacity to change and the job of the coach is only to create appropriate conditions for this to occur. My only concern with this position is that it may mean not addressing the elephant at all in the coaching process. In the developmental coaching that I am suggesting the coach would not neglect this task. The main idea behind this focus on the elephant is to help the client become more familiar and comfortable with it rather than just focusing on controlling it, which some clients initially aim for. At the same time the role of the partnership between coach and client when dealing with this challenge is crucial. The coach is committed to making all interventions explicit to the rider of the client even when they are from the category of working with the elephant.

Another potential issue that may be considered a controversial feature of developmental coaching is the probability of a tension between organizational and individual agendas (Cox and Jackson 2010). The long-term intention of developmental coaching to enhance the wider human capacities of the client may be fully compatible with organizational needs. There are organizations that see the provision of developmental opportunities for their employees as part of the psychological contract with them. That gives the organization in return not only the time and skills of their employees but their enthusiasm and creativity in full measure and on a more personal level. They believe that such an investment in their staff is paid off through the quality of their work and the motivation of their people and therefore they readily agree to a wider remit of coaching goals.

There are, however, organizations who believe in a more transactional approach in their relationships with employees. In this case developmental programmes are more prescribed and aligned with short-term gains for the organization. Such organizational interests and the developmental needs of the client can still be compatible, if both are lucky, even with a tight control from the organization. But with the fear of some organizations that valuable employees may be coached out of the organization, developmental coaching may not be an option. In this case clients may become frustrated if they have to dress up their developmental needs into an organizational uniform. This does not mean that the developmental coach should dig a gap between the client and the sponsor. Many developmental coaches care deeply about the organizations as wholes, but their means of contributing to the organizational welfare is through providing a service that is dedicated to those who constitute the organization. I would suggest that apart from the delivery of coaching, one of the tasks of a developmental coach working in the organizational context is educational: to engage in a conversation with the organization's representatives about the purpose, value and means of the long-term development of their staff.

We will finish with the biggest challenge for developmental coaching – the paradox of individual development as such, and the consequent puzzle of how to influence it. There are a number of traditions in psychology and philosophy, for example, Gestalt, which claim that the transformation of the self is only possible when a person is fully oneself as he/she is now. Could this mean that in order for someone to change we should coach for acceptance rather than for change?

Some argue that even the intention of becoming someone that you are not can be an obstacle to change. It may lead to creating an abstract ideal which in turn, just because of its attractiveness, may justify a lack of full engagement with life and with understanding the world as it is. This implies that we may be content, and even proud, just because we have such wonderful goals and ideals to work towards. Krishnamurti calls pursuing an ideal 'an accepted and respected postponement' (1991: 160). If we believe that understanding the self and the world is important for development then the following statement of Krishnamurti becomes of great magnitude: 'you can understand what *is* but you cannot understand what *should be*' (1994: 127).

There is an even stronger argument against the conscious pursuit of development. Lind (2000), for example, describes a 'modern self' constructing fictional goals that are the products of wishful thinking and cultural conditioning. They are assumed to be real and the self is believed to be capable of achieving them. Hillman (1983: 105) calls for the need to see such pursuit as fiction and for therapy to 'heal this goal'. Lind summarizes the consequences of this seeking of radical self-improvement, perfection or transcendence as the most common cause of chronic suffering that also 'ensnares the self in egoism, a false, heroic sense of unity and efficacy, and chronic internal conflict' (2000: 9). In Krishnamurti and in Gestalt we can also find numerous descriptions of the consequences of internal conflict as the result of creating a gap between what one is and what one wants to become (Perls 1969; Krishnamurti 1991, 1994).

On the other hand we all have powerful examples from the literature and from real life observations of people who have made decisions to change themselves and have achieved amazing results. So how should we resolve this tension between self-improvement/development on the one hand and self-acceptance/authenticity on the other in developmental coaching? And a consequent question: should we coach for change and towards becoming what the clients could/should be or for understanding of what they are? In relation to the developmental coaching that I advocate in this book the answer is not straightforward. The most evasive answer would be: 'it depends', but I am going to offer some ideas as to what this might depend on. And hopefully they may help in terms of clarity between the alternative strategies for working with the challenges discussed above.

Organic change and obstacles to it

One of the most important questions that needs to be answered in coaching is whether the change that the client is aiming for is *organic*. By this organic change, rather than an artificial, non-organic one, I mean a change that is fully grounded in the whole organism of the client and is not just 'a head' change – a rider's change. To be more precise, organic change is the one that is already underway subconsciously and closely associated with the natural needs of the organism and requirements of the situation. Sometimes it may not even be registered by the rider, but only discovered later. The conscious goal or intention for such change is just an accurate prediction of what the whole organism is about to do.

Non-organic change, on the other hand, is generated by the rider and based on conscious desires or 'wants' rather than the needs of the whole organism. When the change is not organic, the work of the coach towards supporting it is most likely to be associated with all the negative consequences discussed above or will cause considerable resistance, regular set-backs and breaks in the coaching relationship. When the change is organic, all of these, I would claim, are avoidable.

To explore what the organic change may look like, we need to go back to our three notions of the self or the three centres: the centre of awareness, the executive centre and the identity centre. The core of the organic change is in the executive centre as a representative of the elephant. It implies that a new mini-self is getting ready to be formed to satisfy a need that is important for the whole organism. That is why there is a natural energy behind it. Each new mini-self is always an aggregate of other simpler mini-selves; so not everything needs to be built from scratch. However, in order for it to go live, as it were, most elements should already be in place: channels to receive information from inside and outside the organism, necessary functional skills and motor-schemas to be activated and many links in the brain that can contribute to preparing this mini-self to go live. The final piece of the jigsaw falls into place and the change might happen without any particular help from the coach or even without the conscious awareness of the rider (route A, Figure 7.1).

Examples of such change happen on a regular basis particularly when people start new jobs or roles. The situation might demand new skills or behaviour or even a different attitude towards people and relationships with them and oneself. Providing that the person is not bogged down by various preconceptions or psychological dysfunctions, different pre-existing mini-selves together with careful observation of the situation help to form another mini-self that provides adaptation to this role. We all know the expression 'it comes naturally to him/her'. This is about people whose mini-selves are

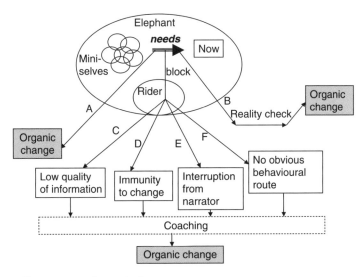

Figure 7.1   Different routes of organic change.

readily available to be used in the creation of other mini-selves. Usually they do not even know how it happens. Even if, in the initial stages of performing, the feedback from the environment is not encouraging (route B, Figure 7.1) it is taken as a reality check, the adjustments are made and the organic change takes place.

By the way, not being able to explain how the change happened does not mean that these people are thoughtless. Thinking as a process is a normal feature of human life and it is not always conscious or very orderly. If we observe our conscious thoughts we can see how changing and often disconnected they are. It is 'simply a stream flowing along of itself', therefore Claxton (1981: 166) suggests that we should see our thoughts 'as transient fragments of print-out from processing that is autonomous and unobservable'. In fact when we become aware of trying to make a change happen, this indicates that this change has encountered an underlying problem.

There could be different routes to organic change when holistic and tacit processing becomes temporarily blocked. And it is exactly those blockages that lead to us becoming conscious of the process of change. Claxton explains how the usually tacit working of mini-selves begins to include conscious processing.

> When all is flowing smoothly, no conscious product intervenes between per-
> ception and action. Only when no ready-made response exists – when the situ-
> ation poses a 'problem' – does conscious deliberation appear. So it is quite true
> that the activity of problem-solving and the conscious experience of 'thinking'
> tend to occur together, but they occur as separate responses to the blockage
> of the tacit flow of activity . . . If the passage between antecedent and achieve-
> ment of a desired consequence is blocked, or does not yet exist, or cannot
> readily be found, activity begins to concentrate at a point in the network

and may reach a level required for consciousness of the impasse. Once this happens, channels of conscious, verbal reason may become active, and we experience ourselves as 'thinking', 'deciding' or 'intending'. These conscious products may relate quite closely, or not at all, to the resolution of the impasse, and the resultant actions that actually occur.

(Claxton 1981: 166–9)

When the change is blocked and we are aware of it, coaching may become a viable option. It may not miraculously identify a point of blockage and offer a precise intervention to release it – this is beyond the reach of science so far. But skilful accumulation of attention and energy around the issues associated with the blockage could be helpful. Depending on the nature of the blockage some more specific strategies could be used that we are going to consider here. In general terms these blockages suggest that something is still missing in the working cycle of the mini-self. It could be at any section of this cycle: input section, action section or communication between them. Something could just be missing or some interruptions may be hindering the change, but if it is organic then there is a strong probability that it will happen.

I am proposing that there could be four types of blockages or obstacles to organic change (C, D, E and F on Figure 7.1), which could be addressed by means of developmental coaching:

- low quality of information at the input point;
- immunity to change (Kegan and Lahey, 2009);
- interruption from the narrator;
- no obvious behaviour routes exist at the action point.

You will see that apart from the immunity to change, a concept which was developed by Kegan and Lahey (2009), the other three are closely connected to the three notions of self that we discussed in Part 1 of this book.

Low quality of information at the input point

To start from the input point, the problem may be with the *quality of information* (route C, Figure 7.1) that comes through to the centre of awareness. Our channels may just be clogged up with noise or information might be distorted by various filters. If they are cleared, and better quality information gets through, the change might happen. To understand the nature of the filters we should look at the basic sense of self that allows us to make quick and precise orientations in situations, to establish boundaries between the organism and the environment and to judge a situation that may present a danger to the survival of the organism. But this sense of self is so basic and implicit that we rarely pay attention to it or value the freshness of perspective that it is associated with. As human beings we have acquired many more properties and abilities that have inevitably taken a larger part in our lives. Interestingly though, with further developments, such as for example linguistic and cultural, we have obviously gained a lot, but we have lost as well. One of the losses is in the area of perception. The channels of communications between the organism and the environment have become overloaded with language structures, beliefs, expectations, interpretations, and so on. It is difficult now to see things as they are rather than how they appear through the noisy and clouded channels. Therefore the challenge of the developmental coach is to facilitate the change in the quality of perception by the whole organism internally and externally. We look at the nature of perception and the way to improve it in Chapter 8.

Immunity to change

Immunity to change is the title of the book by Robert Kegan and Lisa Lahey (2009), in which they propose that many people who sincerely want to change may not be able to because they are directing a lot of productive energy towards a hidden competing commitment. Their individual beliefs or broader mindsets may create a natural but powerful immunity to change. For example, the client may genuinely want to empower others and to delegate, but instead find himself jumping in and sorting the problems by himself. His competing commitment may be to be personally useful with a big assumption behind it that he might not be deeply satisfied when he is in a second line of action.

I believe that using the terminology of this book, 'competing commitments' can illustrate the multitude of mini-selves and the role of the rider in difficult cases. Sometimes different mini-selves do their useful jobs in their own ways and may even satisfy the needs that contradict each other. But if both of these mini-selves are needed for a change to occur they have to become compatible. The 'big assumption' may represent a mini-self capable of inhibiting the links between other mini-selves needed for a change. The task of coaching should be in the first place to make conscious the concerns of contradicting mini-selves. Secondly, in order to 'disarm and pacify' the big assumption a better 'container' has to be found for both mini-selves that can hold them at the same time, making compatible for example 'empowering others' and 'being an individual hero'.

Although Kegan and Lahey describe the immunity to change as an effective anxiety-management system which protects us from the constant but unrecognized anxiety of, for example, losing control or putting important relationships at risk, it appears that the container they propose is cognitive. According to them the same mechanism that protects the individual from anxiety is 'preserving our existing way of making meaning' (2009: x). Therefore in practical terms Kegan and Lahey propose an exercise of four columns (2009) to identify a 'big assumption', to make it 'an object' for a person, which may lead to a new, more 'spacious' mental structure, able to accommodate a wider range of links. In our example, the definition of individual hero could expand into someone who is a hero by the virtue of empowering others.

I think that immunity to change could be a serious blockage to organic changes (route D, Figure 7.1) particularly for the shift needed from one developmental stage to another. My guess, however, is that some mini-selves may be simply missing, if the gap between the needed change and the developmental stage of the client is too big. In this case the work of the coach may involve not only a cognitive work with beliefs: uncovering hidden commitments and 'big assumptions', but building a more solid foundation for change by developing new mini-selves. The coach also needs to be careful not to confuse just a rider's wish for a real commitment required for an organic change.

Interruption from the narrator

Another obstacle to organic change may be *interruption from the narrator*. We said before that the stories told by the narrator are not as potent as mini-selves, especially when they do not correspond to any real mini-self. If they do reflect an actual mini-self they may play a more prominent role in the functioning of the whole organism by creating conscious links between different memories and behaviours. They can also be an obstacle to an organic change if they deny any role of a particular mini-self in the stories created, weakening that mini-self. Therefore we can suppose that formulating a meaningful and powerful story (self-model) that is anticipating a new but not completed mini-self may activate a missing link in the brain. This may bring this new mini-self to life and allow the organic change to happen. We will discuss mechanisms for this in Chapter 8.

No obvious behaviour routes

Finally, the blockage to the organic change may be at the action point of the emerging mini-self just because there is *no obvious behaviour route* that may allow the action to be materialized. For example, if the client wants to reach the top of his career, or to become better at building relationships with the opposite sex, or to make his life more meaningful it is not clear exactly what actions need to be taken. It is also possible that a mini-self for such action is just not developed yet. In this case there needs to be a different type of work done with both the elephant and the rider forming a new way of cooperation. First this may look like what coaches normally would do: identify the strength of the motivation, divide the big goal into sizeable chunks, find behaviours that move the client in solving small tasks and evaluate the progress. In addition, developmental coaches may engage with the elephant of the client to facilitate the organic change. In Chapter 8 we will look at the main mechanisms of this work involving the whole elephant with the unconscious, automatic, emotional mind and the body.

Some or all of these four types of blockage can be present when the organic change is delayed. Unfortunately, precision in the diagnosis of these blockages is a challenge that has not yet been resolved by science. Therefore the coach may need to work in all these directions in order to provide the help needed for the organic change to happen.

Non-organic change

Now let us look at what happens if the change is non-organic, a change that is not grounded in the whole organism of the client and comes mainly from a rider. Figure 7.2 describes the potential consequences (K, L, M and N) that might be observed as the result of non-organic change being initiated in coaching and beyond.

In reasonably free and normal individuals (K) non-organic change finishes in the same way as it starts. The commitment that is not grounded in the elephant wears off

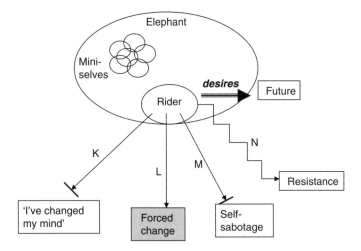

Figure 7.2   Different routes of non-organic change.

pretty quickly. Other needs and commitments take over or we simply forget about this intention or experience this as 'I changed my mind'.

If we are not free (L) the change may be forced by authorities or circumstances. The mini-self would form and can be stable for a long time – we are adaptable by nature. However, there would be a lot of needs suppressed and organic changes unfulfilled. As a result the elephant may become dull and unhappy. Sometimes it remains stuck and sometimes it grows the strengths to break the chains.

The non-organic change can also be successfully sabotaged (M). This is the fate typical of most New Year resolutions and a great example of the futility of the rider's attempts to overpower the elephant. Some examples of self-sabotage can be striking. People develop a real illness in order not to follow their intention to become fit; relationships they decide to mend suddenly become spectacularly and irreparably broken; the time for a telephone call crucially important for the intended project inexplicably and unforgivably forgotten, and so on.

Much has been written on resistance (N), particularly in psychotherapy – a phenomenon that is also present in coaching. It is mainly expressed in the process of relationship with 'the change assistant': therapist or coach. Examples of resistance in coaching are usually described as the cancelling of meetings and resisting advice (Peltier 2001). Peltier goes as far as to say that 'many hard-charging executives and most males resent help and advice' even if they are paying for this advice (1999: 38), which makes me wonder why they ask for coaching in the first place. Resistance could also be demonstrated through 'forgetting to do homework', disagreements and arguments with the coach, objections to trying exercises, tests, and so on.

From a psychoanalytic perspective, resistance is the material to work with as this can teach clients a great deal about their conscious and unconscious forces. From a behavioural perspective, client resistance is often viewed as the result of incorrect assessment or using techniques inappropriately and not in a timely way. From an existential perspective, client and therapist can work creatively with resistance and use it as a topic for exploration. In the context of the distinction between the organic and non-organic change, resistance may suggest a goal associated with non-organic change. However, it can also be a sign of a legitimate break of the coaching relationship caused by incompatibility, lack of experience or inappropriate imposition of particular goals, methods or style by the coach. Simplistic views on resistance often imply that it should be eliminated or overcome. A developmental coach though may see resistance as a sign of non-organic change and in this case would let the client go until he is ready to work on organic change. If resistance is the result of flaws in the coaching approach, there are even stronger reasons for termination of contract, unless this could be rectified through changing the strategy and the close use of supervision.

In the light of such crucial divisions between organic and non-organic change it is important to think how we can learn to discriminate between the two. As we said before, organic change is determined by the organism as a whole. The organism is constantly working to evaluate the situation we are in now taking into account the needs that we have and abilities that are currently developed. Non-organic change is initiated by the rider in response to external pressure or in response to desires that are not intrinsic to the needs of the organism, and sometimes are even against it. One of the best but unconventional ways to illustrate this difference is beautifully described by a sage:

> Needs can be fulfilled, but desires cannot.
> Desire is a need gone mad.
> Needs are simple, they come from nature;
> Desires are very complex, they don't come from nature.
> They are created by the mind.
> Needs are moment to moment,
> They are created out of life itself,
> Desires are not moment to moment,
> They are always for the future.
> They are not created by life itself,
> They are projected by the mind.
> Bhagwan Shree Rajneesh, *When the Shoe Fits* (Osho 2004)

The coach might just feel whether the change is organic or not, or she can explore this together with the client. Sometimes clients cannot explain where their goals come from, but the energy behind them could be well illustrated by the body if we pay attention to it. If the change does not feel organic the coach still has an option to work with this client, coaching him on other smaller units of change. That could also be useful for the organism, so preparing the soil for the organic change.

Summary

To summarize this chapter, we introduced the idea of developmental coaching as a process that involves working with an individual as a whole organism. Describing the main challenges of developmental coaching we introduced the idea of organic change. The idea of organic change may help to discriminate between some alternative solutions for presented challenges. Four types of obstacles to organic change were described that are closely linked to the three notions of the self that I have introduced in this book. These will be explored further along the three main mechanisms of change. They are the important elements of the theory of developmental coaching, but also present some very practical challenges:

- how to coach if we do not see things as they are;
- how to coach if there is no free will;
- how to coach if what we think about ourselves is just a story.

8   Mechanisms of developmental coaching

In this chapter we will be looking in more detail at the three mechanisms of developmental coaching. They correspond to the three notions of self introduced in Part 1 and are offered as ways to address the obstacles to organic change as discussed in Chapter 7: 'low quality of information', 'no obvious behavioural route' and 'interruption from the narrator'.

Working with the quality of perception

> The range of what we think and do
> is limited by what we fail to notice.
> And because we fail to notice
> *that* we fail to notice
> there is little we can do
> to change
> until we notice
> how failing to notice
> shapes our thoughts and deeds.
>
> (Goleman 1997: 24)

Using our slightly mechanical analogy of 'input – processing – action' in the functioning of the organism and the working of the executive centre, a first potential problem to organic change is a low quality of information input. Therefore I will start with the first mechanism of change in developmental coaching suggesting the need to increase the *quality of perception* both internally and externally. Although we don't see things as they are according to Kurt Koffka, this ability can be enhanced, allowing individuals to engage with their environment in a more effective way.

There are well known, and on the surface simple, ways that are traditionally suggested for this task: active listening, observation skills that include noticing external and internal signals, particularly from the own or others' body language, mindfulness practices, and so on. These are all very useful indeed. However, in addition I suggest that in order to increase the quality of information received we also need a much better

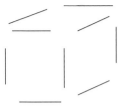

Figure 8.1   What do you see in this picture?

understanding of the nature of perception. We need to know what we are up against when we try to improve it – what prevents us from seeing things as they are.

Perception is a big topic in psychology. A number of interesting phenomena have been discovered that show unusual and useful abilities of our perceptive function. For example, an interesting ability of perception is to fill the gaps (James 1890; Ramachandran and Blakeslee 1998). If you look at (Figure 8.1) you can easily see it as a cube, but strictly speaking it is not. Your perception added missing details to the picture and coined it as a cube. If you see a car parked behind a tree, you see a whole car – not two halves of it with a tree in the middle. We simply take this ability of perception for granted. This means that the brain does not ignore some lack of information, but responds by providing various details from memory, logic or imagination. This is a great ability, but as usual, the negatives are the extensions of the positives. Connected to this ability is another one: to transform what we see into something that is simply not 'there'. Our perception exaggerates discontinuities and invents edges and contours which are non-existent, because our previous experiences and beliefs can skew and colour what we perceive.

Psychologists have also found that our conscious perception is closely linked to attention (James 1890; Mack and Rock 1998; Velmans 2000). The effect of inattentional blindness for example, shows that if we pay attention to a specific task, this greatly inhibits our ability to notice quite significant objects in the perceptive field. The most dramatic example of this effect is the film *Gorillas in our Midst* (Simons and Chabris 1999). Before watching it the audience is given the task of counting how many times a group of students in this film pass the ball while actively moving around the hall. After that, the observers are asked if they saw anything unusual; typically the answer is no. I once attended a presentation where this film was shown before I knew about this effect and was horrified at what I had missed when this clip was shown again. In the middle of the game a person dressed in a gorilla suit walked through the hall, stopped in the centre, thumped her chest and left (Blackmore 2003). You can see variations of this film on YouTube.

No less striking is the effect of change blindness that is associated with the way we simply look, moving our eyes and sometimes blinking (Rensink et al. 1997; Simons 2000; Blackmore 2003). It was found that surprisingly large changes could be made to the object of observation without observers noticing them if the change occurred *during* an eye movement. The object could disappear, be replaced by a different element, change colour, change position and we would not notice it if the image flickers or even when we blink. We are usually convinced that we would notice such changes but experiments again and again show that we grossly overestimate this ability. In the film 'Dan Dennett on our consciousness' (www.ted.com/index.php/talks/dan_ dennett_on_our_consciousness.html) there are many examples of change blindness which are very convincing. This effect, as many others, makes us question the power of conscious perception in the external world.

Unfortunately, we do not have direct access to internal information either. There are so many processes inside our body of which we have very little awareness, unless we study bodies for professional reasons. Our digestive, immune or even central nervous systems are functioning without our knowing about the intricacies of their work. In this case, however, I am sure you would agree with Claxton who says that 'too much information is anathema, and that refers not just to emails but to the "moment-to-moment reality" of my own body and brain' (2004: 131). All of this is happening unconsciously and should probably stay this way, because our unconscious is extremely skilful in both the internal and external worlds.

There are different views on the role of the unconscious in the functioning of the organism. Some claim that the unconscious is 'stupider' than we are (Kihlstrom 1996). Others, however, are absolutely convinced that the unconscious is wiser in many circumstances and in tasks even including problem solving (Lewicki et al. 1992; Claxton 1997). Lewicki, for example concluded after his experiments, that non-conscious information processing was not only faster but structurally more sophisticated. In my view the arguments and research in support of the second view are stronger. They suggest that a great deal of what we do is done swiftly and accurately, and independently of what we consciously perceive. Sometimes even 'what we think we "see" is not what guides our actions' (Milner and Goodale 1995: 177). This is clearly shown in experiments with people who have brain damage and also in experiments with normal subjects. Aglioti et al. (1995), for example, found that although in experiments with visual illusions the perceptual system was fooled, the motor system wasn't (Blackmore 2003: 42). Subjects were making mistakes judging the size of the object which was deliberately misleading, but when asked to pick this object up their movements were absolutely precise.

Perhaps the role of the unconscious at the input point becomes so prominent because the power of our conscious perception is limited. Nearly all recent discoveries show what Helmholtz (1821–1894) said a very long time ago, that normal perception quite generally represents 'the conclusions of unconscious inferences'. Experiments with perceptual illusions in particular confirm this idea. There are very clever ways to trick the unconscious process of the mind/brain into making 'inferences' that are reasonable but in fact wrong (Velmans 2000; Blackmore 2003). Illusions, though, are not just games; they are modelling our 'normal' functioning but make the nature of perception more obvious. They show that our belief in the power of our usual perception might be an illusion in itself.

In coaching we are also affected by all these limitations of perceptions. We rely on what we see and hear, normally without questioning it. But we often see what we want to see or we do not hear what we are, for example, afraid to hear. Our pre-existing concepts and expectations, our beliefs and emotions, our needs and hopes, are all playing the role of colourful filters in our perception of the world. We see this happening in our clients and as coaches we aim to provide, as we say, another perspective for seeing a particular situation. What it might simply mean is that there are holes in their perception and we intend to address this.

Can we aim then for a perfect perception? Is this possible? Buddhists say that 'when the mirror is completely spotless there is no distinction between the world and its reflection' (Blackmore 2003: 414). According to them this is possible. But what does this idea of perception as a spotless mirror actually mean? It appears that we should have no expectations, fears, hopes, which distort our perception. Although this might not be possible to the level of perfection, the task of helping our clients to become more perceptually capable is a worthwhile one nonetheless. 'Dispelling illusions – "cleansing the doors of perception" in Blake's fine phrase – makes experience sharper, values clearer, action more effective, and life less contaminated with unnecessary pain, confusion and negative emotion' (Claxton 2002: 219). This sounds like a reasonable goal for developmental coaching. According to such goals the coach needs to work with conditioning and self-deception which interfere with a better quality of perception.

Conditioning

> There is no perception if that perception is through an image.
>
> Krishnamurti, 1996

We human beings are able to learn from experience – an ability that allows us to adapt to a changing world, to survive in difficult situations, to make use of the feedback that we constantly receive from our environment. This type of learning is no different from the learning done by other species. We, however, have an amazing advantage over animals in terms of learning. Because of language we are able to receive knowledge in a 'ready' form, to learn not from our own mistakes but from the mistakes of others. In our time of unbounded access to information we learn from the immense pool of knowledge, pass it to others and contribute to it generously. However, with this great advantage comes the special type of problem which animals seem to avoid. With the use of language we are in danger of numerous misinterpretations, anxieties and even neuroses. Similarly, by getting 'second hand knowledge' we open the gates for conditioning.

What does conditioning mean? We often believe that we are prone to being conditioned only in childhood. This is partly true: childhood is obviously a prime time for learning and being influenced for all sorts of good reasons. But it is useful to remember that we are never free from being influenced at any age. We are conditioned by the culture of organizations, by circles of friends and by society as a whole in subtle but also in quite direct ways.

> Minds pick up beliefs from family and society that unconsciously infuse perception, showing us a world already saturated with enculturated theory. Some of these beliefs are benign and useful: we call them 'accurate' when in realist mood; 'functional' if we are feeling constructivist. Some were

accurate/functional once but have become anachronisms. Some were never right, but we bought them nonetheless.

(Claxton 1999: 219)

What are the dangers of conditioning? Various theoretical perspectives describe what happens when we 'swallow the messages from other human beings without chewing'. Transactional analysis discusses this as injunctions and counter-injunctions. The REBT approach (Rational Emotive Behavioural Therapy) explores how this adds to our innate tendency to irrationality, forming various 'oughts' and 'shoulds'. The Person-centred approach describes how our organismic self gradually changes into self-concept through denial and distortion of our experiences. The Gestalt approach discusses a middle zone in our psyche where various influences and thoughts are mulled over and create confusion instead of contacting the environment through immediate engagement.

James Hillman once said that it is impossible to see an angel unless you first have a notion of it and this is what we receive from our cultures – notions of different things that could be helpful in understanding the world but also may become unnecessary filters. There is a danger, of course, that coaching may do exactly the same thing: introduce concepts and notions that may become additional filters to the clients' perception. We cannot avoid it, but at least we can choose to do this in a style of enquiry, allowing clients to question the usefulness of the concept in mapping their experience. An example of a contrasting strategy would be a religiously faithful approach to psychometrics. If traits and categories are presented as hard-wired in our psyche with the mentioning of various authority figures to support the message, this might impose just another filter on the clients' perception that would be difficult to shift.

Jiddu Krishnamurti (1895–1986) is one of the philosophers and educationalists who in my view, writes with great clarity about the role of conditioning and influences from authorities in our lives. Although it seems obvious from what we said before that *un-conditioning* ourselves is important and in Part 3 we will discuss some ideas of how it could be approached for different groups of clients, this may not be enough. Krishnamurti invites us all to look more deeply at the issue of conditioning, suggesting that we are ourselves responsible for being conditioned. If we try to find out why we fall prey to conditioning even when we are grown up and seemingly independent, we can discover that we begin conforming because of our own personal reasons. Interestingly even when we wish to cease to be 'secondhand' people this could also be the result of another type of conditioning.

One conforms instinctively for various reasons: out of attachment, fear, the desire for reward, and so on. That is one's first response. Then somebody comes along and says that one must be free from conditioning, and there arises the urge not to conform . . . Now, is there any essential difference between the desire to conform, and the craving to be free of conformity?

(Krishnamurti 1991: 31)

He suggests that the mind itself is conditioned and any movement of it in any direction produces limited results. 'When the mind makes an effort to transform itself, it merely builds another pattern, different perhaps, but still a pattern ... When the mind is totally aware of this fact, as it is totally aware of a poisonous snake, then you will see that the movement of thought comes to an end' (1996: 54). According to Krishnamurti, it is only through understanding the nature of the trap that one can be free of it.

I can also see that what Krishnamurti advocates as 'choiceless awareness' is in a way a perception in pre-cognitive sense, with no bias coming from conditioning, no images, even no concept of anything that is perceived (1996: 54–7). This is a perception that does not create a division between the observer and the observed and does not lead to the wastage of energy. In this sense cleansing the doors of perception is a movement towards a very simple pre-reflective sense of self as we discussed in Part 1. It may need what Claxton calls 'perceptual re-education' (1994: 11).

Self-deception

> Self-deception is an alienation of self from itself, a peculiar type of illness related to the selfhood.
>
> Murphy, 1965

Steven Pinker has said the one great thing that psychology has achieved is 'documenting the human propensity for self-deception, self-serving biases, cognitive dissonance, and defence mechanisms of the ego – the source of much of the complexity, and tragedy, of human life' (2008: 184). Not everyone, however, seems to be concerned with self-deception. People filter information and act accordingly for all sorts of reasons. Research shows that we take credit for successes but deny blame for failures (Zuckerman 1979), accept praise uncritically but receive criticism sceptically, looking for a reason to dismiss it (Wyer and Frey 1983; Kunda 1990). We persuade ourselves that our good traits are exceptional while our flaws are common and shared by many other people (Campbell 1986; Suls and Wan 1987).

There is a significant body of literature (Gur and Sackheim 1979; Ames and Dissanayake 1996; Lewis 1996; Goleman 1997; Fingarette 2000; Mele 2001) that offers useful insights into the psychology of self-deception in individuals, explaining cases of self-deception based on cognitive incompetence, faulty thinking, irrational beliefs and unconscious psychological mechanisms. Some of the authors argue that self-deception is more a cultural phenomenon maintained by the narrator, rather than a natural phenomenon situated in the individual mind. This also suggests some similarity with conditioning in creating an extra filter to perception that comes from the narrator. It appears that self-deceivers engage with the world in some particular way, and yet refuse to identify themselves as this person, denying the fact of such an engagement. While during conditioning the filters to perception of reality are polished by influential others, in self-deception this job is done internally.

The paradox of self-deception is in somehow managing to pretend to myself that there's nothing there to be seen, just because I know well that there is something unbearably distressing to be seen. However, it may not be as puzzling as it seems according to Fingarette (2000), if we carefully consider how our minds work in the light of recent neuro-scientific findings. Fingarette claims that the way the mind produces self-deceptive states is the same as for non-deceptive ones.

> Just as I can avoid focusing my attention on the potentially distracting sounds of the passing cars, and do so without focusing my attention on the fact that I am doing this, so too I can take account of something potentially emotionally traumatic, and for that reason avoid turning my attention to it, and do all this without turning my attention to the fact that I am doing it.
>
> (Fingarette 2000: 169)

Fingarette also suggests an interesting explanation of the mechanism of self-deception using the term 'spelling out' the experience. Self-deception is present if we have a reason not to spell out the experience and then adopt a policy of not spelling it out. However, when we assess the situation that requires from us to notice this policy, we also do not spell out this assessment. We create a story, consistent and plausible, that allows us to keep these policies in place (2000).

Forms and features of self-deception are numerous. Some can be very dramatic when, for example, the owner of a business does not see that it is gradually collapsing until it is too late to do anything about it. On a smaller scale nobody who is honest with themselves can say that they are free from self-deception. Some of us, even when we are able to perceive it, find compelling reasons to justify it. For example coaches might say that a degree of self-deception is even necessary in our job. This is one potential explanation: at the heart of coaching there is a belief in human potential. However, in some cases when coaches experience doubts in their clients' ability to achieve a desired outcome they may select and use only information that supports the former belief. This in turn may help them maintain their energy and motivation, and instil confidence in their clients. Another explanation suggests that a degree of collusion may also be helpful in developing and sustaining the mutual acceptance between coach and client which is considered important for all successful coaching relationships. It seems then that some degree of self-deception may serve us well. At the same time, exactly because of the fact that it may serve us well, this phenomenon should be watched as carefully as possible.

With this thought in mind I conducted a small scale research project called 'Self-deception in coaching'. I interviewed six very experienced coaching supervisors about their experiences of encountering self-deception in coaches. A very interesting picture has emerged which, in the first place, includes various manifestations of self-deception in coaching, for example:

- pretending to be non-directive with no agenda;
- extending coaching unnecessarily;
- not noticing overstepping boundaries with psychotherapy;
- not noticing ethical dilemmas;
- exaggerating success;
- not noticing own good work;
- attributing success to themselves only, rather than to other factors;
- forgetting the organizational client;
- colluding, particularly with powerful or famous clients.

Among the reasons for these manifestations that supervisors identified were: fear (of failure, of not being a good coach, of rejection); personal interest or gain; attachment to or enhancement of a particular image (e.g. a perfect coach). Apart from these internal reasons for self-deception the research participants also identified a number of external factors that contribute to this phenomenon in coaching. For example, the current situation in the coaching field that includes lack of clarity in terms of standards and accountability; no mechanisms that allow clients to register their concerns; high levels of competition for contracts; uncertainty as to what coaching is as such and what constitutes a good job – all of these put pressure on coaches and create situations in which they genuinely do not notice the above manifestations of self-deception in order to sustain a positive image of themselves as professionals. In the conclusions we will come back to this issue for coaches. Here in Box 8.1 you can find a case in which you can explore in what way the coach might deceive herself and speculate about potential reasons for this.

BOX 8.1   Case study: self-deception in a coach

Kate, a coach in your supervision group, is describing her work. Her client is a CEO of a middle-sized company. Her coaching contract with him has already been extended twice from the initial six months and the third period is coming to an end. The client suggested an extension again and Kate is pleased about this. The client is the one in the company who makes decisions about the coaching provision for himself and for his direct reports. Kate sees this as a good contract; they have a great relationship. The client reports that he derives a lot from their work. She also finds him a very interesting person.

Kate brought this case for supervision because it was her turn in the group; he was one of the three remaining clients that she hadn't yet discussed. She also has a quiet period in terms of new contracts that she could bring for supervision. Although she was confident about her decision to extend the contract she wanted to check with the supervision group if her decision was justified.

Kate's personal situation:

Her business is in a reasonable state, but less so than it used to be. Kate is in a relationship that is gradually coming to its natural end. The separation seems imminent. She seems to talk less and less with her partner. She is also not very active socially.

- What could be the nature of Kate's self-deception?
- What made you think so?

So what, as coaches, might we be aiming at by increasing the quality of perception in ourselves and our clients? One of the most important things that we would like to develop is a higher level of awareness in action: an immediate real-time 'dance' of individual and situation, which allows the quick detection of hints, threats, traps and surprises. It is a dance without over-thinking and 'selftalk'. It may not even need much comprehension. According to Claxton (1999) we are addicted to comprehension, because we believe that comprehension precedes competence. However, for this level of awareness it might be better to stop trying to understand, but simply to pick up patterns. And another, perhaps the ideal, facet of such perception is beautifully described by Hesse:

> At the moment when desire ceases and contemplation, pure seeing, and self-surrender, begin, everything changes. People ceased to be useful or dangerous, interesting or boring, genial or rude, strong or weak. They become nature, they become beautiful and remarkable, as does everything that is an object of clear contemplation. For indeed contemplation is not scrutiny or criticism, it is nothing but love. It is the highest and most desirable state of our souls: undemanding love.
>
> (Herman Hesse, adapted by Claxton 2002)

We will return to the topic of self-deception in each practical chapter in Part 3 and also discuss it in relation to coaches themselves in the conclusions to the book. Self-reflection and feedback from others can be a good start for us to minimize it, but supervision is the best way to explore the most stubborn elements of it.

Working with the elephant

> Your body is not a machine, rather a wonderfully intricate interaction with everything around you, which is why it "knows" so much just in being.
>
> Gendlin, 2003

> We think that, if we do not notice something, it has no effect on us. We think that our deepest interests are served by pursuing those things that we are aware of wanting. We think that, if only we could figure things out carefully enough, most of life's difficulties could be smoothed out.
>
> Claxton, 1994

We do think a lot and believe that our actions and behaviours are the product of this thinking. In fact, although thinking is important for many areas of our life the influence of it on our everyday behaviour, learning and sustained changes seems to be exaggerated as we have discussed in Part 1. Any coach can provide many examples when coaching may seem successful as the result of conscious decision to change or a great cognitive insight or skilful reframing, but soon the client is right back to where he started. Even life-altering epiphanies tend to fade in days or weeks (Miller and C'de Baca 2001; Haidt 2006). Haidt (2006: 26) therefore, claims that 'lasting change can come only by retraining the elephant, and that's hard to do'. He argues that different developmental programmes are successful not because of the initial insight or transformational shift but because they keep people involved with the programme long enough to retrain the elephant.

Interpreted in a simplistic way this conclusion might mean that if we aim for sustained change, the only useful way is to arrange long enough coaching or training. Even the core condition of coaching – a good relationship with the client – may be interpreted from this perspective as a clever way to keep the process sufficiently long and comfortable for the elephant in order to retrain it. However, the philosophy of many types of coaching would not fit with this perspective mainly because of the idea of the client's self-determination. This position is also very strong in developmental coaching. To be fair to Haidt, he suggests a role of the rider in this model as an advisor to the elephant, but it sounds like a pretty marginal role. From another angle, the focus on changing the elephant as the emotional and unconscious mind embedded in the body may bring coaching too close to psychotherapy. However, the consequences of this for coaches, such as losing a separate professional identity or the need to be trained accordingly, do not seem attractive.

In order to avoid the above potential pitfalls for developmental coaching I suggest another look at what we know about the experience of flow (Csikszentmihalyi 1975, 1993). It is a highly desirable optimal state of experience in which we become deeply engrossed in a sufficiently challenging activity; it becomes intrinsically rewarding and time seems to disappear. Coaches and clients experience flow in coaching (Wesson and Boniwell 2007) and they are inspired to develop such states in various areas of their lives. Interestingly, flow is usually described as a state of consciousness, but according to Blackmore (2003) it would be much better described 'as a state in which the distinctions between conscious and unconscious processing disappear' (p. 284). Using the terminology of this book we would say that in flow the elephant and rider are in perfect harmony. In addition to this Csikszentmihalyi also suggests that it is not only enjoyment that rewards flow. He claims that every flow experience contributes to the growth of the individual. He gives a reasonable explanation for this using the concepts of integration and differentiation for increasing the complexity of the organism (1993: 237–8).

This phenomenon suggests that there is an opportunity for perfect collaboration between the rider and the elephant. Taking on board this possibility we will look at the general mechanisms of developmental coaching that may allow for a better interaction between the rider and the elephant in the process of organic change. This is particularly important in circumstances where there seems to be no obvious route to achieving a change that is needed or that something is missing in order for a new mini-self to emerge. We will look at two mechanisms that may promote a successful collaboration between the rider and the elephant. One is '*soft thinking*' (Claxton 1999: 146) in addition to traditional hard reasoning, and the second mechanism is better *communication with the emotional body*. Each of these mechanisms, although seemingly rooted in different sides of the rider-elephant divide, are explicit in their intention to meet in the middle and thereby increase the harmony of working together.

Soft thinking

Hard deliberate thinking and concentrated efforts are necessary in some circumstances, but we tend to overestimate their value. We are taught to work hard and not to give in to the demands of a 'lazy' elephant even if it requires a well deserved rest. We are also trained in and respect scientific thinking. This involves analytical thinking (collecting and evaluating evidence) as well as critical thinking (comparing, contrasting and identifying problems). However, De Bono (1969) criticizes both of these modes as reactive, which do not promote creativity. Claxton's view is even more drastic: 'deliberate concentration is ridiculous, for it presumes that my consciousness knows better than my whole organism and it confuses nerves with muscles' (1981: 159).

> As soon as attention is deliberately concentrated in a certain degree, one begins to select from the material before one: one point will be fixed in the mind with particular clearness and some other consequently dis-regarded, and in this selection one's expectations and one's inclinations will be followed. This is just what must not be done, however . . .
>
> (Freud 1912/1958)

This may be quite puzzling for those who see thinking in a traditional way: as a focused concentrated effort to be rational and logical. Instead Claxton advocates a different type of thinking which is more harmonious with the elephant – *soft thinking* or thinking with a soft focus. It implies 'looking at' rather than 'looking for' (Claxton 1999; Claxton and Lucas 2007). It is not hard reasoning with the inhibition of other parts of the mind. It does not lead to what Claxton and Lucas (2007: 42) call a 'premature evaluation', forcing out new, unstable and fragile ideas that come from the unconscious. Claxton and Lucas (2007) suggest that sometimes we fail to solve difficult problems not because we don't think enough, but because we think badly. They say that many real-life problems are 'much more like tangled fishing nets than they are like mathematical equations' (p. 80). For this reason they need a wider and softer focus or several foci on everything together: main intention, a problem to deal with and any related issues. The challenge is to keep this multi-focused attention gently but continuously and simultaneously activated.

Another interesting feature of soft thinking which is more harmonious with the elephant is simply *slowing down*. Research shows how creativity that is always welcome in coaching is enhanced when people are simply asked to slow down. When research participants were prevented from delivering the answers to a problem for some time they came up with better ideas (Rokeach 1950; Parnes 1961). This research gave rise to a method of enhancing creativity based on the conscious requirement to keep on thinking, even when the first flush of the most obvious ideas has passed (Parnes 1961; Claxton 1999). The logic of this method suggests that the brain naturally follows the most conventional routes first, activating more established mini-selves. However, with activation gradually spreading further, less obvious routes and connections emerge that may bring different mini-selves to life.

The ability to hold a problem in mind without actively deliberating on it is the key to soft thinking (Claxton 1999). However, the current pace of life which is determined by deadlines and commitments, leads to a mode of work in which ideas are not 'springing forth but painfully squeezed out' (Claxton and Lucas 2007: 42). Coaches often say that the actual fact that our clients can have a space to slow down and to look at the situation from different perspectives (with a soft focus) is the key to successful coaching. They could be absolutely right about this. We also, as coaches, need to be careful and not fall into the same trap of 'squeezing out' the result of coaching as soon as possible, because 'the situation dictates it'.

Gentle questioning around the edges of the issue is also important as it may help to activate less obvious links between the different mini-selves. The questions do not have to be those 'powerful' and penetrating ones that coaches are often inspired to ask. The insight may come from simple probing questions identifying sometimes just one word which might be included in different mini-selves and so making a useful connection. It is interesting at the same time that Dennett (1983) questions the value of asking myself questions, suggesting that doing this could be as effective as tipping myself for making myself a drink. If he is right, questioning by the coach is a different kettle of fish and so this external intervention may help to make the resources of one mini-self available to another and give rise to a new mini-self in the process of organic change.

Communication with the emotional body

The actual idea of communication between the rider and elephant implies two-way traffic: to and fro. It is important within the same individual, but also a task for the coach, who wants to enable this two-way traffic for their client. We will start from the rider actively receiving information *from* the elephant. The very first and obvious information from the body comes through *emotions*. The actual word emotions sometimes causes an uneasiness in some people especially if it is about strong negative emotions: anxiety that prevents performance or the taking of necessary risks; anger and irritations leading to the escalation of conflicts; fear of not knowing or contributing to actions that we might regret after the event. Coaches themselves, for example, might insist on defining the goals for coaching as soon as possible in order to cope with some of these fears.

This suspicion towards emotion is a relic of an attitude particularly prevalent in organizations. In some organizations emotions are still treated as inferior in comparison to reason. However the simple observation that typical organizational problems look like tangled fishing nets suggests that to untangle them, logic is not sufficient. Damasio (2000), for example, argues that far from being an inferior kind of knowledge, emotions and intuition actually form the vital glue that holds the different elements of intelligence together. Without the ability to hear, heed, respect and act on our hunches we may become the ultimate 'articulate incompetents' (a term suggested by R. Bernstein, quoted in Rowan, 1986: 17, and Claxton 1999).

A number of other modern theories of emotion appeared. They persuasively question the assumption that emotions are a disruptive force for rational thought and effective action (Plutchik and Kellerman 1980; Izard 1993; Oatley and Jenkins 1996; Frijda 2000; Gray and Watson 2004). New tools, measurements and interventions have been developed and introduced in organizations that focus specifically on emotional qualities. They are based on a standpoint that implies that there is no pure cognition; it is always brushed with emotion: 'Everything that is real is emotional; the rational is our subsequent linguistically structured elaboration of that reality' (Buck 1991: 136).

Other authors suggest seeing emotion as the readiness to respond to a change in the situation often associated with a threat (Oatley and Jenkins 1996). From this perspective, particularly negative emotions are important as a self-preservation response and a vital biological process.

> When we meet a hitch, when our knowledge and know-how let us down, or when our own goals and interests conflict, feeling afraid (or sad or angry or shocked or disgusted) is part and parcel of the way we are built to respond. The core negative emotions signal that the brain-mind is responding intelligently. It is doing its job, in the face of an upset, an interruption or a temporary loss of comprehension and control.
>
> (Claxton 1999: 39)

Therefore seeing emotions as an invaluable source of information about the coaching process for a client as well as a coach is rational. It is even intelligent, and that is how a developmental coach would treat any expressed emotion. Emotion is a message from the elephant to the rider and to the coach about how the whole organism is doing and therefore to dismiss this message out of a prejudice is simply unwise.

The elephant's language is mostly *non-verbal* and therefore the rider needs to pay attention to various *signs* that may not be easy to articulate: physical feelings, images and dreams, guesses, fleeting thoughts, hunches and the aesthetic sense. In terms of the latter when it is most difficult to articulate what is liked and why, trusting the elephant may be the only solution. More than that, articulation may not even be helpful as we tend to think. In one of the research experiments (Schooler and Fiore 1997) two groups of participants were asked to make various choices, for example, to choose a picture for the wall in the study room. One group was asked to think very carefully about their choices so they could explain them later. The other group was asked to make their choices intuitively. At the end it appeared that people who made their choices intuitively were more satisfied than those who made their choice deliberately. This means that if we are required to focus on only those features of the situation that can be verbalized, we should not be surprised if we end up feeling that something has been left out of the equation. The developmental coach will respect any sign from their own and their client's elephants without any undue expectation to articulate them.

The approach developed by Eugene Gendlin (1962, 1999, 2003), which is called '*focusing*' is a step even further: not only accepting, but inviting the messages from the elephant, looking not only for unarticulated, but pre-logical, pre-conceptual, just felt dimensions of experiencing. Gendlin (1962) uses the word 'experiencing' rather than 'experience' to emphasize 'the raw, present, ongoing functioning' rather than concrete experience (p. 11). He and his colleagues have discovered a key factor in one of their large-scale studies of psychiatric patients. Those who talked in a fluent, articulate way were less likely to make significant progress than those who were more hesitant and introspective in describing their experiencing. More successful research subjects were listening attentively to their body, trying to give voice to their 'plant-animal-human body's self-sensing of a situation' (1999: 234). They had longer pauses in their narratives and felt clear signs of a physical sense of release when they managed to find the right words or images to capture their 'felt sense'.

> A felt sense is not an emotion. We recognize emotions. We know when we are angry, or sad, or glad. A felt sense is something you do not first recognize – it is vague and murky. It feels meaningful, but not known. It is a *body-sense of meaning*. When you learn how to focus, you will discover that the body finding its own way provides its own answers to many of your problems.
>
> (Gendlin 2003: 10, added emphasis)

Gendlin (2003) developed a process that allows anyone to train themselves to listen to the felt sense. It takes some time to develop the skills of recognizing this feeling, but with space and time allocated to it and ideally with the help of a trained partner everyone can master this process. It is not a therapeutic process as such and it can be successfully used in any one-to-one work including coaching, if this fits the practitioner's philosophy and style.

The next side of communication between the elephant and rider is how the rider can send a message *to* the elephant so that this message is not ignored. There is also an important question if and how the rider can actually influence the elephant and what can a coach do to facilitate this. The first challenge is communication with the elephant, because the normal conceptualized speech of the rider is not the language of the elephant. But images, music, poetry, touch and metaphors are. That is why some people believe that poetry has more capacity to change people than psychotherapy. Our elephants are receptive to such means of communication and so coaches would be advised to be inventive if they want to involve the elephant of the client in the process. The *uses of imagery and metaphors* are certainly among the skills of the developmental coach. It is also the elephant of the client that is sensitive to the *relationship* with the coach. They have to feel safe and accepted. And if the coach is curious and genuinely interested even in the cryptic messages of the elephant this *attitude* is usually rewarded.

The elephant sometimes needs *advice and feedback* about how it is doing. Although it deserves credit for much of the work we do, the elephant's job is the moment-by-moment affairs of the organism. It is not its job to predict what will happen far ahead and to plan for the future. This is the job of the rider and so the rider can play the role of an advisor to the elephant by taking a long-term perspective.

We learned in Part 1 that it is the organism as a whole that makes decisions and choices and acts on them. However, when we make a separation between the rider and the elephant there is a temptation to see it as a separation between our reason and the animal part of our nature. The role of the rider if this were the case may be translated into: how can we get reason to influence our animal nature? This is not a distinction that I make in this book. My view on the elephant is much wider than that. However, some examples provided by Haidt (2006), who seems to be advocating the former view, are very useful and interesting for coaches to consider. For example, he suggests that the elephant has a 'like-o-meter', a simple mechanism that makes quick judgments whether it likes or dislikes anything that we experience without the involvement of the rider (2006: 26–7). Because it is run by the pleasure principle, 'the elephant has a tendency to overindulge . . . so the rider needs to encourage it to get up and move on to another activity' (2006: 96) maybe by flashing up to it a mental picture of the long-term consequences of such pleasures. Haidt argues that there is a lot of evidence now that the elephant reacts 'to bad things more quickly, strongly, and persistently than to the equivalent good things' (2006: 29) because of the need to protect ourselves according to the survival principle. This tendency needs some adjustment if we care not only about survival but also our quality of life.

Developmental coaches may find it useful to keep in mind the tendencies of human nature that we have inherited in the process of evolution. For example we are familiar with the alert reaction to 'negatives' when debriefing our clients on the 360 feedback exercise. With rare exceptions the focus is often on the negative feedback. Evolutionary devices for survival and reproduction such as competitiveness, demonstrations of strength and power, tactical submissiveness or possessiveness (Richard 2000) can also be observed in the everyday behaviour of our otherwise highly civilized clients. And of course, the necessity of such behaviours needs to be questioned by the rational mind in the light of many other factors and values. However, my notion of the elephant here is wider than just the animal nature of the human species. It is more in tune with understanding the body as being in a constant intricate interaction with the rest of the world as suggested by Gendlin (2003) in the quotation at the beginning of this sub-section.

My notion of the elephant is also different from the Freudian idea of the Unconscious with a predominantly pathological meaning associated with it. Although it explains a lot of interesting and sometimes disturbing phenomena and therefore is useful for a range of purposes particularly in psychotherapy, it is still too narrow for explaining a much wider role of the elephant in the functioning of the organism. Freudian Unconscious implies, in evolutionary terms, a reasonably recently acquired range of deep seated beliefs and defences that are designed to shield the person from a painful memory of a trauma or to protect the story of the self as constructed by the narrator. The fact that such beliefs and unquestioned values are unconscious can be illustrated with the experiments. Nosek et al. (2002) have shown, for example, that we can be heavily prejudiced against particular types of people even when the rider would furiously deny this. However, these beliefs and stereotypes are the result of conditioning and therefore fused with the filters that prevent the elephant from receiving decent information from the environment. When these filters are already in place, then we need the rider. In order for the organism as a whole not to act on these prejudiced choices the rider's conscious and rational input is very welcome.

A good rider learns to predict the behaviour of the elephant and this knowledge may create a better harmony within the organism as whole. An immediate reinforcement of 'positive behaviours' by acknowledgment and appreciation is as good a method of influencing your own elephant as it would be for a real one. It is important to remember that in relation to long-term goals, a beautiful image of a desirable future may not work for long for the elephant. It fades pretty quickly and would need constant reminding. But we do know that the elephant feels pleasure whenever it takes a step in the right direction. Therefore it is not the promise of future success, which as we know does not bring a lasting pleasure, even when it is reached, but rather a well designed process with regular feedback that would make work on change more attractive to the elephant.

As far as the issue of *control* is concerned it may appear that the rider is in charge of the elephant, but this view is much more controversial than the role of the advisor as we have just discussed it. There are different positions in relation to this question as presented in Part 1. The summary at its end could be read as 'No, there is no such control'. This is the answer that is the least believable by common sense but the most supported by recent studies. However, this position is not that simple even according to Libet (1985) who famously showed that consciousness comes too late to influence action. Taken simply, if it comes too late it cannot control. However, Libet himself suggests that consciousness may still intervene to veto the unconsciously initiated action, providing a kind of conscious 'free won't'.

Claxton provides an interesting explanation as to the nature of this 'free won't' rather than 'free will', which I will describe using our terminology. While the elephant is preparing to respond to the situation according to the existing mini-self and on the basis of the preliminary diagnosis, it still makes survival-sense to continue scanning everything else that is going on internally and externally. If this checking does not find anything new, the mini-self starts and concludes the action. 'But if elaborative process-ing discloses (or "imagines") a hidden cost of the projected action, it can be aborted before it is implemented' (Claxton 2002: 221). As there is a clear link between vetoing an anticipated course of action and consciousness of some hidden dangers, Libet (1999), Gregory (2005) and some others believe that we possess 'free won't' rather than 'free will'. How would this help us in thinking about the mechanism for change in develop-mental coaching? I would say that it highlights an additional incentive for the contin-uing development of observational skills together with abilities to consider various per-spectives, rather than an opportunity to control the elephant in the moment of action.

Another angle to the role of the rider in relation to the Libet's experiment suggests that while the intention to act studied by Libet may be initiated unconsciously, *prior conscious intentions* may still play a role in action. This does make a lot of sense if we remember that dividing an organism into the rider and the elephant is quite an arti-ficial division. The ego, consisting of various mini-selves, is responsible for the action and when many mini-selves were formed, consciousness could have been very much involved. In the same way through reflection and thinking about particular mini-selves new neural links are established and they can be activated when the organism becomes involved in the next action. Therefore, the rider may not be able to 'control' the ele-phant in the moment of action but it may well contribute to how the elephant will act in the long run.

At the same time not all reflection and thinking turn out to be helpful. Some reflec-tion may be turning over old ground, activating only the routine and old connections. This low effect is quite possible if we are reflecting on our own. That is why the role of the coach is so important. The observations and questioning by the coach around the relevant mini-selves are designed to spread the network of neural links as widely as possible in order to improve a mini-self or may even create a form of scaffolding for a brand new mini-self. As you can see, this is again not about control, but about *influence* coming from the rider.

Coaching is said to be about action. That is why we have so far mostly looked at the relationship between the rider and the elephant in relation to action. But some coaching could be about how we feel. Sometimes clients want to keep doing what they do, but want to feel differently about it. In this case nobody would minimize the role of the rider in influencing our feelings.

And finally in this discussion we need to look at the issue of personal responsibility. This is one of the agendas of coaching even when coaches say that they do not have any agenda. Some coaches, however, are quite explicit that there are two fundamental intentions at the heart of all coaching interventions: *awareness* – helping clients to become aware of what is going on within and around them so that their understanding is enhanced; and *accountability* – encouraging greater levels of personal responsibility for their engagements in the world. But if the rider is not in charge how can we take responsibility for our actions? If we identify ourselves with our conscious rider then it appears that we are not free to make our choices in each particular moment as much as we think we are.

One simple solution to this conundrum is to dismiss what has been discussed on free will and carry on as usual believing in the common sense view which is quite reasonable in relation to morality. Another choice I might have is to see this weird truth but not to identify myself with the rider – to see myself instead as the *whole organism*. It is the whole organism that acts and my conscious thoughts may well influence it in the long run. That is why I am responsible for my actions even if I know that I have not really chosen them consciously in each particular moment. This might be an ultimate existential challenge and the only freedom that we consciously have – to take responsibility for the actions of the organism as a whole, even with the realisation that these actions were not consciously chosen. We can choose to carry on influencing our elephant and working in collaboration with it in order to influence the world and we can also choose to love our fate instead of feeling a victim of it.

What can we do then as coaches for other people if we hold this view? We can help them see this fact if they wish to. We can help them face their responsibilities even if they don't wish to. And we can be there for them in their struggle to find their own way to live with their fate.

Working with the multiplicity of self-models

> Man is divided into a multiplicity of small I's. And each separate small I is able to call itself by the name of the Whole, to act in the name of the Whole, to agree or disagree, to give promises, to make decisions, with which another I or the Whole will have to deal. This explains why people so often make decisions and so seldom carry them out . . . It is the tragedy of the human being that any small I has the right to sign cheques and promissory notes and the man, that is the Whole, has to meet them. People's whole lives often consist in paying off the promissory notes of small accidental I's.
>
> Gurdjieff, 1949

> The great epochs of our lives are at the points when we gain courage to re-baptize our badness as the best in us.
>
> Friedrich Nietzsche, *Beyond Good and Evil*

When we turn inside or observe our behaviour we normally can produce a description of who we are and what we do. This is possible because the rider has a great ability to create various stories using its special function of a narrator. Self-models or various versions of 'me' are created by the narrator. These self-models are conscious stories or theories of self that we think we are. We can see a combination of these self-models as *a centre of identity.*

It appears that the narrator, being a linguistic function in the rider, has developed in evolution together with our ability to use language. The choice of the word 'narrator' rather than the real author indicates that it is not easy to pinpoint the actual author of each story of self whenever it is created. As we are influenced constantly by the culture, by people in our closest environment, by the unconscious needs of the elephant, so all of these in combination should be recognized as the author. The conscious mind can only produce a narrator. The narrator's role is to describe the story of what the actor (a whole organism) is like in each particular situation, or try putting together a story of a lifelong self when looking back at the past. It is not particularly difficult to notice that every time the narrator presents a slightly different story of who we are, depending on the role we play, the mood we are in, just the time of the day or maybe to whom we are describing ourselves. Therefore, some people may sense that there could be many versions of 'me', some may be closely attached to just a few, and some people continue to believe that they are always consistent in describing themselves.

This is not, by the way, a completely new way to understand diversity in our behaviour and our personalities. In philosophy the idea of the multiplicity of self-models can be traced back to Nietzsche. It is also present in one way or another in many psychological theories, such as Berne's ego states or Perls's top dog and underdog. In abnormal psychology the effect of multiple self-stories was studied in order to understand and treat pathological multiplicity: MPD – multiple personality disorder. Some contemporary authors have written on how we can understand and make use of this view of ourselves in everyday life, work and helping relationships. The reader can look at two books that are exclusively devoted to this topic. One is by John Rowan (2009), *Sub-personalities,* and the other by Rita Carter (2008) *Multiplicity: The New Science of Personality.*

However, what is not always clear, including in these books, is whether these self-models are the same as the actual mini-selves. The assumption is often made that the ways we describe ourselves, not just may correspond to the way we engage with the world but actually are the same thing. The notions of the mini-self and self-model can help to understand that this is not the case. For example, I may be in fact a reliable person and present myself as such. But I may tell a story of myself as a reliable person in spite of the evidence to the contrary, when in fact my mini-self responsible for the organism being reliable is simply underdeveloped. At the same time there are millions of mini-selves that are not represented as self-models. The mini-selves facilitate actual ways of engagement with the world, self-models are just stories of how some of these engagements may be, even if there is a perfect harmony between some of them.

In Chapter 7 we also discussed the idea that *interruption from the narrator* could be one of the obstacles to organic change. What could make these stories become an obstacle if they are just stories in comparison to real mini-selves? If they do not correspond to any real mini-self in the long run they may present a problem in relationships with other people involved. If I continuously let people down because of my issue with reliability, while thinking about myself as very reliable, at some point I may start losing customers, friends and important opportunities. On the other hand, if the stories do reflect the actual mini-self they may play a more prominent role in the functioning of the whole organism by creating conscious links between different memories and behaviours.

There are already good ideas in a variety of different theoretical and practical traditions of helping, including coaching, that deal with the multiplicity of self-models even when the multiplicity as such is not explicitly acknowledged or emphasized as important. We are going to make use of them in the following practical Part 3. Here we need to start with the main tasks of such interventions:

- accepting the fact of multiplicity;
- matching a self-story with a real mini-self;
- working on the synthesis of self-models.

Accepting the fact of multiplicity

Sometimes people feel uncomfortable thinking about themselves as a multiplicity of stories. One of the reasons for this could be a potential association with MPD (multiple personality disorder) or a thought of a famous example from literature such as Jekyll and Hyde. To refute this fear we need to say that in contrast to these pathological cases, in which one personality acts independently of another, our multiple self-models do remember what each mini-self actually did while 'leading the show', unless it is the morning after heavy drinking. Our 'normal' self-models 'are more like conjoined twins than entirely separate individuals' (Carter 2008: 21). They share the memory of the major events – only interpretations of them may change to fit different stories.

Another reason for being cautious about accepting themselves as multiplicity might be expressed by those who are taken by the existential approach and an idea of authenticity which is often (and mistakenly) understood as being true to yourself. In fact, authenticity, as defined by existentialists, is not incompatible with the way I describe the self in this section. For Sartre, for example, there is nothing to be true to. Instead, some existentialists see authenticity as a radical openness to the world, oneself and others with recognition of one's personal vulnerability and mortality and with the acknowledgement of the ultimate uncertainty of all that is known (van Deurzen-Smith 2002). Other existentialists would say that the self needs to be continuously chosen, rather than found and kept in its 'true' form (Kierkegaard 1959).

However, even for those who are sceptical about multiplicity, this way of seeing oneself is not new. Everyone observant enough can see that children are natural multiples. Babies can mimic nearly everyone around them and young children will play different roles depending on the situation, what they want from adults and what games they are playing. 'The illusion of unity doesn't kick in until they learn to see themselves as though from the outside – in other words, to be self-reflective. Until then there is only the "I" of the here and now, quite unconnected with the "I" of yesterday or the "I" that will be around tomorrow' (Carter 2008: 95).

Social psychologists also argue that the constantly changing and technologically overloaded life that we live as adults is also challenging for us in this respect. It involves us in different social worlds and various virtual communities, exposing us to a constantly growing variety of opinions, values and lifestyles of others. This is influencing us in different ways and creating ever more multiple selves. However, because the speed of life keeps increasing, many of these interactions and their consequent stories are incomplete narratives. 'There is a populating of the self, reflecting the infusion of partial identities through social saturation ... One begins to experience the vertigo of unlimited multiplicity' (Gergen 1991: 49).

People differ, of course, in how they might deal with this multiplicity. Some just simply do not see it. And this is possible, because at each particular moment I can only see myself as one self-model. It is not possible to be synchronically multiple (Strawson 1999). It is exactly like the well-known tricks of perception used in Gestalt psychology. You can see a vase or two profiles whenever you switch your focus of attention, but you cannot see them both at the same time. Similarly, people just do not notice how they move into a different story of self, because they cannot run two stories at the same time, unless they discuss these stories in a reflective way.

Strawson (1999, 2009) suggests that those who can reflect on who they seem to be in different moments could be divided into Diachronics and Episodics. Diachronics may see the multiplicity and tend to create a cohesive and reasonably consistent narrative that links together their past and will be there in the future. For Episodics it would have little sense that the self that they are now experiencing was there in the past and will be the future. They would be more flexible and not investing in any particular narrative. It might be interesting that Diachronics will tend to be in the quest for discovering the self or creating one. For Episodics the self just happens. So the nature of awareness of multiplicity I believe would be different for these two types. Diachronics may be more inclined to work on the rational synthesis of self-models. Episodics would be more curious about the variety of self-models, however weird they might be, adjusting only to the requirement of the situation:

> I am often confronted by the necessity of standing by one of my empirical selves and relinquishing the rest. Not that I would not, if I could be both handsome and fat and well dressed, and a great athlete, and make a million a year, be a wit, a bon-vivant, and a lady-killer, as well as a philosopher; a philanthropist, statesman, warrior, and African explorer, as well as a 'tone-poet' and a saint.
>
> (James 1999: 73)

Whoever you are, it seems that awareness of the multiplicity of self-models is a useful thing. We could learn about the style of the narrator: what type of story and in what situations it tends to present itself. In this case we would be able to predict our behaviour and to take some extra steps when necessary. For some of us such careful planning is not a luxury. Considering all the assets of different self-models may be the only way they could start anything new. 'Some of us have to hold a meeting every time we want to do something only slightly difficult, in order to find the self who is capable of undertaking it' (Midgley 1984: 123).

John Rowan (1976) gives a wonderful description of how we can benefit from the awareness of the multiplicity of self-models particularly if we are concerned with what we see as a weaknesses in our character:

> Once we begin to think in these terms, many things become clearer – we can start to see how our sub-selves torture each other, how they play games with each other, how they play into each other's hands, and often how little they know each other. And once we know our sub-selves, and give them names, and find out what their nature is, what their motives are, they become powerless to harm us. A shadow is only strong when it is dark; once some light is shed on the scene, it changes colour and may disappear altogether.
>
> (Rowan 1976: 151–2)

Another example from O'Connor (1971) describes how seeing and accepting multiplicity can give additional strength to a client facing a difficult facet of himself and allow him to take a step further in the process of change:

> If I say 'I am jealous', it describes the whole of me, and I am overwhelmed with its implications. The completeness of the statement makes me feel contemptuous of myself. It is little wonder that I fear letting another know when my identity with the feeling is such that it describes the totality of who I am ... If I respect the plurality in myself, and no longer see my jealous self as the whole of me, then I have gained the distance I need to observe it, listen to it, and let it acquaint me with a piece of my own lost history. In this way I come into possession of more of myself and extend my own inner kingdom.
>
> (O'Connor 1971: 23)

Moreover, it has been said that recognizing the many self-models in ourselves can protect us from illness. In an interesting piece of research by Linville (1987) college students were asked to select from the list of various personality features those that they could attribute to themselves. The result has shown that the students who selected more of these qualities, which were at the same time quite distinct from one another, were less likely to suffer from headaches, backaches and infections when they were under stress. They also reported fewer signs of depression. Explanation for this remarkable result was quite logical. Any stressful event can affect only one or two self-models at the same time, but not the whole group of them. And if these self-models are quite distinct there will be more uncontaminated areas of our life that could act as buffers to stress in any one area (1987).

Finally, accepting multiplicity is also good for a coach in the process of understanding the client. We would give up on quick judgments of the type 'If he is like that then there is no hope' or 'If he is like that there will be no problem, he can certainly manage this', just because we had a glimpse of a particular self-model. We would listen to the client with attention that is not restricted by the judgment that that is all there is. It would be an intention for listening that I cannot express better than has already been done by Rowan (1976):

> We can wait for the dialectical movement which is going to bring the next sub-self out into the picture – maybe a directly opposed one. And this makes the job of the listening much easier, because we have given up the impossible task of understanding a person better than she does herself. We can genuinely give ourselves up to following the energy to see where it leads today.
>
> (Rowan 1976: 152)

Matching a self-story with a real mini-self

If accepting the multiplicity of self-models or self-narratives seems worthwhile to you we can look now at the next step in working with this multiplicity. It would involve helping the narrator to write stories that match real mini-selves or at least do not contradict them. We already suggested in Chapter 7 that the narrator can become an obstacle for an organic change if it does not provide any representation of a particular mini-self in the whole set of created stories. If a mini-self is being 'ignored' it may be denied access to relevant memories that could be activated for its benefit – it may miss out on new opportunities for strengthening and development. For example, if a client has a talent for leading groups, but his narrator, being heavily influenced by an old and unfair testimonial or by a real fear associated with it, never includes this facet in his story, this is not good for encouraging change. This story, constantly repeated to oneself or worse, to the client's employer, and not challenged by other memories that may contradict it, may result in preventing this client from seeing and taking new opportunities for organic change. That is why coaches ask their clients again and again to tell them what they do well – to keep the real mini-self in the client attended to and connected with others. This is particularly important in relation to those mini-selves that are not acknowledged or poorly expressed.

On the other hand we have similar grounds to speculate about a positive influence of self-stories in the process of development. Forming a meaningful and powerful story or self-model that is anticipating a new but not completed mini-self may serve as a missing link in the mind/brain. It may help to form new connections in the neural network and to involve other mini-selves in this work. This might bring this new mini-self to life and allow the organic change to happen. For example, the client may choose to mentally rehearse a different image of himself performing a particular task that he could not have done before. He would become accustomed to the sense of the risk and associated fears, which may allow the neural activation to spread to other areas of the brain, and all of this could be useful in performing the task in reality.

There are a number of coaching approaches that specifically ask the client to mimic a person whom they admire for what they want to learn to do. Apparently the brain can be fooled into learning something even from the fake experience. Modelling real situations in any learning environment is used for the same reason. With the current development of technology and new forms of social life people can experiment, even with creating completely new personalities or avatars and through this, try out completely new behaviours and new stories of themselves.

However, we need to be aware of a number of concerns and even pitfalls associated with the process of creating better harmony between the stories of 'me' created by the narrator and the real mini-selves. First of all, we need to know that the narrator, unfortunately, is not very trustworthy, because it has an agenda. The narrator must tell a 'good' story, which has to make sense and to be coherent. So if the situation is complex and muddled, the narrator will fabricate the tale to make it 'work'. Usually we do not notice this but we can, if we are sufficiently attentive. We can notice that the narrator 'adjusts' the memory to make each story more accurate and coherent than it was originally. The narrator has a tendency not only to straighten the story line, but also to dramatize it, particularly if the story is planned for public consumption. The self-models presented by the narrator are also slightly skewed for another reason. 'All things being equal, the Narrator's job is to present 'Me' in a favourable, or at least a sympathetic, light' (Claxton 1994: 118). If we want to understand ourselves and our clients better we need to watch for this tendency of the narrator.

At the same time, for better or worse, this is what we have to rely on when we try to understand ourselves or our clients. If we seriously distrust the narrator and simple observation of behaviour, another option is to put our trust in psychometric tests. You can guess though, that the whole idea of psychometrics does not sit particularly well with the multiplicity of self-models to the same extent as with a multitude of mini-selves. If multiplicity of self-models makes sense to you then the results of psychometric tests can be useful but would need to be looked at in a different light from the one they normally suggest. The main problem with personality testing is a big claim of identifying the essential nature of the person as if different characteristics of the person are just facets of one and the same self. According to the approach adapted in this book there is no essential self, only a combination of facets and these facets can be in quite complex relationships with each other.

How then can we see the results of personality tests from this perspective? There are type tests and trait tests. If we take MBTI (Myers-Briggs Type Indicator) as an example of personality tests which aim to identify our type of personality, we can say that it is constructed with sufficient flexibility. It can accommodate a different interpretation of the results by the person even if his/her interpretation is at odds with what the test showed in the first place. This means that one self-model can change our mind (another self-model's mind) even in the gap between the time of filling in the questionnaire and the time of interpreting the results. A review of eleven studies on the reliability of this test results showed that the number of respondents who were put in the same category on the second testing was between 24 per cent and 61 per cent (Druckman and Bjork 1991: 97). It does not, however, diminish the value of this test if we look at the results as an expression of one story of the self presented by the narrator at that particular time.

Trait tests on the other hand, as 'Big Five' or 'Big Six', are in principle fuzzier than type testing. They do not produce definitive results and, I would say, for a good reason. These tests are claimed to measure the likelihood of a person being, for example, open to experience 80 per cent of the time and not open for 20 per cent, which in itself is quite indicative of the multiplicity rather than the singularity of self. The researchers and testers themselves are not happy with this changeability of the traits according to circumstances. They begin suggesting that the predictive value of trait testing is much improved when people are asked to do the test within a particular frame of reference. This fits exactly with the multiplicity approach. And in fact when people did the Big Five test in each of their roles (for example, parent, student, friend) they rated differently on every one of the tested dimensions in each particular role (Sheldon et al. 1997; Carter 2008).

It is important to mention here that the researchers of personality have a very different task to coaches. They work with a wider focus of interest and their intention of understanding human nature by means of testing is fully justified. The focus of developmental coaches is deep rather than wide and so they need to work with psychometrics in a different way. The type of questions they might ask in relation to such data is:

- Which self-model(s) of the client speaks to me through this data?
- Why is this story chosen by the client's narrator? Why is this story important now?
- What self-model(s) are in the shadow of this data?
- How does this client avoid experimenting with a different story?

Another 'small' trap that we as coaches may fall into is to confuse the transformation of the client with the transformation of the story they tell about themselves. Although the latter could be useful in it-self, overestimating the power of the narrator may just lead to a snowball of wishful thinking and leave the client exactly where he was before. In a real transformation the change in the identity centre follows the change in the executive centre.

Finally, it is useful to remember that the stories of the narrator in relation to the real mini-selves are important provided they are not taken as referring to any underlying reality. They are nothing but words and memories. These stories do play a role in the whole functioning of the whole organism, but this role is not as grand as the narrator tends to describe. If we keep in mind this 'delusion of grandeur' and allocate a more modest role to the narrator in the whole organism then there will be no need to banish it completely as some spiritual traditions tend to imply.

Working on the synthesis of self-models

If we accept the multiplicity of self-models and work towards a better match between the real mini-selves and the narrator's stories about them, the next and more ambitious task may be to create a better synthesis of self-models – a coherent story of self that incorporates many various self-models. This is a task for the narrator that could be facilitated during the coaching process.

A good start is probably to have a fairer picture of the necessity of this task. Creating a synthesis of self-models in the identity centre is not a main task for the survival of the organism. The executive centre will continue working for the benefit of the individual even if the identity centre is quite loose and not very efficient. If we see self-models as employees in the identity centre we could say that some of them may be doing a good job together with their counterparts from the executive centre, but some may be no good. The job of the whole organism will still be done even under this condition.

At the same time if there were to be more order in the identity centre the job of the organism might be done better and we would feel much happier about it.

There are different ways of approaching the task of creating a better order in the identity centre. One potential way is to choose a particular set of self-models that we would prefer to see in ourselves and to try supporting them as much as we can. The benefits of this approach are that the narrator tells a consistent story, selects appropriate feedback to maintain this story and keeps attention on relevant connections with the executive centre. There may however be several problems associated with investing too much in one particular way of seeing oneself:

1   If I am attached to a particular set of self-models this may prevent me from new learning: if I see myself as, for example, not capable in ice-skating I may not even try to learn it.
2   I may need to invest a lot in what can be called 'impression management'. If one particular image is so precious for me I would want others to see me in the same way. Much energy will be involved in creating and maintaining this image for my-self and for others. I may become very vulnerable to any sign of people changing their view about me.
3   I might tend to identify myself with the things and people that are associated with this particular version of 'me'. The danger of this is that losing this connection may become a life tragedy. For example, if the only way I see myself is in my role as a bank manager, and if I lose this job – I am lost as a person and do not know anymore who I am.
4   Such a focus on my particular image may cause a distorted view of others. I may project my suspicions and insecurities onto other people in a similar way as the following joke implies:
    •   I am frank; you are outspoken; he is rude.
    •   I have a large frame; you are heavy; she is fat.
    •   I am appropriately cautious; you are fearful; he is paranoid.
    •   I am discriminating; you are prejudiced; she is bigoted.
    •   I merely assert my point of view; you push yourself on others; she walks all over people.
    •   I change my mind because I am flexible; you change yours because you are wishy-washy; she changes hers because she has no convictions.

Another approach to creating order in the identity centre is interestingly enough, to give up on any order. We could accept the fragmentary nature of the self and choose to see ourselves more like open systems that keep changing by themselves. This approach would help to keep a lighter touch on who we think we are. If our behaviour is not as coherent and consistent in different situations as we might wish it to be and if we surprise ourselves and others by the 'self' that pops up, we might say 'I don't know what came over me' or 'I must have been beside myself' (Claxton 1994: 124). Seeing our fluctuating nature may not be as tragic for us as in the first approach. The sense of self will continue expanding and may include 'the areas of psyche that are less predictable and more mysterious' (Claxton 2004: 137). However, as some conflicts between different self-models could also become more acceptable, these conflicts may continue to happen indefinitely.

Yet another approach is to use rationality in constructing a creative synthesis of self-models that may eventually lead to a better harmony within the identity centre and maybe eventually to a more efficient executive centre. An example of such an attempt is psychoanalysis that promotes coordination between different parts of the psyche and potentially a resolution between ego and counter-ego. In a similar but more experiential way the Gestalt tradition offers many different interventions that promote an active communication between different self-models and their mutual engagement, using for example a famous 'two chairs' exercise. The four columns exercise by Kegan and Lahey (2009) that we have already mentioned in Chapter 7 can be used as an exercise for creating more harmony between different and even contradictory commitments as representatives of their associated self-models.

Creating a synthesis of self-models, however, is not an easy task. In Fingarette's account of the existential position on the self (2000) I found a definition that is very close to what we understand here by self-models. He says that the members of the community of self are 'rudimentary but unified complexes of reason-motive-feeling-aim-means-and-moralistic reactions' (p. 84). Seeing self-models in this way helps to understand that to create a union or to come to a reasonable compromise between some of them might require a high level of rationality and soul searching. That is why some philosophers say that the self has to be seen as an achievement, a synthesis and to choose oneself as an ethical agent is a spiritual act (Sartre 1956; Kierkegaard 1959; Murphy 1965; Fingarette 2000). The problem arises when this work is done, but an individual finds that he is still powerfully inclined towards a particular engagement which is incompatible with an achieved synthesis of self-models. The only solution in this case is self-deception: the person 'refuses' to see a mini-self and corresponding behaviour as an indication of a failure of the achieved synthesis. 'It is from this perspective, so insistently favoured by Sartre and other Existentialists that we see how someone, by reason of lack of spiritual courage, attempts to save his integrity at a price of surrendering, however indirectly, the very integrity that he cherishes' (Fingarette 2000: 138).

It is possible that some clients may need to face this level of work in coaching. Therefore developmental coaches would benefit from the knowledge of traditions that developed different ways of creating some sense of order in the identity centre. In Part 3 we will discuss some further ideas for this purpose.

In conclusion

I am fairly certain that while you were reading this chapter you did not find that all passages fit well with your experience of coaching. Or maybe some ideas were fine for some clients but not fine for others. You are absolutely right because these mechanisms were only discussed so far as general principles and their applications are not yet sufficiently elaborate. These mechanisms must be applied in a different way for different people at different stages of life and for different problems that need to be tackled. The framework for this differentiated approach will be suggested in the next chapter.

9   Developmental framework

All our lives long, every day and every hour, we are engaged in the process of ac-commodating our changed and unchanged selves to changed and unchanged surroundings; living, in fact, is nothing else than this accommodation: when we fail in it a little we are stupid, when we fail flagrantly we are mad, when we suspend it temporarily we sleep, when we give up the attempt altogether we die.

Samuel Butler, *The Way of All Flesh*

In Chapter 8 we described the features and general principles of three mechanisms of developmental coaching: working with perception, the elephant and the narrator. However, it is clear that these general principles require adjustment when we work with different people at different stages of their lives and for the different challenges they face. That is why coaching is a creative process – it is impossible to give an exact recipe for each particular case. It does help, at the same time, if in the sea of all possible variations and differences we can identify some patterns and apply recommendations according to them.

Various theories indicate patterns according to which people can be grouped to-gether if they share some particular features. For example, personality theories suggest dividing people into groups according to their personality features. If we use MBTI we are grouped into, for example, ESTGs or INTPs and a coach might have an idea of what to expect when working with us. Cognitive-developmental theories offer another way of dividing us in groups as we discussed in Chapter 4, so we can be in the groups of those with for example a Socialized Mind or a Self-Authoring Mind. Both of the above sets of theories, and corresponding practical approaches, imply assessment, sometimes complex, of the features that are crucial for their principle of 'slicing the pie'.

In this chapter I will suggest my own way of addressing the issue of individual dif-ferences that I believe makes sense specifically for coaching. At the core of this approach is the idea of development, in this case, of the ego (executive centre of the organism as a whole). Four separate groups of differences associated with the development of the ego are suggested. However, I will be making a case that for the purpose of coaching we do not need assessment of where the client is according to any scale – instead we can work with developmental themes that are brought by clients themselves. It is these themes that would indicate the mix of different features in each client and will help to shape an individual approach to coaching.

I would like to start by supporting the idea that development is a prominent phenomenon in our lives as individuals. As we discussed in Chapter 4 it is impossible to ignore very impressive research indicating the evolution of individuals throughout their lives that is reflected in the research and the theories of Maslow (1954), Loevinger (1987), Graves (1970), Wilber (2000) and many, many others. Some of them draw parallels with the evolution of human kind and use this to postulate changes in the self of each individual.

> ... the process by which individual organisms mature from conception to full growth resembles the way the entire species evolved over millions of years. The statement that 'ontogeny recapitulates phylogeny' refers to the fact that, for instance, human embryos in the womb pass through phases in which they first resemble fish, then frogs, then pigs, and other mammalian embryos – as if the mind-bogglingly slow process of evolution of the human race was repeated, in fast forward, in the course of a few months, by each baby.
>
> (Csikszentmihalyi 1993: 236)

Csikszentmihalyi also suggests that perhaps the same principle holds true for the development of the self in us as human beings after birth. He even advocates the need to accelerate this process because of his warning that we may not have the luxury of slow development nowadays when 'we are capable of destroying ourselves and the environment with increasing ease' (p. 237).

In our everyday life we meet people who grow as individuals throughout their lives. They make changes in their values, their lifestyle – and in many other areas. In our work as coaches we also witness clients who not only resolve their problems and reach their specific goals – they make significant changes in what is considered to be the core of who they are. When they look back at who they used to be they realize that they have developed and are now more able to engage with and influence their environment in a harmonious way, and are becoming more capable of looking after the internal needs and aspirations of their whole organism. Although stasis and regression also happen, it is difficult to deny that we develop, even as adults.

Development and the executive centre (ego)

In the theory of developmental coaching proposed in this book changes in adults that are counted as 'developmental' have to be manifested in new behaviours. This means that these changes take place in the executive centre. The executive centre or ego, as we discussed before, is a network of mini-selves through which the organism engages in numerous experiential cycles and is able to function in the world. Information from individual needs, motives and states of the organism is linked with information from external conditions and opportunities and this activates certain patterns of response. The functioning of the ego is mainly subconscious, but with more complex tasks, consciousness may also become involved. When the organism faces new challenges or develops different needs new mini-selves are created sometimes as a combination of existing mini-selves.

Any significant change in the organism is manifested in many different ways: the perception of a situation becomes clearer, a qualitatively different relationship between the rider and the elephant is established and the narrator produces a story of the self that reflects the actual functioning of a new mini-self. However, we should attribute the main role in determining the maturity of the organism to the ego, because it is the executive centre that, at the end of the day, executes new behaviours.

Unformed ego

The ego could be developed to various degrees, from unformed to fully formed. When the ego is fully developed the mind/brain can act or refrain from action if necessary in a way that reasonably satisfies the organism as a whole with all the multiplicity of its needs and tasks. When the ego is not fully developed there are needs that remain un-satisfied and tasks unfulfilled. For example, the person may have an ability to perform a task but would instead of carrying it out, freeze because of a fear of failure. They actually need more help or guidance from others. Some people cannot take responsibility for their particular actions or inactions in the past which may cause an inadequate assess-ment of the current situation and thus result in a chain of actions not in the interests of the whole organism.

Another sign of the unformed ego is unsettled relationship to other people. Some-times an individual isolates themselves in order not to let others get to know them and so protect themselves from being easily hurt. Most often they get fused with another person or group or organization, losing the sense of boundaries between themselves and others. It is important to say that the description of an unformed ego does not explain the whole character of the person. Those with unformed egos can be kind or mean, adventurous or down to earth, intellectual or practical, serious or playful, and so on. What seems to be characteristic is a higher dependency on others which results in a reduced sense of control over their environment and themselves. The areas of mind/brain that are associated with the views of other people, norms and rules, and so on, are highly represented in the workings of the mini-selves.

Formed ego

The sign of a fully formed ego is the capacity of the whole organism to take ownership of the past, withstand anxiety about what future holds and build relationships with others without losing the sense of who they are. The shift from Unformed ego to Formed ego is probably the most critical change in the majority of adults. The description of a person with a Formed ego would match with the way we usually describe a real adult. This is a fulfilling stage that creates a sense of achievement and freedom in spite of the many responsibilities that could be assumed. Life, however, does not become easier with a Formed ego. The pressures of life will remain and may even grow, because people with a Formed ego may willingly face and even create challenges to test their ego. But they will feel less like the victims of circumstances and some may even enjoy challenges.

It is important to notice that this state of the ego may not say much about the nature of their responsibilities or the direction of their initiatives. Their choices may be constructive or destructive, but they are made according to their own criteria that can be rationally explained. Although this stage of the ego is an achievement it is associated with some developmental challenges. The sense of control and self-ownership may lead to an overestimation of what is possible and realistic for the organism, which may result in a lack of attention to and even abuse of the body when working to achieve some specific targets. The sense of independence from other people coupled with self-righteousness may lead to misunderstandings and conflicts in relationships.

Reformed ego

The Unformed and Formed egos as described above are not the end of the story. In Chapter 4 we discussed the cumulative description of the three stages in adult development (Table 4.2) drawn from a number of relevant developmental theories. The third category, which we call a Reformed ego, represents capacities of the ego that go beyond those of the Formed ego. They describe a much more harmonious relationship between the elephant and the rider, manifested in the ability of the organism to tolerate the ambiguity of some needs and tasks, thus minimizing energy wasted on conflicts between the various mini-selves. Instead of investing in 'being right', at this stage people become increasingly interested in authenticity, which could be described as congruence between the executive centre and the identity centre. There is more awareness of the quality of information received by the brain/mind at this stage. People notice how they are influenced by language itself, let alone more explicit brainwashing devices. They also become more aware of how they deceive themselves and how the stories created by their narrator keep changing.

Ego with a soul

We also need to consider a level beyond the three mentioned above. We know that a number of developmental theories postulate and provide significant evidence for at least one more level that suggests a different picture of the world and consequently a different relationship between the various elements of the self (Wade 1996; Cook-Greuter 1999; Wilber 2006). Individuals interested in this picture of the world look for a different dimension of development that includes their spiritual needs and aspirations. This developmental route is much less understood and so not as predictable as the others. Although more and more people are now interested in this side of life, the opportunity of studying it is limited by the tiny proportion of people who seem to be demonstrating capacities different from the three other stages. There is an argument though that the traditional scientific methods are insufficient for understanding the deeper significance of this route to development. We might need not only different research strategies to study them, but potentially a new paradigm.

However, as many people nowadays aspire to this level of development I believe that we cannot ignore the needs of these people in developmental coaching while waiting for a new paradigm to emerge. Therefore I have added to the framework another stage of development that will be called 'ego with a soul'. I have to admit though that the topic of soul is not easy to discuss for many reasons. The list of reasons could start with a problem of defining spiritual (Wilber 2006). I will say more about these difficulties in Chapter 11, but at this point I want to emphasize the complexity of this stage because of the diversity of people that it might include, for example:

1   people who demonstrate unusual capacities (these capacities may indicate a stage reached by a few);
2   people who have had special (spiritual) experiences (these experiences could indicate a state which may happen to a lot of people);
3   people who have deep interest in the spiritual (an inclination that could be shared by anyone).

1   *The first* group is of those who demonstrate unusual acquired capacities of the organism beyond those previously described and which may appear spontaneously or as the result of spiritual practices. For example, there is documented evidence that long-term meditators can control their responses to various stressors much better than we normally do. Their abilities can increase with the length of meditation and this can be registered on special equipment (Kasamatsu and Hirai 1969; Blackmore 2003). Some rare individuals seemingly demonstrate that they can consciously control and even stop all brain waves as if they were asleep or even dead (see video clip on YouTube: Ken Wilber Stops His Brain Waves). Cook-Greuter (1999) in her study identified many remarkable characteristics of this group such as an entirely new way of perceiving human existence and consciousness, acceptance and affiliation with all manifestations of life, equanimity, and an unassuming presence. Even those who have not reached such a state but persevere with their practice say that they become more loving and compassionate. On the other hand, the latter effects are mainly internally judged and can be easily questioned by sceptics who also argue that hard data, for example, on the effect of meditation on relaxation or special powers is inconclusive. Blackmore (2003) and Fenwick (1987: 116), however, remind us that people meditate for a much deeper reason – for greater understanding of the world – and so the 'proof' of their developed capacities is not their concern. Although it is difficult to imagine these people asking for coaching, there could be coaching clients who aspire to such levels of development.

2   *The second* and much wider group is of people who occasionally have unusual experiences that may happen spontaneously or as the result of spiritual practice. Some may even have such experiences quite often. They could vary from important and moving to profound and highly significant in terms of their development as the following example demonstrates.

> I was walking across a field turning my head to admire the Western sky and looking at a line of pine trees appearing as black velvet against a pink backdrop, turning to duck egg blue/green overhead, as the sun set. Then it happened.

It was as if a switch marked 'ego' was suddenly switched off. Consciousness expanded to include, *be*, the previously observed. 'I' was the sunset and there was no 'I' experiencing 'it'. No more observer and observed. At the same time – eternity was 'born'. There was no past, no future, just an eternal now ... then I returned completely to normal consciousness finding myself still walking across the field, in time, with a memory.

(Hay 1990: 50)

This is a beautiful description of such an experience, but we can see that the different notions of self are difficult to discern. For example, what we understand in this book by 'ego' could not be switched off as the person experiencing this was still walking. We could say that the narrator was switched off and possibly something else was happening, but the ego was still in place. In other literature these experiences are called ASC (altered states of consciousness), peak experiences, epiphanies, transpersonal experiences, etc. In coaching people may wish to find a way to have such experiences more often or to make sense of them or integrate them in their current view of the world.

3   *The third* group includes many of us who are looking for a meaningful explanation of what the world may be like and what life is all about. It could be a traditionally religious route or a quest with a high respect for science but without disregarding that which is important in our lives. My belief is that this group is constantly growing and it is quite likely that some of our coaching clients may be open to a conversation that includes this dimension as well.

It is obvious that there could be people who belong to all three of these groups. Some might be in just one or two and some – not in any of them. Only the first group could be treated as a stage, but we are not going to exclude the other two from our developmental framework and I will explain later why we can do this. Altogether, according to the described four stages of ego development, the developmental tasks of the person and the corresponding focus of coaching are described in Table 9.1.

Table 9.1   Developmental tasks and foci of coaching

Stage of ego development	Developmental task	Focus of coaching
Unformed ego	Developing a healthy ego	Coaching towards a healthy ego
Formed ego	Living with a strong ego	Coaching the ego
Reformed ego	Developing beyond the ego	Coaching beyond the ego
Ego with a soul	Developing the soul	Coaching the soul

Coaching according to developmental themes

From our experiences of coaching approaches based on the theories of adult development we know that the process of coaching people who belong to different stages of development should also be different, because each stage has its specific characteristics. To illustrate this we can use an example of coaching that involves the 360 degree feedback exercise. This exercise is designed to enable people to gain an insight into how they are perceived by others. In the case of an unformed ego the person is already very much influenced by others. Their view of themselves is practically an internalized view of how others see them. Therefore, if this view is fully confirmed in this exercise it would not make any difference to their development and so does not offer much for a coach to work with. If they receive feedback that they perceive as worse than they had expected it may be too overwhelming for them. The task of the coach in this case would be to help them cope with the psychological trauma rather than to focus on development. Quite differently, the 360 degree feedback could be most useful for those with a formed ego. As they are confident in their own view of themselves their attitude to feedback will depend on how rigid this view is and if they are interested in development. If development is important for them the feedback would give very rich information to work with. If their view is rigid they may simply dismiss feedback incongruent to their view. In this case it is an indication that there is a need for much deeper work. Those with a reformed ego may be curious about 360 degree feedback, but the importance of this exercise will depend on what role it plays in other strategic areas of their life. It is even more difficult to predict what role this exercise would play in coaching the soul.

So far, this developmental framework has been described in a way that is no different in terms of its central idea from the other cognitive-developmental approaches. However, I promised a different approach which implies working with developmental themes. To argue for the value of this approach I will start with a consideration of potential problems with traditional developmental approaches which focus on identifying the stage the person is at. These problems prompted me to look for a different stance on working with individual differences. I will also revisit some specific differences between coaching and other forms of understanding and helping people which support this new proposition.

Problems with traditional developmental approaches to coaching

One of the first concerns about developmental theories is relationship between stages and environment. It is well accepted that individual differences result from the interaction of the person's stage of growth with their current psychical and social circumstances. However, critics of developmental theories claim that what seem like stages are the result of incidental growth and social expectations and sanctions, as programmed by the culture, the community and the family and so may differ in different environments. For example, Gilligan (1992) successfully challenged Kohlberg's (1969) stages of moral development when applied to girls rather than the boys studied by Kohlberg. She argued that cultural and biological roles of girls are different. At the same time she identified a different stage-based progression for them in terms of moral development. Even Loevinger (1987) herself admits that looking at the pool of data available 'there is neither warrant for discarding the idea of stages nor for construing development as a strict progression along a narrow, logically defined path' (p. 242). All comes down to one's methodology that determines the range of admissible results. However, she still argues that each person progresses from one stage to the next as a result of their own pattern of interests and various circumstances. In the same way other proponents of the developmental approach agree that different groups of people in different circumstances will change according to different patterns, but they maintain that these patterns are still developmental. This concern is relevant in the same way to the stages of ego development that I suggest. I could argue that ego in my theory is about the most basic structure in the mind/brain/organism interaction with any environment and so the stages of ego development should be less affected by cultural expectations than, for example, the stories of the narrator. At the same time, it is still an assumption that can be questioned.

Another concern with developmental theories is the idea of overall development which divides various authors. Some of them, for example Loevinger, believe that developmental theory should indicate commonality. 'If the stages really reflect a common "deep structure", the stages of those variables should all proceed in tandem.' (1987: 242). Not surprisingly, there are claims from authors (Loevinger 1987; Beck and Cowan 1996; Wade 1996; Laske 2006a) who believe that their theories describe such a structure. The fact that all of them are somewhat different unfortunately works against their arguments. Wilber (1999, 2006) on the other hand, argues that the overall mixture of developmental lines does not follow stages, insisting that 'each individual's unfolding will be a radically unique affair' (1998: 122). Although the idea of an overall developmental structure is appealing I side with Wilber because of seeing the actuality of working with each individual client. Whatever each theory suggests the picture describing an individual is messy, as in Figure 4.1. When we encounter an individual client, we may need to work with a variety of developmental lines such as interpersonal, cognitive, emotional, moral, and so on. This requires addressing each area of development with an open mind in spite of the indication of a particular stage in some of the others.

My next concerns with traditional developmental theories are related to other realities of coaching practice. These theories were not conceived to serve coaching practice. They were developed in order to gain a better understanding of individual differences, for example, how different people make meaning of their life tasks and how the way they think and make meaning changes over time. The purpose of this work was scientific: to observe, describe and explain the differences between people in relation to the developmental aspects they chose to focus on. Therefore, all of these theories implicitly or explicitly involve diagnostics of studied aspects and stages of their development. It is understandable and completely justified that the methods for identifying and measuring at what stage an individual is, are very complex. On the other hand, it is difficult to envisage that any coach could be trained in such a way as to be able to assess their clients against such developmental frameworks. So, even without discussing some potential methodological issues with their diagnostic tools, the quality use of these approaches is restricted by the need for a serious, maybe even lifelong training in the diagnostics of the stages.

Some final practical concerns are connected to the whole idea of the developmental agenda in coaching. The thought of an overall development which could be measured in the client can become a temptation for both a client and a coach to establish it as a plan for coaching. One of the consequences of this is the pursuit of an abstract ideal and so a diversion of energy from those real life situations that clients may need to deal with. It is also possible that continuous comparison with a higher level of development may undermine a client's belief in themselves and their current abilities, so diminishing their self-efficacy. And yet another, and probably the most important concern is that this pursuit may also create an illusion that qualitative developmental shifts can happen with sufficient motivation and effort. Although motivation and effort are important in coaching their power should not be overestimated – the type of development that we discuss here is a very complex process that involves enormous numbers of known and unknown internal and environmental factors. It can take years just to recognize some shifts. Therefore, setting up an explicit task of moving the client through developmental levels or stages in a short-term coaching contract is, to say the least, irresponsible.

An alternative approach

Consideration of the above issues suggests that we need a different approach to working with the developmental framework that is not only compatible with coaching but is designed specifically for it. Initially, in order to do this we need to acknowledge what all the authors of developmental theories agree with and what is also confirmed by research: people can move a stage up or down from the one that is identified as a centre of gravity when significant change to the organism happens. Secondly, people can occupy different stages in different areas of their life, for example the ego may seem formed in the area of work, but show all the signs of being unformed in personal relationships. Hughes and Flowers (1978) have identified six domains in which people may demonstrate completely different stages of development without experiencing internal conflict: sex, work, religion, politics, social situations and family/marriage. Thirdly, developmental theories emphasize *internal* predispositions to development. However, there are many factors in the environment that may stimulate significant changes, such as a new workplace, a new relationship or just a matter of time available for change. When changes of such a nature take place it appears that the issues that people have and their needs and priorities in life also change. According to these needs and priorities they bring different issues for coaching and formulate different goals.

At the same time reviewing many developmental theories I noticed that there is a pattern in themes that is characteristic of each particular stage and it is consistent even for different individuals. Thus I assumed that particular issues and associated goals of an overarching nature could be associated with each stage of ego development across different individuals. I call these issues and goals here '*developmental themes*'. These themes are not only about goals – they are about the challenges that people face in life, what they find difficult, what their life circumstances demand from them.

For example, the issue of confidence and self-esteem is typical for the first stage of ego development. It often becomes an overarching topic for coaching people with an unformed ego, because their well-being depends on how they are seen and valued by others. Kegan (1982) even suggests that strictly speaking 'self-esteem' is not an applicable term for individuals at this stage, as their 'esteem' does not come from their sense of 'self', but rather from the received and unexamined opinions of others. At the next stage the topic of self-esteem is not as prominent. It may sometimes present as

Table 9.2 Potential developmental themes (enhanced for selected stages on the original Wade's (1996: 263) table of transitional dilemmas)

Stage	Core assumption	Transitional dilemmas	Corresponding challenge
Unformed ego/ conformist	The universe is fair, so I can ensure my security by being good.	Life is not fair.	Learning to stand on one's own feet.
Formed ego/ achievement	I can be the master of my fate through my own initiative.	Some forces cannot be controlled.	Learning to see things from many perspectives.
Reformed ego/ authentic	I need to be all that I can be to fulfil my purpose in life.	I can only realize my potential by giving up myself.	Learning to live with paradox and see through constraints of language.
Ego with a Soul/ transcendent	I seek to be one with the Ground of All Being.	Seeking or not seeking the Ground keeps me from it.	Learning a new way of being.

a concern about confidence in relation to a particular task or performance but does not have an overarching nature and is most likely an indication of a need for better judgment about ambitions and reality. It is unlikely that the theme of self-esteem will reappear for the reformed ego and the ego with a soul.

Some of the developmental themes are not just characteristic to a particular stage, but also emphasize a major developmental challenge that needs to be overcome in order to proceed to the next stage. Wade (1996) for example, describes the main assumptions and transitional dilemmas in relation to stages that are similar to ego-development proposed in this book. I have added some corresponding challenges to her suggestions to illustrate these major developmental themes that could also be addressed in coaching (Table 9.2).

Developmental themes are what clients bring to coaching, formulated from their own perspective of their overarching needs and challenges. At the same time these themes can be identified as characteristic to four developmental stages as described. This approach therefore, eliminates the need for formal assessment to discern the stage the individual client is at. Instead it allows for full engagement with the theme chosen by the client, but with the knowledge and understanding that this theme is developmental.

The task of the coach

A developmental coach would approach a new assignment initially in the same way as any other coach: identifying the clients' needs, exploring their situation fully and clarifying his goals. These are the most important tasks which should not be minimized by the focus on the client's stage of development. However, as she proceeds she will also develop a sense of the state of the client's ego from taking into account the goals and issues they both identified, the challenges the client faces and the difficulties he experiences. The task of the coach is to engage with whatever theme is presented, but noticing at the same time a pattern in these themes. The job to do between the sessions is to explore these patterns and consider relevant coaching strategies through reflection on the previous sessions, preparation for the coming sessions and discussion of these cases in supervision.

For example, the pattern of an unformed ego which requires coaching towards a healthy ego may be identified if the client expresses insufficient belief in his ability not only in relation to a particular task at work but also in other areas of life. He may find it quite challenging to disagree with significant people in his life. He may wish to develop a sense of control in himself and his environment and to have tangible results. You as a coach may feel that he gives you too much power in your relationship and an unlimited opportunity to influence him.

In terms of selecting coaching interventions coaches may choose to use any appropriate tools and methods that they are familiar with. There are traditional approaches particularly useful for some specific developmental themes. For example, Cognitive-behavioural coaching and Transactional Analysis have good methods suitable for coaching towards a healthy ego. The Existential approach on the other hand fits well with coaching beyond the ego. In addition to these approaches the developmental coach would be also considering the three main mechanisms that we discussed in Chapter 8: working with perception, the elephant and the multiplicity of self-models.

This approach is flexible, because clients can bring in themes that belong to various groups. It is possible that circumstances offer the challenges that may shift the focus from the themes of one stage to another. For example, illness may affect the theme of achievement that began unfolding but had to be put on hold and the client now may require coaching towards a healthy ego. The same illness may accelerate the developmental process and the client may begin to question the theme of achievement indicating the need for coaching beyond the ego. The loss of a partner may revive a theme of aloneness and revisiting a need to belong and to be in a relationship. This may affect the process of living with the ego and would need coaching towards a healthy ego. A new job and the expanded range of responsibilities may temporarily awake doubts about the capacity to manage them, so the issue of confidence may become prominent again even though it had been resolved in the past. Coaching the soul could be a part of any one of the other three types of coaching if the client's interests in spirituality are explicit.

It is important to notice that although much of the thinking and reflection on developmental themes and relevant coaching strategies is done outside the coaching session, if necessary the coach is prepared to be absolutely transparent about this with the client. In spite of the fact that the ego is mostly unconscious, the developmental coach works explicitly with the rider in order to increase its participation in the process and to help the client to take responsibility for potential changes. The outcomes of development may affect the client in many different ways and not all of them may be considered by him as positive at different stages of the process. Therefore the responsibility of the coach is to work in partnership with the rider of the client and let the client be in charge of this process. When other parties have a stake in the result of coaching they also need to be aware, as fully as possible, of potential outcomes.

To summarize the nature of the approach:

- Developmental coaches need to identify developmental themes presented by the client as typical to one or more of the ego-development stages.
- The coaching process and the role of the coach in relation to each of these stages may differ.
- The coach is prepared to be explicit about her view on development and the coaching process.
- The implications of the process and the outcomes of resulting changes are made explicit for all parties involved.

Evaluation of this approach to coaching

I want to emphasize again some particular features of this approach to coaching, and to illustrate at the same time how it is different from the traditional cognitive-developmental theories and their adaptations to practice.

No assessment

Developmental coaching as introduced here does not require diagnosis of the client's state of development. The thematic approach to the task of coaching implies that the coach starts from the client's presented theme, keeping in mind that the theme in itself may be developmental. The coach may use the methods of the traditions they were trained in if these traditions have the necessary tools for the presented theme.

No temptation to impose a developmental agenda by the coach

The developmental coach will stay faithful to the themes presented by the client without an assumption that the client needs to progress in terms of overall development. A useful reminder of this which I like is: 'amongst the many things from which a practitioner's clients need protection is the practitioner's hopes for the client's future, however benign and sympathetic these hopes may be' (Kegan 1982: 296).

No judgment

Coaches are usually sensitive to assessing and categorizing their clients which goes against an implicit characteristic of coaching as being non-judgmental. Other developmental approaches, by the very fact of presenting developmental scales, imply judgments. These judgments are fairly justified when they aim to facilitate a better fit between the environment and the individual's capacity for dealing with it. However, it may still create unease in many coaches. Developmental coaching as proposed here shifts the weight of judgment from the person to the developmental theme and leaves more space for manoeuvre when themes from different stages are presented.

Working with the whole individual rather than a developmental line

Other developmental approaches usually focus on one developmental line. The focus of the main cognitive-developmental theories, for example, is mainly on the structure of meaning-making. The developmental approach presented here is interested in the whole organism in action and therefore in the ego of the client which is mainly unconscious. The emphasis is then on working with the whole individual: an elephant as well as a rider. Meaning-making and working with assumptions are important but not the only and not the central focus of this process.

Respect for complexity

Developmental coaching is based on a theory which appreciates the complexity of the human psyche and the organism as a whole in the constant interaction with the external world. It warns against a too light approach to designing and suggesting interventions to 'move' clients from one stage to another, thus creating the illusion that significant developmental shifts can be induced by sufficient motivation and effort. In this I agree with Berger's warning about hasty judgments of developmental stages, particularly in organizational contexts (2006: 96).

And finally . . .

The differences of developmental coaching to some others in the field begin from the very perception of the client and follow into a corresponding principle of coaching. It is easy to demonstrate this in comparison to some other potential standpoints:

- If we see the client *as a problem* we may try to mould him into someone else.
- If we see the client as someone who *has a problem* we may try to fix the problem.
- If we see the client as someone *in the process of development* we may try to help him to move to the next stage.
- If we see the client as someone who is *facing a challenge connected to a developmental theme* we help him to engage fully with this theme keeping in mind its developmental significance.

And thus we may be able to contribute to the well-being of our clients if they wish to learn how 'to derive spontaneous joy and deep satisfaction from living their lives. Not from gaining riches and honours, but from the very process of living, from developing skills and overcoming challenges – from being a part of the evolutionary process that leads to higher levels of harmonious complexity' (Csikszentimalyi 1993: 215).

PART 3
Coaching according to the developmental framework

10 Introduction to Part 3

In this section we will be looking at each stage of the developmental framework separately, keeping in mind a practical question: what a coach might do differently with each group of themes if they want to coach developmentally. We will be focusing here on:

- typical issues and tasks when working with the developmental themes of each stage;
- relevant approaches and interventions for each stage;
- the role of the coach and the nature of coaching relationships in each stage.

In terms of typical issues and tasks we will discuss what is most characteristic for each stage, what themes these clients might bring to coaching and how these themes can be recognized as developmental. We will also try to identify what is most difficult for these clients and what developmental challenges they suppose to overcome.

In terms of relevant approaches and interventions we will be looking at the three main mechanisms of developmental coaching: improving perception, working with the elephant and with the multiplicity of self-models (Chapter 8). The details of working with each of these mechanisms will be different for each stage of developmental coaching. I will be drawing on a number of different approaches to coaching (Palmer and Whybrow 2007; Cox et al. 2010) that have a proven history of application in the context of coaching as well as counselling/psychotherapy and other areas of one-to-one work with clients. I acknowledge that there could be as many different styles and approaches to coaching as there are coaches. I hope you will use this developmental framework to reflect on your work and enhance your skills. I also hope that the richness and diversity of your experiences may eventually add many more specific details to the practice of developmental coaching.

I would not like to give an impression that it will be easy to decide to which stage each developmental theme might belong. Although I will include many examples in each chapter at the end of the day it will be only your own decision that can be trusted. A discussion with your supervisor can also help. You could start practising this straight away using the following exercise (Box 10.1). Although natural drivers are not developmental themes the exercise may still be useful. Drivers are more general motivational forces that are present in each of us to various degrees. In comparison to them, developmental themes are more concrete and related to specific tasks in clients' lives. However, the exercise could be used as a starting point for thinking about the relationship between developmental themes and stages.

BOX 10.1   Mapping typical drivers with the ego-development stages

Try to map some of the typical drivers from the following list to the four ego-development stages discussed. Use the number of the driver to allocate it in one of the circles on Figure 10.1 where you think it is more likely to belong. Each driver may be also placed on the overlaps between the stages.

1   short-term hedonism (to be content, to have good things in life);
2   security (financial, reputation);
3   OK-ness;
4   success, achievement;
5   actualization of all potentials (skills, abilities);
6   balance/homeostasis with environment (e.g. minimization of conflicts, healthy and eco-friendly lifestyle);
7   existential concerns (dealing with anxiety over mortality, issues of freedom, relatedness);
8   self-understanding and personal growth;
9   excitement, joy of being alive;
10   transcendence.

Repeat the exercise when you have finished reading Part 3. Compare these two ways of mapping:

• Which driver was the easiest to allocate? Which was the most difficult to allocate? Why?
• What has changed between your two ways of mapping? Why?

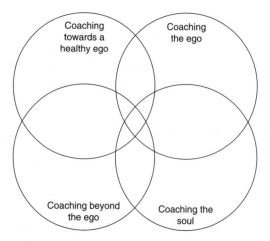

Figure 10.1   Allocating drivers in relation to developmental stages.

I am sure that you understand that it is not possible to put together a list of all potential developmental themes and to group them according to the stage of ego development. Human nature is too complex and we are too unique to create a neat structure of all possible combinations of developmental themes, drivers and stages. However, I hope that the structures already suggested, and examples that will be provided in this section, together with your own knowledge, experience and intuition, will help to make your coaching more developmental.

11 Coaching towards a healthy ego

...he who has made one blunder after another, and still lies in middle life among the failures at the foot of the hill, is liable to grow all sicklied o'er with self-distrust, and to shrink from trials with which his powers can really cope.

William James, 1890

That which we do not bring to consciousness appears in our lives as fate.

C.G. Jung, *Collected Works*

Many authors of developmental theories provide statistics that suggest that the shift from unformed to formed ego is the main developmental shift in adults, through which a large proportion of the adult population progresses. This means that there is a high probability that many clients will bring themes of this nature to coaching. This implies the need to give sufficient attention to understanding what coaching towards a healthy ego may look like. In order to discuss this to the depth it deserves I will choose one theme that is most prominent for this stage. I will justify this choice and suggest in more detail how and why the coach may choose to work on this theme.

Typical issues and tasks of this stage

First of all let us quickly revisit what the unformed ego means. When the ego is not fully developed the mind/brain can engage in many tasks but may not be able to accomplish them to the extent that reasonably satisfies the organism without the help of other people. Some mini-selves are formed, but some are lacking in terms of the quality of information input, the capacity to process it or a behavioural component. Emotions play a dominant role in the functioning of mind/brain in response to difficulties, particularly when there is a need to bear ambiguity and the uncertainty of situations. The sense of control that may come from the ability to evaluate rationally main factors involved in the situation is limited. Because of this there may be some needs unsatisfied or tasks not initiated or not completed. Therefore, those with an unformed ego genuinely require clear guidance, explicit rules and more support from others. They could depend on others for such help and could be highly influenced by their views. They may find it difficult to take responsibility for their particular actions or inaction in the past and feel that they have insufficient control over their environment and themselves.

This description may remind you of a child. However strange this comparison with children may sound, it makes sense if we see a fully grown up person as someone with a formed ego. Of course, it has little to do with age. The ego can be formed pretty early in some young people, but a lot of adults can remain with an unformed ego throughout their whole lives. At the same time the roles of people with unformed egos in society can be very important; they may have their own children and be very good citizens. They could be making many decisions, but these decisions are made with a high proportion of input from the values and rules of others, assimilated by the mind without questioning. It may not be obvious but the egos of these people still need to learn to function independently in order for the whole organism to stand on its own two feet. As a sense of control over oneself and one's environment is important for a person's well-being, they may know that they need to be more independent than they currently are and this could be a source of low self-esteem.

Typical themes that could be brought by these clients for coaching are:

- making a decision on important areas of life;
- standing up for themselves when unfairly treated;
- identifying their position in situations that involve a number of stakeholders significant for them;
- taking on a role that requires a higher level of responsibility than they feel they can cope with;
- work-life balance issues related to the lack of prioritizing or inability to say 'no';
- accepting the consequences of their actions and decisions;
- taking responsibility for the team;
- taking control over their own well-being;
- a need for confidence building;
- performance anxiety;
- issues of self-esteem.

The main need of the ego behind these themes is *to be able* to act, to perform; but the rider, instead of helping, could stay in the way. For example, performance anxiety in the unformed ego is often associated with high self-consciousness. This is a state of the organism when the rider takes the central stage in the functioning of the mind/brain, activating attention to multiple, often incompatible actions and their negative consequences. It often happens when the cost of error – especially social costs – are perceived as unbearably high and shame and guilt seem unavoidable. All of these lead to what Claxton (1999) describes as a system crash: flow of action is reduced to nothing; action becomes crude and jerky; perception becomes flighty or fixated; emotional alarm signals anxiety of not knowing what to do for the best. Claxton also explains this in brain terms: 'The more anxious and upset one becomes with one's own performance, the less neural activation there is left over to generate the skilful engagement of the muscles, or the accurate perception of the senses' (1999: 173).

Looking at the list of themes that could become the focus of coaching towards a healthy ego it appears that some themes are concerned with how the client feels and some are about action and performance in a general sense. In some 'doing' themes a fear, for example, of taking on a role that requires a higher level of responsibility may be fairly justified. It could be related to a realistic judgment of potential demands that can actually be beyond the current abilities of the client. It is possible, at the same time, that this theme can be brought by clients with a fairly formed ego or even a reformed ego. What we are going to discuss as useful strategies in this respect would be of help in these cases, too. However, I want to make a case for the issue of self-esteem as one of the central themes of an unformed ego and will explain how it could be used as a typical example of coaching towards a healthy ego.

Self-esteem is conceived of as one of the main needs of the individual (Maslow 1954), but maybe not for its own sake. I would like to suggest that the need for self-esteem is just another side of the need to belong, to be part of the group, to be accepted by important others. They are linked because the ego cannot cope without extra help. Research (Leary et al. 1999) convincingly shows that self-esteem is quite strongly correlated with anxiety over social rejection and exclusion. Leary et al. examined other explanations of why people strive for self-esteem, for example, buffering against anxiety and uncertainty, promoting goal achievement or just for its own sake, but provide good arguments to dismiss each of them as insufficient. Their explanation instead is based on the most basic understanding of human nature: 'Because solitary human beings in a primitive state are unlikely to survive and reproduce, psychological systems evolved that motivated people to develop and maintain some minimum level of inclusion in social relationships and groups' (Leary et al. 1999: 89).

If we see the need for self-esteem and the need to belong as intrinsically the same it is much easier to explain why they are prominent at the same stage of ego-development and why they create an impossible situation for a person at this stage (Figure 11.1). The unformed ego naturally needs more support, whether from other people or from clear rules and guidelines created by others. The executive centre is not ready to cope with new and difficult situations without relying on memorized accepted norms or actual suggestions from others. The problem is, as we already said, that this would be normal for children, but for adults there is another 'rule' or expectation which dictates that they should be able to take care of at least themselves and perhaps of others without help. This creates a discrepancy between how the client perceives himself and what

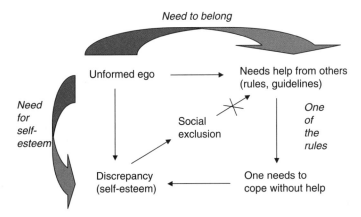

Figure 11.1 The problem of self-esteem in an unformed ego.

he believes is expected from him. In this case self-esteem may be experienced as a gap between what one is 'supposed to be able to do' and what one can actually do. That is why adults and particularly men sometimes feel ashamed of admitting the issue of low self-esteem; it is like admitting to not being grown up. If the client brings an issue of low self-esteem he may be concerned with not being accepted by others because he cannot fulfil one of their important expectations.

This conceptualization of self-esteem in turn fits with the results of research on and the explanation of self-esteem by Leary et al. (1999). They argue that self-esteem works like a *sociometer* 'that monitors the degree to which the individual is being included versus excluded by other people and that motivates the person to behave in ways that minimize the probability of rejection or exclusion' (Leary et al. 1999: 88). This requires the client to behave according to the expectations of others and so can reinforce the need to be grown up, but the ego is not ready for this. By not fulfilling an expectation a person might be socially excluded, which may lead to a problem with getting help if necessary which is paramount for an unformed ego. So the person is now in the middle of an impossible knot.

The choices that people have in such situations is either to ignore the expectation of being independent and accept the role of someone who is often in need of support, which used to be an option for women; or to find a niche in which they can learn to perform appropriately, fulfilling the expectations of others and not move too far from that niche. Yet another option is to take risks but to act as if one is fully independent, coping with all the difficult feelings associated with this. Brookfield called these feelings an 'Impostor Syndrome': 'We wear an external mask of control, but beneath it we know that really we are frail figures, struggling to make it through to the end of each day. There is the sense that around the corner is an unforeseen but cataclysmic event that will reveal us as frauds' (1995: 230).

From the perspective of other people, those with unformed egos may appear indecisive and may be perceived of as a 'pushover'. Sometimes they are recommended to attend assertiveness training and to learn how to stand up for themselves. As they are influenced by the standards and rules of others without much discrimination, it is inevitable that some of these standards may in fact be unattainable, unreasonable or become outdated. The coach can help them to discriminate what sort of support is beneficial and useful to keep and what they can do already without. However it is important, at the same time, not to create a dangerous gap in their support system, because the unformed ego depends on appropriate help. To expect them to act completely independently is wanting too much too soon.

In terms of a possible course of action, if low self-esteem *is* an indicator of social exclusion there seems to be no point in changing it artificially. It would be like fixing the indicator that shows that the level of fuel in your car is low, instead of going to a petrol station and filling it up. If self-esteem is boosted just by praise and indiscriminate support, the individual may lose touch with how they are actually perceived and may lose the support they need when necessary. Contrary to popular belief simple positive affirmations (for example, looking in the mirror and telling yourself that you are successful) are not very useful. They may temporarily inflate self-esteem but it can be easily burst if something unexpected happens.

We can speculate that it would be better if people were accepted as being what they are at this particular stage – unformed egos. In this light high self-esteem in childhood and adolescence would be an anomaly. It may be the result of very strong defences. Or it could be high, even when the ego is unformed, because the child has been unconditionally included in the family environment. In early childhood this might be sufficient, but later the inclusion is required from peers and wider groups. The acceptance of the family may not feel enough because the young person is aware that the family know him/her only from one perspective.

In children this issue is simpler for another reason: they experience high self-esteem if included and low self-esteem if excluded. They would do anything just to fit in. In adults the unformed ego is more complex. They do not feel OK even if they are accepted. The narrator paints an image of the way this acceptance should be and this creates a conflict with the actual acceptance. First of all they want to be accepted by people who are important to them and capable of understanding them. But the rider's irrational logic may follow like this: 'Yes, I am accepted but this is just because they don't know me yet', or 'Yes, I am accepted, but this is just because they are not capable of recognizing who I really am'. So 'I want to be accepted by people I respect, who *can* see me for who I really am, but I want them to see me in the way I *want to be* rather than who I *am* now, which I don't like'. This is pretty much impossible. So what options do people have if they do not want 'cheap' acceptance? They might work like crazy aiming for real achievements, which might be a positive side of low self-esteem and a good route to a formed ego. Others may just focus on the fact of acceptance and develop in a slow but more natural pace.

More recent writers (Epstein 1973; Brown et al. 1988; Baumeister 1993, 1999; Mruk 2006) describe two other angles on the nature of self-esteem: the self-consistency motive and the self-enhancement motive. The self-consistency motive drives people to seek out information that confirms what they already believe about themselves – whether good or bad. Once established, such self-opinion may be difficult to discard or refine, and a coach could meet with considerable defences if they attempt to disrupt the established 'self-view'. The self-enhancement motive instead drives people to acquire information that tends to show them in a positive light, discarding information which may cast an unfavourable shade upon themselves. Self-esteem is therefore fraught with the possibility for distortion (Claxton 1994; Dunning 2006) and various theoretical traditions and studies document the many ways we may defend ourselves against threats to our self-evaluations (Hamachek 1987; Goleman 1997; Fingarette 2000).

To summarize, self-esteem is a sign of how well we are doing in terms of social inclusion just in case we need support for our unformed ego. We can also see self-esteem as essentially a problem of discrepancy between the actual state of the ego and the internalized expectations of others or unconscious envy for a formed ego. If we were satisfied with being unformed egos there would be just two main tasks to fulfil. The first one is to learn how to ask for help when we are in trouble and so to be included in the circles where such help is available. The problem with this task might be that the rider might refuse help out of pride. And the second task is to work and develop our executive centre further which would involve realistic appraisal of ourselves and our situations, meaningful accomplishments and overcoming adversities. In addition to these we are going to explore in what way the three main mechanisms of change that we described in Chapter 8 could be part of coaching towards a healthy ego.

Improving the quality of perception

What are the particular reasons for the need to improve the quality of perception in the unformed ego? One of the features of the unformed ego is that information that comes from emotions and the inner world dominates the information that comes from the outer world or supplied by the rider (Winson 1985). Internalized values and rules take precedence over the external reality 'creating strong effect and conviction of truth without any confirmation from the environment – feeling over fact – and then having the neocortex [rider] rationalize that choice' (Wade 1996: 123). We said, however, that the ego needs support from others at this stage and that is why the rules and values of others are accepted and followed without rational evaluation as Figure 11.2 metaphorically illustrates. It is obvious that finding ways to overcome excessive *conditioning* is one of the most important tasks for the coach at this stage. However, it has to be done with care and with the awareness that the ego's reliance on others at this stage is justified.

The coach may invite the client to question the legitimacy of some strong beliefs and values when working with any developmental theme at this stage, including the issue of self-esteem. One way to start with this is to point out that we all experience objects in our environment in different ways depending on our intentions, values and other perceptual filters. A good example to illustrate this is to imagine how different people see the same house: estate agents, an artist, a person looking for a house to rent or someone coming to visit a friend. This can show how we are responsible for the way we experience the world (May 1969: 224). It may be easier then to invite the client to look at similar filters to perception that may be unreasonable or outdated.

Figure 11.2 The power of conditioning.

Another important ongoing feature of the coach's work is to inquire frequently what the client's own thoughts and feelings are about the issues in question. When the client makes decisions or judgments it is useful to explore if there is a difference between those that came from their intuition and the ideas and guidelines received from others. It is important to keep in mind and make it clear to the client that this questioning is not meant to undermine the authorities from whom the ideas and beliefs originated, but to enhance the client's ability to read each situation as fully as possible by themselves. This helps the organism to have a better quality of information and to develop confidence for the independent processing of information. At the same time the client's need to remain associated with the 'authorities' that issue rules and recommendations, is respected.

The main reason for *self-deception* at this stage is self-protection. The ego is not fully developed and awareness of this is something that the client might wish to avoid. Other examples of self-deception could include simply not 'noticing' information that is threatening to the system of beliefs that they have introjected from others and identified themselves with. It is interesting however, how positive qualities are attributed to the groups that one wishes to belong to, but negative qualities automatically become allocated to those who are outside these groups. Diversity and complexity in others and in situations is confusing and so translated into a more 'black and white' picture. They find it difficult to notice 'unacceptable' feelings in themselves and are quite likely to project them onto others.

Drawing their attention directly to such discrepancies as examples of self-deception is not advisable. It is possible that these subconscious strategies are in place to protect the organism from knowledge that cannot be used as yet and from extreme emotions that could overwhelm the person. It might be a legitimate defence against anxiety and if these defences are pushed against they may only become stronger. In the same way, a direct appeal to integrity and moral concerns will only strengthen self-deception. They already have an extremely strict internal critic in their rider – that is why they seem to hide the truth even from themselves. If the coach wants to work developmentally she should create a climate in the sessions that is safe for the client to continue exploring the issues in question. This could keep the relevant areas of the mind/brain activated and may gradually allow relevant information into awareness. If this does not happen the coach has to accept this as a limitation of the unformed ego and use different ways to develop the ego.

Working with the elephant

I believe that the main task in coaching towards a healthy ego in relation to the elephant is to involve it in action. When the ego is unformed there are natural fears that the organism may not be capable of performing certain functions. Many irrational fears come from the rider who is concerned about having its inadequacies exposed. This may lead the person to be overcautious and thus continue only with habitual behaviour and withdraw from new, more risky actions. However, the ego develops through action, when new links in the mind/brain are activated and so new mini-selves are formed and tested. Therefore the task at this stage is to help the client to dwell less on potential negatives but to take action in steps that are manageable for this state of his ego. In this case the ego is developing when mini-selves are completed and strengthened in action, what we usually call 'accumulation of experience'. The rider can observe this and develop a sense of confidence and control over particular tasks. This in turn generates real autonomy in the organism and the ability to manage life tasks independently from other people's help when necessary.

However, when we talk here about control this does not mean control of the rider over the elephant. It is the sense of control that the rider can feel as the result of the organism as a whole being able to manage the tasks of successful engagement with the environment. It may seem to contradict the ideas of the existentialists that advocate the need to take responsibility for choices in our lives. I do not see, however, their views as an invitation to develop the will power of the rider over the body. The autonomy they advocate is the autonomy of the organism in its environment, which implies that the executive centre can function reasonably independently from others in providing for the needs of the organism. It is the whole organism that makes choices and so the rider should take responsibility for them.

There are types of training, such as martial arts, that could be seen as aiming at strengthening control of mind over body and are very successful at that. I am sure, however, that people who are trained in these centres are no different from others. They undergo all four stages described in this book and many of them would be at the stage of the unformed ego even if they can withstand significant pain or break a wooden brick with just their bare hands. At the same time they may be highly dependent on their community and masters in all their engagements with the world. In fact, many exercises they go through are designed to move them towards a formed ego. At the beginning of their training it is not even the will of the disciples that is responsible for an act, but that of the master who orders them to act. Just by obeying the master they complete an act which is designed to show them that their organism *can* perform it and this is intended as a strengthening of their ego.

Authors like Assagioli (1993) suggest various exercises specifically designed to develop a strong will by, for example, mobilizing energies, strengthening commitments and the actual act of volition. I believe, however, that it is the whole organism that gets strengthened, not just the conscious will. These exercises provide good proof for a person of what is possible and so can prevent the rider putting a veto on the actions that it overcautiously believes are impossible. Assagioli also, in comments on his exercises, expresses an appreciation of what we call here an elephant and suggests some ideas for how to cooperate with it.

> Not to arouse resistances or rebellion in the unconscious, or in other constituents of the personality, is a general caution applicable in the use of all techniques, but particularly in the use of techniques for the development of the will. One method of guarding against arousing such resistance is to advise the patient not to use a technique too seriously, nor in a way which is pedantic or annoying to the unconscious. Instead, the aim must be to win the cooperation of the unconscious through amusing and interesting it – and that is the specific attitude of play.
>
> (Assagioli 1993: 137)

It is advisable for coaching a healthy ego to use *soft thinking* to create a relaxed atmosphere in the sessions that could allow the client to look at the situation without rush and with a soft focus, as we discussed in Chapter 8, particularly if the theme of coaching requires making important decisions. The intention is to calm down the rider who may be frantically scanning all the possible negative consequences of the choices under consideration and instead allow it to give voice to a more rational and detached part of itself. Gentle questioning around the edges of the issue can help in keeping the mind/brain activated and may encourage some new links necessary for decision making and the initiating of action.

In terms of *communication with the emotional body* the main tactic of the coach is helping the client to receive messages from the elephant about the emotions that prevent risk taking but at the same time to convey the messages that encourage it. The developmental coach would pay attention to the elephant, observing body language and all the cues from speech about what is going on under the surface of the client's behaviour. Recognition of these is important, not in order to work with these feelings or to give them particular attention, but to show the elephant that it is understood and to win its trust. If this is the case there are more chances for the messages from the coach and the rider of the client to be received. The core of the message is to encourage the elephant to try and initiate an action which may involve certain risks for the client. Here are some examples of messages that may appeal to the elephant:

> *The turtle only makes progress when its neck is stuck out.*
>
> Rollo May
>
> *A ship is safe in harbour, but that's not what ships are for.*
>
> William Shea
>
> *Even when you fall on your face, you are still moving forward.*
>
> Indian folklore

Two things are particularly important in such endeavours. The action that the client is prepared to take should be reasonably congruent to his abilities. And the elephant should not feel completely alone in actions that are considered risky.

Working with the multiplicity of self-models

Many of the themes that clients bring to coaching at this stage are about action and decision-making and this is what coaching is for. All of them at the same time have strong connections with the sense of identity of the client. People with unformed egos often suffer from the fragmentary nature of their self. Their self-models are a joint creation of their own narrator and many other people in their lives who have significant influence. If the number of 'external contributors' is large, the narrator is desperate to create an acceptable and coherent story of who they are. It tries to make sense of powerful emotions experienced by the organism and strong or half-sensed desires or various inconsistent ideas and values that come from other people who are influencing them. This is not an easy task, because the ego is not strong enough to act on its own and the rider is confused and self-critical. As a result inconsistent feelings may be split from each other and 'bad' emotional states and 'bad' parts of the self may then be projected outwards into the external world and 'got rid of' into other people. In this way, only good parts are kept as 'mine', generating some feeling of worthiness. Conflicts with others are often avoided, but when they happen they need to be quickly forgotten rather than made sense of, because this might threaten important self-stories.

Taking all of the above into consideration, the work in the identity centre during coaching towards a healthy ego needs to be concentrated on the level of the rider. The developmental coach can help the rider to see how confusing the narrator's stories are and to begin to untangle at least some of them. In particular, the rider needs a) to tame a self-model 'internal critic' and b) to see the logic and value of multiplicity. The sign of progress for clients with an unformed ego would be an emergence of a highly populated but organized and logically consistent identity centre, in which the voice of the client's rider matters more than the voices of various outside influences. We can then say that the narrator is embracing the rider in the process of establishing the identity of the client (Figure 11.3).

Accepting the fact of the multiplicity of self-stories is thus a step forward in the process of clearing up the identity centre. This is the work that is also needed in relation to the issues of self-esteem, helping to shift the focus of stories from the typically negative.

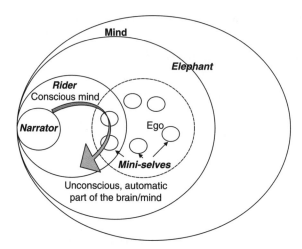

Figure 11.3   Embracing the rider for establishing self-identity.

People with an unformed ego tend to disregard stronger and more able selves because their internal critic is relentless in its job. If they accept the idea of the multiplicity of self-models they will see that in addition to their old and possibly negative stories they can also have other self-models. That is why one of the first things that coaches do when they work with issues of self-esteem is to ask people to create a list of what they are good at. This usually works as the beginning of a recognition that different aspects of the self could be brought to the fore and so different stories of the self could be created. Acceptance of multiplicity also prevents the skewing into an exclusively positive dimension, which could lead to an unrealistic and ungrounded sense of self.

Introducing the idea of the 'community of selves' is not difficult. People often identify, for example, two voices in the mind that are not in agreement. Transactional Analysis provides a useful approach to see oneself as Child, Adult and Parent and could serve as an introduction to multiplicity. John Rowan's book, *Subpersonalities* (2009) contains many interesting ideas and examples of eliciting many self-models. The following fragment is an example of self-models that have emerged during his work with subpersonalities and that have allowed one person to understand herself and to gradually accept different aspects of herself:

> *Freem:*
> Monster, enormous, fat, lazy, apathetic, self-destructive. (Freem was originally very beautiful.)
> *Madman:*
> (Compound of man and madam.) Parent, moral, critical, demanding, ambitious, competitive, mocking.
> *Child:*
> Very dependent, demanding, intense, desperate at times. (Forms torture pattern with Madman and Freem.)

Professor:
Tall, intellectual, interested in everything.
Creative:
A creative self, able to invent and solve problems.
Ruth:
Stable, understanding, sensitive. (Used as front.)
Gina:
Attractive, happy-go-lucky.
Bulldog:
Aggressive, rebels against Madman and everyone else

(Rowan 2009: 49–50)

In order to *match a self-story with a real mini-self* the coach can encourage the client to be more observant of his experiences in the world in order for the self-stories that he creates to be grounded in what is actually happening in his life. It is interesting that although this task implies being realistic and grounded, conversations about dreams and different actors in one's dream can promote this work in a less threatening way. It has been said that actors in the dream are the product of our subconscious and so may reflect aspects of ourselves. Gendlin (1986), the author of *Focusing*, also wrote a very interesting book *Let Your Body Interpret Your Dreams* (1986), in which he gives some examples of questions that could be asked in order to explore this possibility:

- What feel-quality does this person [in the dream] give you? What sense comes in your body?
- If no quality comes, ask yourself: What is one adjective I could use for that person?
- Now think of that adjective or feel-quality as a part of you. If *that* is part of you, what part would that be?
- You may or may not like this part of you, or know much about it. But let it be here for a moment, anyway.
- Does the dream make sense, if you take it as a story about how you relate to that part of you?

(Gendlin 1986: 11–12)

It would be useful to identify or create a self-model which can take the role of the Inner Coach for the client with an unformed ego. This would be an immensely useful self-model to have. What does need to be in place for it to be created? It may start from the generalized model in their mind of an instructor – an expert in the field of their work, a mentor, a coach. This self-model may represent knowledge and advice that are not yet embedded in the client's spontaneous performance. The client may be shifting in their mind from the Inner Coach to Flowing Performance during their act or both can be activated at the same time, as if the Inner Coach is sitting on the client's shoulder. This enables attention and habit development to be guided by 'good advice'. It could be said that that's what 'knowledge' is for. This Inner Coach must be patient and thoughtful, and not judgemental, impatient or overwhelming. The model of this Inner Coach is derived and can be distilled from observation and imitation of a range of 'mentors'.

Their 'voices' and 'manners' are obviously crucial (Claxton 2007). The actual coach can help the client in the process of distillation of this model and reinforce it by asking the client to reflect on the experiences with the Inner Coach present.

One of the most difficult tasks of working with the multiplicity of self-stories is creating *the synthesis of self-models*. When the ego is unformed this job could usefully start just with contemplating such synthesis. I would suggest a modest attempt to approach it: to notice a tendency of people at this stage to hold poor stories of self. Often these stories have many voices of other people instead of the client's own and so may benefit from gentle challenging. If their stories show an overall victim feel, it would help to elicit more positive aspects in them or at least to notice a new story line emerging – a promise for a new and more empowering story. As a practical exercise in this direction I can recommend the 'Four Columns Exercise' by Kegan and Lahey (2009), which helps to identify competing commitments that prevent him from engaging fully with the task. The coach may work with the client to realize that both commitments are in fact different self-models that can be integrated and useful for the overall wellbeing of the client.

The role of the coach and the nature of coaching relationships

When the ego is unformed clients are doubtful about their abilities not only in relation to a particular task at work, but also in other areas of life. They may find it challenging to disagree with significant people in their life. You as a coach may feel that they give you too much power in your relationship and an unlimited opportunity to influence them.

I do not think that it would be sufficient for a coach who works with these clients to rely mainly on the usual probing and questioning and on giving them a lot of positive feedback. These clients genuinely need more support from the environment and from the coach. This makes the role of the coach quite controversial at this particular stage. A traditional conceptualization of coaching implies drawing from the resources of the client and being mainly a catalyst to his process. The client is seen as someone who is, if not already successful, at least very capable and resourceful. In this case coaches have to see the client as being at the beginning of such a journey and still in need of explicit support. At the same time they need to show respect for him to help to develop self-respect as a foundation for further development. What makes their role even more difficult is their awareness that strictly speaking they cannot be there for the client when he may need more active support. So what is the role of the coach and what type of coaching relationship can fit this balance of power and this state of the client's ego development? In my view this role can resemble the one of a good parent, who gives more support if necessary with a view to gradually minimizing it and shows patience and trust for the developmental process to happen, however slow it may be.

In terms of the more specific features of this role the coach can approach the themes of the unformed ego as follows:

- demonstrate to the client that she is there for him as much as possible to give him support when he needs it;

- help the client in learning to ask for help from others;
- help to identify unreasonable demands from the environment;
- help to identify unreasonable demands from the Inner Critic to be what he cannot yet be;
- help to work on social skills – to have more opportunities to be included in groups important for the client in different areas of life;
- help the client to expose the real ego in reasonable portions (e.g. shame attacking exercises used in cognitive-behavioural coaching which involve asking the client to perform an act that is innocent but embarrassing – to prove that the ego can handle it in spite of social disapproval);
- help the narrator to embrace the rider while attempting to create a better order in the identity centre;
- help the client in developing an Inner Coach;
- demonstrate that the client can be liked for what he is even with an unformed ego by a person who can really understand him (person-centred approach);
- help with the work of building a formed ego – to stand on his own two feet using the mechanisms of developmental coaching described above in this chapter.

Other types of coaching can also be usefully applied for the themes of this stage. Psychodynamic, Cognitive-behavioural and Person-centred approaches can be particularly useful. For example, in the Psychodynamic approach the intention of the coach would not be uncovering historical truth about the past but negotiating with memory and constructing a better story of the self as it is now (Lee 2010). It is even possible to conceive that if the client struggles to create a coherent image of himself, he may temporarily identify with a more positive image that the coach might see emerging in him.

The cognitive-behavioural approach (Williams et al. 2010) could be useful because of the strength of its behavioural component. It has excellent activities to elicit and humour unfounded fears preventing the client from acting. It also offers a lot of practical ideas of how to assist clients to relax, reduce anxiety and overcome phobias by using, for example, progressive relaxation and systematic desensitization. Many useful exercises were developed as 'homework' by Ellis (1999). They prompt the client to take risks in measured and manageable steps, developing confidence and increasing self-respect that is borne out by actual behaviour.

Humanistic psychology and the Person-centred approach in particular are in my view the important foundation for coaching towards a healthy ego. If the coach is able to offer unconditional positive regard to the client, irrespective of their actions, achievements, values or their stage of development, this can allow the client to reclaim self-respect and a deeper sense of their own needs (Joseph 2010). It may appear that this approach can potentially conflict with an externally-derived, for example, organizational agenda, and may not be compatible with the overt goal achievement orientation dominating the traditional coaching literature. I believe, however, that the growing confidence and self-respect of the client as the result of this approach, are necessary to fulfil the expectations of others and will be paid off in the long run.

12 Coaching the ego

I wasn't satisfied just to earn a good living. I was looking to make a statement. I was out to build something monumental . . . Money was never a big motivation for me, except as a way to keep score. The real excitement is playing the game.

D. Trump

The formed ego is a comfortable stage to reach in comparison to the unformed ego. This is why people tend to stay in this stage for a long time or even revert to it if the pace of development seems too fast and risky. There are now enough mini-selves to look after the main functions of the organism without explicit support from others and enough self-understanding to accept oneself in principle. People with formed ego are not afraid to stay apart from the crowd. From this platform a formed ego has a genuine interest in truth, self-development and the improvement of the world, from small teams to whole societies. As they can predict the behaviour of their elephant better they are particularly interested in their future and potential changes.

How can the coach recognize clients with a formed ego? First, it would be clear that they can safely differentiate themselves from their immediate contexts, whether familial or organizational, and so can assert and express their individuality as much as they need and want. They do not get confused about their identity even if they belong to various groups. Secondly, they can manage tasks which are important for them, relying on their own resources or can take responsibility for the help they might need according to their own evaluation. They make decisions for themselves and can do it for others even if there is risk involved. Thirdly, they can reflect on themselves in a more rational way and discuss those qualities that they are not particularly happy with in a more detached way. They are interested in the reasons, goals and causes of their own behaviour and that of others, particularly for the purpose of making changes in the future.

At the same time, their rational competence and independence from others may cause them to feel that they are special and don't need others or they may feel they have a right to influence others for their own purposes. Their conviction could be quite contagious and they could be argumentative, opinionated and critical of others. Their newly developed capacity to stand on their own two feet may lead to a strong drive to be successful and in the process they may become vulnerable to over-extension and exhaustion. Money and status may become more important than usual as a measure of success. Their increased interest in human nature and themselves from the rational and pragmatic standpoint may lead to excessive and unjustified trust in psychometric testing and various inventions for influencing people.

Executive coaches may find that this description fits many of their clients. This would not be surprising because when the ego is formed the person is capable of taking responsibility not only for themselves but also for others. They can also be ambitious and competitive and so motivated to pursue their goals on the wider scale which leadership provides. They could be very thoughtful and conscientious as leaders, but their style can 'inhibit thinking outside the box' (Rooke and Torbert 2005). As leaders they may also find it difficult to delegate and to be sufficiently diplomatic when issues that are important for them are at stake.

Typical tasks and issues

This stage describes people who, on the bigger scale of things, can be masters of their own fate through their own initiative. What their ego seems to be striving for is *to be efficient* at the same time. However, the developmental challenge for this stage is discovering that not everything can be controlled and learning to see things from many different perspectives which includes the internal perspective of their own body.

Now we need to consider what themes these people are likely to bring to coaching, keeping in mind that some of the themes at this stage may also be relevant to other types of clients. For example, the topic of the lack of time for everything that needs to be accomplished could be relevant both for the unformed and the reformed ego. As Claxton and Lucas (2007: 55) vividly describe, 'one of the essential survival skills these days is to decrease the length of time between opening an email and deleting it (and even better, judging which ones you can delete without even opening)'. However this topic may be more typical for a formed ego, because of the scope of tasks that the formed ego is keen to manage well.

Typical themes that clients could bring for coaching for this stage are:

- coping with a heavy workload which is often self-chosen, e.g. the theme of time management;
- achievement of long-term personal goals according to inner standards and values;
- choosing the most efficient strategies in making decisions;

- working towards more recognition or specific promotion;
- resolving interpersonal conflicts which may be the result of a forceful assertion of their rights and needs;
- dealing with the strong drive for success with the underlying fear of failure;
- problem solving;
- self-understanding for self-motivation;
- developing attitudes and skills for effective leadership or collaboration with others;
- learning to delegate;
- dealing with stress.

You have probably noticed that these issues sound very like the typical themes we meet in traditional coaching. And it is mainly for this stage, out of all four introduced, that the traditional coaching models could be fully applicable. For example, the goal setting element of the coaching process is very important. It has been said that you *are* what you attend to and this is particularly relevant for the formed ego. Goals direct all attention at this stage and so need to be chosen or crafted wisely (Figure 12.1). It could be useful to keep the goals under review and encourage flexibility. If the goals are not set in stone they would allow for an overview of a changing situation and for the emergence of new mini-selves.

Similarly important is the attitude to problem solving if this is the theme of coaching. The enthusiasm of the formed ego for problem solving should be watched for and potentially tamed. The formed ego has a tendency to be single-minded and to look 'within the box'. The coach needs to keep in mind that not all problems have to be eliminated. Rather they need to be explored from different perspectives. One of the useful approaches, for example, is to ask the client to imagine that it is not his problem, which would help to create a distance from it and allow a different perspective on the situation.

I would like to explore one particular theme from the above list that could be quite important for formed egos, even if it is not presented by the client directly – the issue of stress. Without an elaborate discussion of the definitions of stress, this is just the usual way of understanding it: when we perceive a situation as creating demands greater than our capacity to cope with them, we perceive ourselves as being under stress. The core word in this sentence is not 'demands' or 'capacity' or even 'stress', but 'perception'. Sometimes we may overestimate the demands; sometimes we

Figure 12.1   Paying particular attention to the goals of coaching

may underestimate our capacity. Sometimes even our conceptualization of stress can be questioned – it is inevitably subjective and may lead to various consequences. The way we understand stress may be helpful for us in dealing with it, but there are several myths about stress (Nuernberger 1996) that may lead us into psychological traps.

One of such myths is: *stress is something that happens to me.* According to this myth stress comes upon us like a storm, it is unpredictable and there is nothing we can do to stop it. But unfortunately, there is no way that this thing that we call stress can be found somewhere out there and eliminated. If this were possible it would have been done a long time ago judging by the amount of research and effort that have already been put into solving the problem of stress. This is a myth that is more typical of the unformed ego. If the client believes that their stress is created mainly by external pressures and demands he becomes a victim of it. The coach may find it very difficult to help the client who feels powerless and unwilling to change his view of the situation.

Another myth is: *there is good stress and bad stress.* This is a myth that is more typical of the formed ego, who may mistakenly believe that there could be a good stress or that we need stress to achieve high performance. It may be associated with the old managerial philosophies that justify fear and pressure as a motivation for work and study. However, none of the experts in stress can define differences in good and bad stress except in terms of the consequences. 'Saying that there is good stress and bad stress is like saying there are good heart attacks and bad heart attacks. Bad heart attacks are fatal, while good heart attacks only damage your heart, giving you the opportunity to have another' (Nuernberger 1996: 6). In the formed ego, stress can be self-inflicted by taking on too much too soon for many different reasons. Although it can bring good results, it is too costly as a long-term strategy. We can say that this myth is the result of the confusion between being stressed and being challenged and it is important that the coach does not collude on this with her client.

Yet another myth is: *I don't have any stress.* Clients with formed egos are very prone to overestimate the strength of their organism and not notice the limits of its resilience. One of the roles of the coach is to point this situation out and to challenge clients who think of themselves as a superman or a superwoman. Coaches also need to be careful in relation to this because they often have a vested interest in the success of coaching and may (inadvertently) put an extra pressure on the client.

In relation to understanding stress and enabling the client to build his own sensible strategies for development, the coach can help him see stress as a prolonged reaction to a perceived 'threat'. This threat could be physical or psychological and the elephant gets ready for fight or flight. This is a reasonable reaction when it helps to deal with real and immediate dangers, but such a reaction is unsustainable in the long run. It is also important to notice that the 'prolonged' element in this definition of stress is usually associated with a psychological threat. For example, the client might have a belief that he must do well in any task he faces in order to sustain his self-respect. With such an ambition any new and difficult task becomes a threat. The developmental coach can use plenty of stress-management strategies, such as visualization exercises, various relaxation techniques and time-management adjustments. However, unpacking and examining stress-producing beliefs similar to the one above could be the most radical intervention with a more lasting effect.

Relevant approaches and interventions

The overarching ambition of the client at the stage of coaching the ego is to improve their effectiveness to a great extent. Therefore all three main mechanisms of facilitating a change in the client discussed in Chapter 8 are crucially important. The efficiency of mini-selves depends on the quality of information that is received and a good collaboration between the rider and the elephant. A reasonable interpretation of what is happening by the narrator is essential, because self-image and reputation are important for a formed ego.

Improving the quality of perception

> Truth waits for eyes unclouded by longing
>
> Tao Te Ching

In terms of improvement of perception in Chapter 8 we have discussed two main approaches to minimizing obstacles to seeing things as they are. They include understanding conditioning and minimizing self-deception. While the priority for the unformed ego was to work on conditioning, when working with the formed ego the task is reversed. More attention should be given to self-deception. It does not mean, of course, that the formed ego is completely free from conditioning – at no stage, unfortunately, do we reach this ideal. Nevertheless, the formed ego has some degree of freedom from significant others and the client can look at some values and beliefs assimilated from others in a more rational way. However, with the confidence and the apparent independence of the formed ego new types of filters to perception emerge that indicate self-deception. For example, some of these filters can be associated with self-righteousness. When the ego is formed, people are able to make decisions more easily, relying on their own thinking process, and can own their behaviour even if it is less predictable. They are also capable of taking into account the interests of many other individuals or groups of people with a genuine desire to create the best solution to a problem. When they invest so much in their decisions, then, if challenged, they may become puzzled, disgruntled or defensive. The filter in this case could be created by an inability to detach from their own point of view, which they believe is right.

In the previous chapter we said that self-deception associated with the unformed ego is usually used for protection. The self-deception of the formed ego is more likely to be for personal gain – not allowing things to get in their way. They may become, as it were, 'blind' to certain things because if they were to see these things, this would make it difficult for them to achieve what they want. For example, they may 'close their eyes' to some ethical issues if they are in the way of their goals and can be genuinely surprised when this becomes obvious. While working with the unformed ego the coach tried to elicit what the client's own feelings, views and positions were, as opposed to those received from others. When coaching the ego and assessing the different sources of information, priority should be given to external input and feedback. For example, for the unformed ego the feedback from the 360 degree exercise could be overwhelming and the coach would try to minimize the impact of discrepancies between their

expectations and the views of others. For the formed ego the task is exactly the opposite. The importance of feedback is emphasized and discrepancies are paid particular
attention. Clients with a formed ego could simply miss the point or dismiss it without
proper consideration.

This type of work with self-deception in coaching at the ego stage could be accepted
well by clients. They are already capable of understanding the significance of watching
for self-deception, curious about this phenomenon and wish to develop a thorough
knowledge of themselves. This could be a level of challenge worthy of their attention
in the spirit of the attitude described by Chogyam Trungpa:

> We must surrender our hopes and expectations and march directly into disap-
> pointment ... Disappointment is a good sign of basic intelligence. It cannot
> be compared to anything else: it is so sharp, precise, obvious and direct. If we
> can open, then we suddenly begin to see that our expectations are irrelevant
> compared with the reality of the situations we are facing.
>
> (Chogyam Trungpa 1973: 29)

Working with the elephant

> There is no such thing as a logical method of having new ideas ... Every dis-
> covery contains an irrational element or a creative intuition.
>
> Sir Karl Popper, *The Logic of Scientific Discovery*

The rider in the formed ego stage believes that it is now in charge of the elephant.
The executive centre is functioning well without help and support from others and the
rider can interpret and rationally evaluate the working of the organism. Put together
this can make us think that it is not the maturity and good coordination of the mini-
selves, but the rider itself, by good rational guidance, that keeps the organism going.
It looks, at this stage, as if there is now more coordination between the rider and the
elephant, because more conscious and rational thought is involved in the working of
the mini-selves. So this stage could be seen as the stage of the triumph of the rider.

In some ways it could be quite an innocent illusion that may even have some useful
outcomes, such as taking full responsibility for the past, if it wasn't for an overuse of
the body. What is actually happening is that the rider formulates goals; if they are
in no disagreement with the needs of the elephant the organism pursues them; the
achievement of the intended results follows. But all of this may lead to an assumption
that everything is possible and consequently, to the exploitation of the body and the
exhaustion of natural resources. There could be many examples of this: for instance, a
couple of sleepless nights before the submission of an important project could be an
abuse on a small scale, the needs of the body will take over afterwards. More serious
and long term damage may be caused by a prolonged workaholic tendency.

Sometimes the judgement about the limitations of the body is made quite correctly,
but the course of action that is chosen is overly ambitious: enhancing the body at any
cost. This is fine if no harm is done as the result of it, but there are many examples
of unnecessary interventions by the rider into the working of the organism leading to

irreversible damage. The examples are well known in sport when the capacities of the body are stretched to the limits, leaving people as invalids for the rest of their lives. On the one hand people with formed ego can become gym-junkies; on the other hand, they ignore even the simplest needs of the body for water, movement or rest when they are preoccupied by the goal of the rider say, to finish a project and would not leave their computer until it is completed.

Although the potential for direct control of behaviour by the rider is very small, some psychologists argue that even this small proportion is important and has to be studied. Baumeister et al. (1999) for example, argue that deliberate, conscious and controlled responses to situations may be important to the long-term health, happiness and success of individuals. At the same time they found that the act of volition 'draws on some limited resource, akin to strength or energy; therefore, one act of volition will have a detrimental impact on subsequent volition' (p. 317). They call this effect ego-depletion and trace the first potential explanation of it to Freud. The experiments show that the exertion of self-control causes people to give up more quickly on a subsequent task (Muraven et al. 1998; Wegner 1989). It seems that the rider's effort to regulate the elephant can deplete some scarce resource. Even Assogioli (1993), who advocates the importance of will also warns that overdevelopment of it 'can have injurious and even a destructive effect, especially on others' (p. 141).

It is important to notice that the rider's attempt to overpower the elephant may not be healthy even in the main domain of the rider – thinking. At this stage hard thinking tends to take over *soft thinking*. Without undermining the power and importance of reasoning the coach should be able to support different modes of thinking in these clients. If we don't think enough or our thinking is poor all sort of issues will arise, but sometimes we fail to solve difficult problems because we think too much. Claxton (1999) and de Bono (1982) give good arguments about the dangers of pure disembodied cleverness. They describe, for example, students who are trained with a heavy focus on reasoning as opposed to intuition and what we call here 'soft thinking'. As a result these students can construct a seemingly coherent argument virtually for any point of view and then will have a great investment in supporting and defending this argument instead of trying to find out what is actually going on. In addition, when the image of the person is closely associated with their cleverness they will look for strategies to protect this image. For example, they can learn to pick holes in others' arguments rather than developing their own ideas, which is a more risky strategy. They may also have a tendency to jump to conclusions too quickly instead of taking it slowly and considering more factors and the complexity of the issues (de Bono 1982; Claxton 1999).

In relation to thinking at this stage, the task for the rider is to develop respect for the invisible workings of the organism as a whole and to involve intuition as much as possible in decision making and problem solving. Thinking, even if efficient, is not adequate in many situations. A smart mind can see that intuition is the faculty that can be used when it is stumped and in need of a fresh idea. Intuition 'is a perfectly rational and valuable section of the mental orchestra, for which there is solid experimental evidence' (Claxton and Lucas 2007: 82).

The role of emotion is similar to intuition in relation to thinking. The emotions can be destructive, of course, but it is not useful to blame them for all sorts of sins and to disconnect them every time from the decision-making process. 'Emotions may sometimes be misleading; but to respond by trying to bleach our thoughts of their emotional colours is not bright at all' (Claxton 2005: 28). In their book *The Creative Thinking Plan* (2007) Claxton and Lucas describe an excellent range of ideas and exercises for involving intuition in the process of problem solving.

Another challenging task in coaching the ego is the facilitation of reasonable *communication between the rider and the emotional body* of the client. The triumph of the rider is very easily and regularly undermined by strong emotions that can create havoc in all the great achievements of the organism. Therefore the rider tends to marginalize, minimize, control and do whatever is available to protect itself from strong emotions. Emotions and feeling are often seen as directly caused by outside events and so 'the way to be happy is by fixing the world in place so that it does not go awry and upset me' (Claxton 1994: 194). The default strategy is always to *do* something instead of learning from the emotion. The formed ego's attitude to emotions is very much in tune with the discourse on rationality in societies where emotions are considered dangerous or at least interfering with rational behaviour. The task is to minimize the effect of emotions. Many coaches also work towards this agenda (Bachkirova and Cox 2007). A developmental coach, however, will keep in mind that many emotions could be useful for learning, managing people and essential for getting what one wants. As we said in Chapter 8 emotions are very much involved in and are the vital foundation of our intelligence. In fact, even rational minds in organizations are convinced of the value of emotional literacy and make an effort to promote emotional intelligence (EI) in every manager. Coaches are often among those who implement this agenda at work.

Although the idea of EI is a step forward from naked hostility towards emotion we should not forget that it is still based on the logic of the rider rather than of the whole organism. It is focused on the aspect of the usefulness of emotions. The main features of emotional intelligence are described as: a) being aware of one's own emotions, b) being able to manage one's own emotions, c) being sensitive to the emotions of others, d) being able to respond to and negotiate with other people emotionally, and e) being able to use one's own emotions to motivate oneself. Although these are all useful skills to learn, we need to be aware that on the whole this idea implies that happiness is simply a result of getting what you want and unmanaged emotions are potential impediments to 'success'. It is also more about intelligence rather than emotions as such. A developmental coach would avoid manipulating the client's emotional expressions strictly for the rider or employers' benefit but explore difficult questions about what is going on for the whole organism. We should not forget that EI tests and programmes are also full of value judgments and are based on specific cultural norms (Claxton 2005).

The main point of working with emotion for the formed ego is increasing the number of available perspectives on the world and engaging with the situation. Emotions provide a different and unique perspective in comparison to what is available to the rider alone. Emotions are also a way of communication between the rider and the elephant. So 'coaching with emotion' is a part of the strategy of the developmental coach, which is particularly important for coaching the ego. Emotional literacy and mastery in communication with the body gives clients more options in their engagements with the world.

However, when we are coaching the ego it is useful not to confuse talking fluently about emotions with being emotionally sensitive and emotionally intelligent. The former does not guarantee the latter. The rider can be very crafty and can create a great impression by being very articulate about emotions. The positive change, however, cannot happen only through talking about feelings – there is a need sometimes to express and work through some sticky emotions. The Gestalt approach to coaching is excellent for this purpose, because it would not let the client get away with just talking. At the same time it is useful to remember that clients have a right not to talk about emotions and not to develop them as others or organizations might request. At the end of the day the client's emotions are their own personal matter. Many people with a formed ego choose not to dwell on emotions but persevere with what needs to be done, particularly when faced with adversity. 'Resilience is, above all else, the ability to tolerate certain kinds of feelings' (Claxton 1999: 37). They may postpone the task of working with emotion until the stage of coaching beyond the ego.

And finally, developing relationships with other elephants in a more sensing/ feeling way is another step forward for a formed ego. These clients could become too independent and self-sufficient, losing out on the value of learning through meaningful relationships. Relationships may become more business-like and unnecessarily selective. Others may be exploited within socially acceptable limits. This tendency may be evident in a slightly different way for the feminine formed ego (Wade 1996) with a focus on being in close relationships, but similar dangers could remain even in this context. Although it is still the stage when clients celebrate their independence from others, the developmental coach may need to explore with them how the rider may overlook the value of being accepted by others and caring for them on the level of the elephant.

Working with the multiplicity of self-models

The issue of identity is less painful and more playful for the formed ego. This is a stage when clients are not threatened by new information about them and are interested in making more sense of who they are. Information from psychometrics can be sought but also quickly dismissed and forgotten if considered irrelevant to particular goals they might have. The attitude is of curiosity but with a dose of scepticism: 'I know better who I am'. Information from others is also questioned because of the motives these others might have. When problems or conflicts arise the focus of criticism changes at this stage: while with unformed ego it would be 'what's wrong with me?', with a formed ego it is more likely to be 'what's wrong with others?'

When clients with a formed ego face contradictory information about themselves or find themselves acting unusually, they can easily find various factors in the situation that may be used to explain such behaviours. This does not shake their view of themselves, which can afford to be more adaptable to the situation. Therefore the idea of the multiplicity of self-models can be *accepted* without any problems and even may excite them. They can see the complexity of identifying a stable self in the many roles they play and situations they are usually involved in. The idea of multiplicity may seem to them rational and even useful. They could be particularly interested in the opportunity inherent in this idea: 'to use subpersonalities, rather than being used by them' (Rowan 2009: 202).

If this is the case, the coach may be able to address the various developmental challenges of the formed ego. One of them is a tendency of the formed ego to identify with only strong and successful self-models and being very unkind to himself when his 'self-protective' or 'weak' mini-selves take priority. This is a task of *matching* between the actual mini-selves and the stories that the narrator creates. The Voice Dialogue approach could be useful for this purpose (Stone and Winkelman 1985). It works with a list of prescribed self-models which they call 'energy patterns': The Protector/Controller, The Pusher, The Critic, The Perfectionist, The Power Brokers, The Pleaser, The Inner Child, The Good and Bad Mother, and The Good and Bad Father. Each of them is explored with a list of questions, such as: What is your purpose? What do you do? What do you need? A rich exploration of some of these in coaching could help the client become aware of the different sides of their engagement with the world and corresponding self-models.

In general clients with a formed ego are fairly comfortable in their own skin and not afraid of experimenting with their identity. Some experiments could be designed to help the client to role-play various 'models of me', which could be very effective for the 'mental rehearsal' of skills. The client can explore and experience the feeling of what it would be like to be X so he can consciously build a model of himself and rehearse it. This would be particularly useful in group work. People who can open up to one another in groups and take a risk to be there as their different selves can accelerate their development. This is also possible in one-to-one coaching.

Another challenging task for the centre of identity is to expand the boundaries of the client's identity to include the ego. The rider tends to identify only with voluntary processes. It is much easier to see ourselves only as our consciousness. We do know, however, that 'machinery' of both voluntary and involuntary actions is processed in the same executive centre. At this stage the rider of the client may be capable of accepting this and so helping the narrator to embrace the ego as me (Figure 12.2). The client would benefit from having a more realistic picture of the world and his relationship with it. To experiment with this, a developmental coach could suggest to the client to do something without reason, as if led by the elephant alone. This could be an unusual exercise for the formed ego which invests a lot in its efficiency and tends to act purposefully. Reflection on this experience may feel strange and could be developmentally stretching for a formed ego.

Creating a *synthesis* of the multiple self-models is potentially less complex for a formed ego. A good analogy for this task is the inner team. Building a 'team' out of an internal group of self-models could be seen as a worthwhile task at this stage. The formed ego can be up to the challenge of creating a better '"characterscape", strengthening minors that are generally helpful, curbing those that have got too strong, creating new ones where necessary and transforming those that are a nuisance' (Carter 2008: 220). A developmental coach would be a good assistant in this work. She may even suggest to the client to conceive a leader for this team and explore this self-model. A good practical approach for this task is of course the 'chair exercise' as described in the Gestalt approach. Rowan, however, is quite sceptical about the potential unification of

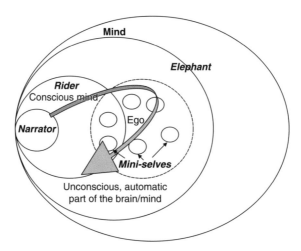

Figure 12.2 Embracing the ego for establishing self-identity.

self-models 'because of the very strong social pressures within our very complex culture, which makes it hard indeed to avoid some kind of role playing' (2009: 203). Some have argued that it may not even be desirable to have such an aim (Watkins 1986: 106) – a good discussion to have with this type of client.

The role of the coach and the nature of coaching relationships

On the whole, what is characteristic for this stage is that the executive centre is highly capable of doing a good job for the organism in a way that satisfies it in principle. What is necessary now, developmentally, is to learn that this is not the only way to see the world. There could be different perspectives in the perception of the world, there could be different interpretations of one's life tasks and there could be different ways of engaging with them. The role of the coach is to challenge the client not to be satisfied with only one way of seeing, acting and evaluating the results of his actions. This does not mean encouraging perfectionism and claiming that there are no 'good enough' results in their work. In fact, the perspective that the coach could encourage the client to see might be exactly that – there could be such a thing as 'good enough'. But this role of the coach should also be supportive in order not to let the client slip back into a lack of confidence and an unstable ego. So it is the choice of the coach in this work whether to be a challenging supporter or a supportive challenger. Whatever her choice is, the balance should be constantly monitored, because clients with a formed ego will not respect the coach who allows this work to become too comfortable and who does not challenge them.

To summarize the specific features of approaching the themes of the formed ego, the coach would be wise to:

- keep exploring and refining the goals for coaching as the goals are the reflection of what the client was and so should be changing as the client changes;
- challenge clients to explore their myths of stress and observe them in action;
- challenge and explore self-deception in the client, particularly if it seems to be harnessed for some sort of gain;
- challenge the 'triumph of the rider' by pointing out the work that is done by the elephant and the trouble created because of the rider's delusions of power;
- work with the 'soft' skills of the client by showing the value of emotion, intuition and soft thinking;
- help the client to see the value of working with other elephants, their perspectives and wider pictures of reality;
- support the client in his experimenting with different models of who he can be;
- challenge the client to own more actions produced by the elephant;
- help the client in creating a functional team out of the range of self-models;
- challenge the client to see what is beyond the formed ego – using the mechanisms of developmental coaching described above in this chapter.

Other types of coaching can be usefully applied for the themes of this stage. Cognitive-behavioural, Solution-focused and Gestalt approaches can be particularly useful. The Cognitive-behavioural approach and especially REBT version of it can be used for challenging irrational beliefs. The clients with a formed ego are robust enough to face outdated rules and guidelines that were imposed on them through conditioning. Shedding these can strengthen the ego further and liberate it in the process of seeing more perspectives on the realities they face. The Solution-focused approach to coaching (Cavanagh and Grant 2010) would also be appealing to the formed ego because of its concrete and focused way of resolving problems, being an explicit and formally established collaboration between the coach and the client.

The Gestalt approach to coaching (Bluckert 2010) has a lot of potential means to challenge the formed ego, particularly in relation to the 'triumph of the rider'. It provides many ways of inviting the client's elephant to be part of the coaching process, encouraging moment-to-moment awareness of experience. In relation to working with the multiplicity of self-models, Gestalt provides various exercises that allow for active experimentation, prompting different stories of the self to come alive instead of remaining the property of the narrator.

13 Coaching beyond the ego

What is demanded of man is not, as some existential philosophies teach, to endure the meaninglessness of life; but rather to bear his incapacity to grasp its unconditional meaningfulness in rational terms.

Victor Frankl, *Man's Search for Meaning*

When transformation occurs, it is never a result of successful seeking, but always a result of its failure.

Richard Lind, *The Seeking Self*

In this chapter we will explore potential themes that could be brought in by clients indicating a need for coaching beyond the ego. First of all, how did they arrive at this stage? What shift has taken place that made them move away from the stage of the formed ego? People with a formed ego are fairly independent of others, capable of achieving their goals, know who they are and feel more comfortable with themselves. What can drive someone away from or beyond all of this? One potential explanation could start from the fact that the executive centre is now more efficient. This leaves more energy and attention available for the conscious awareness of situations, the organism and the relationship between them. For example, in Chapter 9 we proposed core assumptions and developmental challenges for people at each stage (Table 9.2), which were subconscious to the unformed and formed ego. Now clients have more space to notice these and to be aware of new challenges, which may not necessarily feel positive to them.

Clients at this stage are in reasonable control of situations, but they are aware that they cannot control everything. Their mini-selves are versatile and are able to adapt to various situations, but at the same time these clients can see how inconsistent they are, and how intense an internal conflict between the mini-selves could be. They may feel a strong need to know what they are 'really' like, what they are supposed to be, not as designed by others but derived from their essence. They may even question if there is such a thing as an essence. There is more awareness of the quality of information received by the mind/brain at this stage. At the same time they can see how their minds can play tricks and are aware of self-deception. This is why this stage is called a reformed ego. It implies a more meaningful input from the rider to the executive centre initiating a change beyond the formed ego stage.

Clients with a reformed ego are no longer satisfied with only achieving goals – they also want to know what these goals are for, and what they mean. They can be frustrated by meaningless tasks and demands that could be made on them in organizations. If the unformed ego was self-critical and the formed ego critical of others, the reformed ego can be extremely critical about various states of affairs extending from the personal level to the state of the world.

In the 'thinking department' they abandon the purely rational way of sorting out problems and can see the value of more holistic and organismic approaches. Their preferences change from merely logical to 'psycho-logical' (Cook-Greuter 1999) acknowledging how the same realities are constructed in different ways by different people because of their own personal qualities and values.

They are much more aware of the connection between the body and mind than an unformed ego or a formed ego, and may therefore see themselves as being responsible for potential health issues. This may result in increasing interest in alternative approaches for looking after themselves. They could become more aware of what is going on in their relationships with others because they do not invest so much now in 'being right'. However, in spite of this expanded ability they could be distraught to find the lack of real connections with people or feel isolated.

Typical tasks and issues

Typical themes of this stage that clients can bring for coaching are:

- dissatisfaction with a job and/or a life situation in spite of high achievements;
- exploring a situation of 'not fitting in' or 'not being understood';
- overcoming a life crisis caused by a loss or a significant change in circumstances, for example redundancy;
- inability to find meaning in current engagements;
- excessive critical attitude to many things;
- realization of internal conflicts and contradictions;

- trying to find a way to stay true to themselves in the middle of a complex and problematic situation;
- contemplating a dramatic change in career;
- changing their mindset when leaving an organization and starting their own business;
- intention to see through personal illusions;
- finding ways of meaningfully connecting with others.

These themes all demonstrate the high level of awareness available to clients with a reformed ego. However, there seems to be an underlying dissatisfaction with many things they are aware of. I would like to suggest one potential explanation for the source of these clients' problems: they may stem from a fundamental confusion about the self. First, let us look at the tasks of the ego in service to the whole organism in comparison to the two previous stages:

- *to be able,* when the ego is unformed;
- *to be efficient,* when the ego is formed;
- *to be the best one can be,* when the ego is reformed.

When the ego is either unformed or formed these tasks are the natural expressions mainly of the elephant in its continuous effort to adapt to a changing environment and to have survival and competitive advantages in the game of life. From the stage of the reformed ego the rider begins to play a more active role and tries to raise the game, that is, to become the best one can be.

According to the theory presented in this book we need to look at this task of the reformed ego – becoming the best one can be – from both perspectives: the elephant or the whole organism on the one hand, and the rider on the other. What would 'becoming the best' mean from the organismic perspective? It would imply that the organism is able to respond fully to all the challenges of ever-changing situations using available resources. The resources and capacities of the organism would need to grow organically in correspondence with new challenges and values. In an ideal case there would be no blockages to the changes required, which we identified in Chapter 7 as:

- low quality of information at the input point;
- immunity to change;
- interruption from the narrator;
- no obvious behavioural routes existing at the point of action.

At the same time, as we said, the rider is now able to play a much more active role because the ego is reasonably efficient. There is more energy left for conscious awareness after the rider has made an immediate contribution to dealing with everyday tasks. The rider can now focus on *anticipating and preventing* the appearance of the above blockages and this is what it does. For example, in relation to the low quality of information the rider is now actively involved in minimizing conditioning and self-deception. It is characteristic of people at this stage to actively question their conditioning: exploring previously subconscious assumptions based on cultural, societal and family inheritance;

strongly resisting influences from various authorities; critically evaluating previously held beliefs and values. They are also aware of self-deception and consciously examine potential filters to their perception that may be a cause of the low quality of information from the environment.

In relation to 'immunity to change' they may be well aware of conflicting forces in the executive centre and open to any form of work that would help them to find a way to reconcile different needs. They would see this type of work as challenging but rewarding. In relation to the lack of obvious behavioural routes for responding to the challenges of current situations these people are becoming great learners. They experiment willingly; they take risks if necessary; they are not afraid of making mistakes. They also do not hesitate to ask when in need of help. Any kind of developmental work, whether coaching or counselling, is seen as an opportunity to make progress.

It seems the rider is already on the case, helping the organism to be the best it can be. However, the remaining problem is in the area of interruptions from the narrator. In spite of the high level of awareness of the rider and even its dedication to understanding and development, the narrator is simply confused. And confusion comes, I believe, with the unsubstantiated notions of the self in the various enterprises of this stage. Some of these confusions are associated with movements described in humanistic psychology. For example, Maslow's idea of self-actualization being nearly at the peak of the hierarchy of needs makes sense; it fits with the underlying intention of the reformed ego stage: to be the best one can be. But the element of 'self' in it is rather bewildering: what sort of self is meant to be actualized? Does it mean there is a 'real self' somewhere, which is not yet realized and needs to be uncovered? Is this the self that the person believes he is or is it the self that could be described in a more objective way? There are also many critics of this idea on the basis of it appearing to advocate self-seeking and personal gratification (Frankl 1966; Ansbacher 1971; Friedman 1976; Daniels 2005), who emphasize the following danger:

> With self-actualisation as the ideal, the movement can easily be mistaken for a cult of the self. It would attract self-seeking, immature persons who wish to avoid responsibility towards their fellow men, and who are not prepared to contribute to the whole, exemplifying the pampered style of life.
>
> (Ansbacher 1971: 60–1)

This danger does not exactly fit the agenda of people at the stage of the reformed ego. However, it may still elicit a cause of potential confusion if taken as a main focus of development in contrast to the needs of others and of the environment that they care about. Rogers' (1961) idea of 'organismic self' and 'self-concept', on the other hand, seems less confusing. I think that it is comparable to our concepts of ego and some particular self-models created by the narrator. Maslow's idea would also be less controversial in terms of its relationship with the wider context, if it was about *organism-actualization* rather than self-actualization. The organism does not exist in isolation but is in constant interaction with the environment.

A similar problem is caused by the theme of authenticity that is important for many people at this stage. How authenticity is defined is a puzzle in itself, especially if we try to reconcile its common meaning with the way it is discussed in existential philosophy. A popular understanding of authenticity implies being true to your self or acting according to the 'true' self. This meaning presents the same challenges as mentioned above in relation to humanistic psychology: which self is true? Or which one should we choose to be true to? We could take this meaning of authenticity as an indication of congruence between the executive centre and the identity centre, but it is a huge challenge even to conceive of and I cannot see how it can help one to be 'the best one can be' in action. It may only be something that could potentially make the rider feel better about itself.

At the same time, the way some existentialists discuss authenticity is perplexing but also exciting, because it has a potential to bring us back to the organism and to the organism's engagement with the world. Sartre, for example, argues that authenticity involves a person confronting reality, facing up to it without regret and assuming full responsibility for his actions. It is a not a permanent quality of the person that is established once and forever, but what 'he must maintain constantly by choosing authentic responses to his situation' (Cox 2006: 139). This seems like the role of the rider, similarly emphasized by other existentialists (Taylor 1991; van Deurzen-Smith 2002). Taylor, for example, argues that authenticity 'allows us to live (potentially) a fuller and more differentiated life, because more fully appropriated as our own' (1991: 74).

Confusion still can arise about the actual authorship of choices that we make. It may seem that the rider is in charge. However, the following excerpt from Sartre in my view brings it back to the organism as a whole, because it is the organism in action that is the point of connection with the situation:

> To be authentic is to realise fully one's being-in-situation, whatever this situation may happen to be, with a profound awareness that, through the authentic realisation of the being-in-situation, one brings to plenary existence the situation on the one hand and human reality on the other. This presupposes a patient study of what the situation requires, and then a way of throwing oneself into it and determining oneself to 'be-for' this situation.
>
> (Sartre 1999: 54)

If choices are made in the interplay between the situation and the organism, authenticity is just a challenge for the rider to appropriate these choices, to contribute as fully as possible to them and to take full responsibility for the consequences of action without wasting any energy on regret. It may seem less 'fair' than the idea of the self who is an actual author of choices. So the narrator keeps writing stories of the self as the one who is in the centre of these actions and choices.

However, the rider at this stage can see through many illusions and self-deceptions. It knows, for example, how many inconsistencies and even conflicts there are between self-models and how difficult it is to decide which one of them is 'true'. So the rider at this stage cannot be satisfied with the vague and inconsistent idea of self, can see how much energy is wasted on this confusion, but doesn't know the way out. Paradoxically it has to admit that in order to help the whole organism to be the best it can be is to give up on the self. This is what Wade (1996) called a transitional dilemma for this

Figure 13.1   Impatient for personal and others' growth.

stage: I can only realize my potential by giving up myself. This could be, of course, too much to ask in one go. So a more gradual approach may be to learn how to live with the many paradoxes and existential concerns.

One example of these paradoxes may be the idea of development as such as we already discussed in Chapter 7. Does it make a difference if the rider has a strong intention to grow (see Figure 13.1)? Or there is no need to push the river – it flows by itself? Another example is a paradox about what is often called 'living in the present', which is most clearly described by Schopenhauer: 'The greatest wisdom is to make the enjoyment of the present the supreme object of life because that is the only reality, all else being the play of thought. But we could just as well call it our greatest folly because that which exists only a moment and vanishes as a dream can never be worth a serious effort' (Schopenhauer 2000: 284). What seems to be the least confusing out of these and other existential dilemmas is the issue of death. Although there are different explanations and interpretations of the various implications of death for the way of life, particularly in different religions, it comes down eventually to the attitude that is described below. I think this may reflect the end of reality as it is known to the organism in spite of the various theories of the rider.

> The central fact of my own life is my death. After a while it will all come to nothing. Whenever I have the courage to face this, my priorities become clear. At such times nothing is done in order to achieve something else. No energy is

wasted in maintaining the illusions. My image does not matter. I do not worry about how I am doing. I do what I do, am what I am. That's it. The imminence of my own death is the point around which things turn.

(Kopp 1972: 42)

Relevant approaches and interventions

It is much easier to describe potential approaches for coaching beyond the ego because clients with a reformed ego are already working in nearly all the main directions. They are also incredible learners who only need a mindful companion for a coach to bounce ideas around. The coach in such assignments may learn as much as her clients.

Improving the quality of perception

As we said earlier, clients with a reformed ego already effectively question their conditioning and self-deception. Interestingly enough, some of their problems with perception may come from their excessive reflectiveness. For example, confusion may be caused by the use of concepts, which are always insufficient to grasp reality. They need to become increasingly aware of the role that language plays in perception. It helps in communication, and it also helps in structuring experiences, but at the same time the linguistic apparatus restricts and reduces reality like any map reduces the reality of a territory. The most beautiful way to illustrate this is the 'medicine wheel of mistakes'. I read about it in the book *Son-Rise* by Barry Kaufman (1979). Apparently Native Americans have a tradition of assimilating new knowledge or learning new skills gradually through 'medicine wheels'. Here is the one about attitudes to mistakes, showing how we would normally start and how we gradually change if we are making progress in this matter:

> *North*
> "Learning from our own mistakes"
> *West*
> "Learning from the mistakes of others"
> *South*
> "Learning from the mistakes of our teachers"
> *East*
> "Being willing to make as many mistakes as it takes"
> *Centre*
> "Learning that there is no such thing as a mistake"

The last message shows that we need to break free from the rigid use of concepts if we are to make progress. Even more difficult is the task of freeing the perception from concepts even before they arise in the mind. According to Krishnamurti we stop learning and observing when we name things – naming creates an impression of the job done. To resist this we can play with an exercise suggested by Csikszentmihalyi (1993) that may challenge this tendency and I suggest extending it to coaching (Box 13.1).

BOX 13.1   Looking without concepts

'It's a good exercise to occasionally look at an object that comes into your view as if you don't know what it is, as if you do not even know its name. Can you look at a chair or a lamp in a room without prejudice, as if you were seeing such a thing for the first time, and refuse to think of it as "chair" or "lamp"?'

(Csikszentmihalyi 1993: 83)

Now, if you are successful with this exercise, can you do the same in your coaching session? Try to observe and listen to the client without the knowledge that you already have of him as a person. Could you stop yourself before the concepts of your diagnostic tools spring to your mind?

There is another warning to be mentioned about *conditioning*: meaningfulness is also culturally constructed. We are expected to search for or to create meaning in our lives particularly with age. In some situations these expectations together with an inability to respond to them can become deadly. Yalom includes someone's suicide note in one of his books that gives an example of such situation:

> Imagine a happy group of morons who are engaged in work. They are carrying bricks in an open field. As soon as they have stacked all the bricks at one end of the field, they proceed to transport them to the opposite end. This continues without stop and everyday of every year they are busy doing the same thing. One day one of the morons stops long enough to ask himself what he is doing. He wonders what purpose there is in carrying the bricks. And from that instant on he is not quite as content with his occupation as he had been before.
> I am the moron who wonders why he is carrying the bricks.
> (Yalom 1980: 419)

Similarly, people can devote their lives to searching for truth and feel good about themselves when they are following the expectations of others. They may feel good just because they see themselves engaged in a respectful activity even if they are not making much progress. This seems like self-deception as well as conditioning. Krishnamurti suggests a more radical way of addressing this issue: 'do not bother about truth but rather let the mind be aware of its own prison' (Krishnamurti 1990: 253).

Finally, it is useful to remember that although clients with a reformed ego are certainly aware of the danger that Einstein warned us about: 'unthinking respect for authority is the greatest enemy of truth', they still may continue being conditioned by highly selected, like-minded people. The coach could be also part of this 'exclusive club' and should challenge the client who appears to agree with her too often.

In terms of working with *self-deception* a coach can be as challenging as she can be in principle when coaching beyond the ego. The clients are already cautious about their own filters to perception and would welcome a contribution from a coach. They are able to see that filters come from the rider which tries to protect its image or ambitions.

The developmental task becomes improving the instrument of seeing, which is in this case – the rider's responsibility.

Working with the elephant

The main task for working with the elephant is improving communication between the mind and body in order for the identity centre becoming grounded in the body and the body to become 'me' rather than 'mine'. Wilber (1999) calls this shift in the client's development the 'centaur': the rider and the elephant become one. During this process the quality of thinking in the rider becomes 'softer' and communication between the rider and the elephant moves to a new level.

The reformed ego is already familiar with the art of *soft thinking*. In fact, there may be quite a lot of soft thinking going on, allowing for spontaneity and creativity in decision making. The reformed ego believes in the power of intuition. The coaching process may also benefit from a patient and inward-looking type of working with problems, when attention to them is activated continuously but without high intensity, like being on the 'back burner'. Several foci of work can be simultaneously active. These can generate a creative space which would allow for insight to occur. The developmental coach can encourage what Claxton (2007) calls 'thinking at the edge' (TATE) by a suggestion to 'sit with a question: what do you "know" and cannot yet say that wants to be said?' This is a good invitation to insight. It is important though that insight is grounded in the reality of the situation and the role of the coach is to bring many different organizational and social perspectives to the client's situation. A creative insight is only meaningful if it is fundamentally contextualized.

The clients at this stage are also interested in meta-thinking. They are fascinated by big systems theories which can reconcile various dichotomies for them. In the coaching process these theories need to be used sparingly with a clear focus on practice. These theories and 'thinking about thinking' can be useful but also could detract from experiences and encourage too analytic a style of enquiry.

In terms of *communication with emotions and the body* the most challenging task for a reformed ego is the search for a natural motivational flow in relation to things that need to be done without forcing any choices and actions on the organism. This is an issue in principle important for coaching and there are different views on it. The question that is normally asked is: why do we become active? And the next question would follow: how can we influence this? However, both of them may become redundant if we see the nature of motivation in a different way:

> The wrong way to construe motivation is to see us as intermittently prodded into action by the activation of a need, upon the satisfaction of which we slump into inactivity again. A better way is to see us as continuously engaged in satisfying the need nearest to the top of the pile that seems capable of being satisfied. As soon as it is satisfied, or the situation changes significantly, so that the first activity is disallowed and another permitted, then a new action, directed towards the attainment of a different end, starts up. Everything we

do, even sleep, is an activity, and directed towards some achievement – even though we may not be conscious of what that achievement is.

(Claxton 1981: 186–7)

With this view on motivation the question to ask is not how I can motivate myself or motivate a client to do something that we consciously chose to do; the questions to ask are of the following kind:

- How do I know that this need is more important than others?
- Is it a need at all?
- Is it worth taking energy from what my organism is doing?
- If this is a very important need how can I help the whole organism to see it?
- What am I prepared to lose if energy is redirected to this need?

The implication of such a position on motivation is, in principal, the same as we have discussed throughout this book. If we want to influence this process consciously for ourselves, the best strategy is to ensure that the organism has as full an apprehension of the situation as possible, that the organism is reasonably healthy and there is not much intervention from the narrator. However, the rider at the stage of reformed ego can do something extra. It may keep alive, for the elephant, the vision of needs from the wider context. It can help the elephant to notice the change in the level of energy when a meaningful goal is realised or when the joy of being alive is in focus. Without manipulating or controlling the elephant unnecessarily the rider could show the importance and attractiveness of a new action in order for it to compete with others (Figure 13.2). All of these strategies can also be observed and amplified during the coaching process.

Figure 13.2 Searching for natural motivational flow.

It is also important to notice the strategies of the reformed ego when dealing with adversities and strong emotions, as they differ from those of the unformed and formed egos. The unformed ego may be overwhelmed by strong emotions and would rely on the comfort received from others. A coach would be there to provide an emotional support. The strategies at the stage of the formed ego would involve the rider's attempt to control emotion, maybe by distracting themselves from the source of it. The reformed ego does not hide from emotions. The adversity or crisis becomes a test of the strength of a reformed ego and the ability of the rider to make meaning of it. A person comes out of a situation like this with more understanding of life and oneself and with new qualities such as resilience and courage. As Claxton said 'equanimity can be found by staring distress in the face' (1992: 16–17).

Working with a multiplicity of self-models

There are no difficulties in *accepting the multiplicity of self-models* for the reformed ego. Self-models are much more available to consciousness and the narrator feels free to choose and create many stories in this expanded domain. As Mahrer describes:

> This new freedom significantly expands the array of behaviours which can flow forth from me. I literally can be this potential or that other potential, and I can accomplish this switch with ease. In effect I am free to be each of these potential selves, and in each there is a distinctive set of behaviours. As a result, the total repertoire of behaviours which can flow forth from me is considerably increased.
>
> (Mahrer 1978: 504)

This freedom allows the reformed ego to understand and work with internal conflicts between different self-models. These clients can take ownership of all sides of the conflict in order to feel them and to explore the consequences. The rider at this stage is also aware of how self-models can change. This can serve as a good starting point for understanding the nature of the narrator as a linguistic function and for questioning in principle the reality of the self.

In terms of *matching* self-models with real mini-selves, a good job could be done by the developmental coach helping the client to explore his fundamental values and their relationship to action. Before the ego becomes reformed, values are the property of the elephant. They are interjected by others in the process of conditioning. At this stage values become conscious and can be usefully discussed and challenged. The reformed ego is more likely to have self-models 'allocated' to various values. Exploring how these values manifest themselves in action would be meaningful in coaching beyond the ego.

For example, when some values contradict each other, it is useful to discuss how the client prioritizes them on the level of rational thinking. It is most important, however, to realize how the whole organism prioritizes things in action and what price is paid for this. The following exercise (Box 13.2) is designed for coaches to explore this issue in parts 1 and 2. The additional parts 3 and 4 can be used to reflect on the potential of coaching as a profession to influence leaders. The first two parts of the exercise can be usefully adapted for clients.

BOX 13.2   Working with values

This activity is designed to help you to explore some of your values. The exercise consists of four parts each expanding the levels and angles of exploration.

Part 1

In column 1 of Table 13.1 rank the described 12 values in order of their importance to you, the most important being number 1 and the least important number 12.

Table 13.1   The list of values for exercise 13.1 (expanded and modified from the original by Insckipp 1987: 101–2)

1	*Values*	*2*	*3*	*4*
	Leadership To be a competent and powerful leader: to organise and influence others to achieve community or organizational goals			
	Expertness To be an authority on a special subject: to reach a hoped-for expert level of skill and accomplishment			
	Prestige To be well known, to obtain recognition, awards, or high social status			
	Service To contribute to the satisfaction of others: to be helpful to others who need it			
	Wealth To earn a great deal of money: to build a large financial estate			
	Independence To have the opportunity for freedom of thought and action: to be one's own boss			
	Affection To obtain and share companionship and affection through immediate family, partners and friends			
	Truth To search for the ultimate meaning of self, life and the world			
	Security To achieve a secure and stable position at work and in financial affairs			
	Self-realization To heighten personal development: to realize one's full creative and innovative potential			
	Mission To dedicate oneself to the pursuit of ultimate values, ideas and principles			
	Pleasure To enjoy life, to be happy and content, to have good things in life			

Explore the result of the ranking using the following questions:

- How did you get these values? Did you choose them or adopt them from other people?
- Are there any conflicts between any two values, e.g. Mission/Pleasure, Prestige/Affection?

Part 2

Cover column 1 and repeat the process of ranking in column 2 considering now these values as goals (the values that you are acting upon). The ranking should be determined by how much psychic energy you invest in each goal. Number 1 is the goal in which you invest most of your energy, 12 is the goal in which your investment of energy is the lowest.

Explore the result of this ranking using the following questions:

- How similar or different are your rankings in part 1 and part 2 of this activity?
- Which of the rankings do you think is more characteristic of you as a person?
- How do you feel about the discrepancies, if any?

Part 3

In column 3 rank at least five of these values in the order that reflects what you would ideally like an actual leader in your life to value. Number 1 is what is most important for you in your leader, 5 is important but comparatively less so than 1.

Explore this ranking using the following questions:

- Why do you want this person to have and act on these values?
- What do you predict may happen to their organization if the leader had these values?

Part 4

In column 4 rank at least five of these values reflecting what you believe coaches can realistically influence in leaders. Number 1 is what is most likely to be influenced, 5 is possible but comparatively less than 1.

Explore this ranking using the following questions:

- What do you think this ranking reflects? (capacity of coaches; readiness of leaders; any other?)
- What has to change for ranking in columns 3 and 4 to be more closely matched?

The most difficult task for the reformed ego, as we already mentioned above, is to expand the boundaries of the client's identity to include the elephant. At the previous stage the rider learned to extend its identity from only rational and voluntary processes to include the whole executive centre that works mainly subconsciously. It was an important achievement. Now coaching beyond the ego can help the client to become a centaur, to help the rider/narrator to embrace the elephant, to unite the mind and the body and to see both of them as 'me' (Figure 13.3).

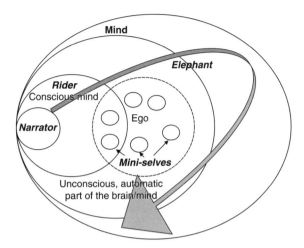

Figure 13.3   Embracing the elephant for establishing self-identity.

This does not mean that the rider would be able to control the whole organism. It would mean actually a much diminished need to control and manipulate it, but paradoxically, this would bring an expanded sense of freedom. This sense can be based on a realization that the organism as a totality can do 'literally millions of processes from the intricacies of digestion to the complexities of neuro-transmission, to the co-ordination of conceptual information' (Wilber 1979: 117). All this is done without the input of the rider and so it can afford to relax and trust the organism. Even the sense of happiness does not need to be artificially manufactured by the rider, who often feels that something is lacking in the present situation. Becoming the centaur means that mental and physical well-being already circulates within the total psychophysical organism. As William Blake said: 'energy is eternal delight, and it is from the body'.

This type of work may require a lot of attention to the body, which may not be appropriate for many types of coaching. However, the coach may recommend some relevant literature. For example, Chapter 8 in Wilber's book, *No Boundaries,* contains many useful exercises for working with the body that clients can try on their own. There is also an excellent resource book by Perls (1969) *Gestalt Therapy Verbatim,* which is specifically designed for individual work with the whole organism. *Focusing* by Gendlin (2003) that we have already mentioned is another useful book for this purpose.

In contrast to the previous stages, one psychological trap that the clients with a reformed ego can still fall into is the pursuit for a *synthesis of self-models.* Although identifying some hidden patterns in the stories of the self could be useful when searching for new meanings and new potential, these clients may be still looking for more than that. It could be a search for a 'true' self which would be against a main developmental challenge of this stage to give up on the self. In a worse scenario a search for a 'true' self may be linked with the search for a meaning in life. This would certainly be a dead end. In this case I would echo the warning about the dangers of self-actualization leading to reduced connections with others. As a counteraction to this James Hillman has some good advice in his famous suggestion: 'It's important to ask yourself, how am I useful to others? What do people want from me? That may very well reveal what you are here for.'

Role of the coach and the nature of coaching relationships

To summarize, a particular feature of this stage is that the ego, after becoming more efficient, has more energy left over for the rider. The rider in turn makes it a mission to help the organism to be the best it can be. On this mission the rider has to struggle with paradoxes, to embrace the elephant in the identity centre and, potentially, to give up on the idea of a self altogether. The nature and the scale of tasks that can be faced during coaching beyond the ego suggest that the coach cannot consider herself to be an expert in all of them. One possible role that the coach could honestly assume is of a 'fellow traveller' or an 'advanced client' in the best tradition of the existential approach. At the same time, I do not want to be prescriptive even in relation to this. For example, if the focus is more on Gestalt type body work, it is possible to imagine a more direct and intervention-based style of coaching. It would of course imply the relevant expertise of the coach and permission from the client. Needless to say, the coach herself has to be involved in her own developmental process with a similar depth and rigour to her clients.

To summarize the specific features of approaching the themes of the reformed ego, the coach may consider the following:

- helping the rider of the client to anticipate and prevent potential blockages to the needed changes and to the efficient functioning of the organism;
- challenging the client's conception of 'the best' in his task of being the best he can be;
- helping the client to untangle his views on self-actualization and/or authenticity if he is in pursuit of them;
- helping the client to explore a way of living with the existential paradoxes that affect his life;
- challenging non-traditional ways of falling into the trap of conditioning;
- exploring with the client the conditions for natural motivational flow;
- exploring the values that are held by the client and their relationship to action;
- supporting the client in his attempt to embrace the elephant as a part of his identity;
- supporting the client in his attempt at reconsidering the nature of the self.

Some already existing traditions of coaching, such as Existential, Gestalt and Narrative approaches can be very suitable for coaching beyond the ego. The Existential coach may be well placed to help the client in facing the essential paradoxes of living, to question their non-traditional conditioning and issues of responsibility in the pursuit of authenticity (Spinelli 2010). In the Gestalt approach to coaching (Bluckert 2010) there are many useful interventions that can help to ground abstract values in the body and to elicit the challenges in the attempt to synthesize self-models. As far as Narrative coaching (Drake 2010) is concerned, the theory presented in this book is not fully compatible with the extent of the power of stories as postulated in this approach. At the same time I can see the enormous potential of this approach for coaching beyond the ego when working with the identity centre. Particularly useful is the emphasis of this approach on generating more experiences instead of rushing to interpretations and meanings and also its emphasis on connecting the stories with social contexts.

14 Coaching the soul

There is the strangest lightness about the heart when one's nothingness in a particular line is once accepted in good faith . . . How pleasant is the day when we give up striving to be young, – or slender!

William James, 1890

To separate the essential from the non-essential is what I call being spiritual.

Franz Marc

This stage of 'coaching the soul' does not mean that the theory described so far has changed dramatically and that instead of a fairly grounded and rationally conceived ego we are going to talk here about the ephemeral and mysterious soul. This chapter is about the ego with the soul. Although it is no lesser challenge, I will try to stay true to my initial intention of developing a theory of working with the self that does not at least contradict what we currently know about human nature.

First of all, what needs to be said is that coaching the soul is much less attached to a stage in comparison to the previous three coaching types, such as coaching towards a healthy ego. It is best viewed as a dimension of coaching that can be relevant to each of the three previous stages. If we look at the diversity of clients who might be interested in coaching the soul we can see the following:

1   Potential clients who demonstrate capacities beyond those available to individuals with unformed, formed and reformed ego: this group can include people who are called mystics and sages and also long-term meditators who can bring their organism on a regular basis to an unusual state of 'no-self'. This group

is unlikely to be a large one in principle and particularly among the coaching clientele.

2   Clients who have had unusual (spiritual/mystical) experiences which might or might not be integrated with the way they see themselves and the world: these experiences could be available to many people. Some clients may consider such experiences as significant and relevant to potential themes of coaching and to the coaching process.

3   Clients who have a deep interest in the spiritual: they could be members of religious communities, have commitment to spiritual practices or pursue this interest in their own individual way. There could be many clients who would fall into this category and consider this inclination as part of their value system. Their themes of coaching may be intertwined with their spiritual values.

There are no clear dividing lines between these groups. Some people may belong to two or all three of them at the same time. We will consider each of them separately, but first we need to discuss what we mean by the 'ego with a soul' and what might be different about it from the unformed, formed and reformed ego.

To start with, you, the reader, may ask: why introduce such a vague and loaded concept as a 'soul'? One simple reason is inclusiveness. In spite of disagreements about methodologies, nearly all estimates of world demographics show that the vast majority of the adult population of the world belong to at least the third category. It means that the concept of the soul is important for perhaps 80 per cent of the world's adults. The vagueness and the beauty of this concept also help to unite all three groups in spite of the variations between them. A traditional meaning of the term 'soul' refers to a spiritual or immaterial part of a human being, regarded as immortal (Oxford Dictionary). Whether believing in immortality or not, the soul is still a meaningful concept for many people, and as a well-known neuroscientist, Ramachandran (2003), once said:

> You know from everything that you hear from science and from neurology, that you are a beast, just a hairless ape which happens to be a little bit more clever than other apes. At the same time, you don't feel like that. You feel like you're an angel trapped inside this body, constantly craving immortality, craving transcendence, trying to escape from this body. And this is the essential human predicament.

Staying clear and logical when considering an 'ego with a soul' is not easy. The more you go into the literature that addresses these topics, the more its language becomes emotionally rich and colourful but also nebulous and the evidence becomes more scarce and unconventional. At the same time the realities behind this and the related concept of 'spirit' are too important for us to dismiss. The current lack of hard evidence in the realm of the spiritual is a problem, but the fact that spiritual phenomena are so meaningful in the lives of so many people in the world is a good reason not to dismiss them and to continue studying them.

> Within the confines of a finite, personal life, the soul is a link to the invisible
> world of essential qualities and perceptions that endow human existence with
> a sense of meaning and purpose. To be soulful is to be filled with deep feeling;
> to be soulless is to be hard and callous. To be inspired is to be connected to
> Spirit; to be dispirited, depressed and anxious is to be out of touch with soul.
>
> (Vaughan 2005: 102)

It is possible that scientists will eventually find a way to understand and explain what
we so far have not been able to. Even now some of them speculate that we might be
hard-wired for religious beliefs. There might be some neural structures in the brain that
make us more prone to spirituality. There are many interesting experiments that offer
unusual and far-reaching explanations. For example, the effect of an 'enlarged self' can
apparently be identified by neuro-imaging (Newberg et al. 2001). Neuroscientists who
studied long-term meditators found two areas of the brain that receive input from the
senses to help us maintain an ongoing representation of how we identify our location in
space. At the point of mystical union that was reported by the meditators overall activity
in these two areas appeared to be significantly reduced as well as input from other parts
of the brain. However, these areas, even when 'cut off', seem to be trying to do their job
and so people end up experiencing a loss of self combined with a paradoxical expansion
of the self. The result is that the person feels merged with something bigger than the self.

The soul as an opening to Reality

While scientists are looking for the explanation of spiritual phenomena I do not see
any reason why developmental coaches should shy away from these topics if they have
meaning in the lives of their clients. 'Coaching the soul' is the term that I suggest
using for this dimension of our work. First we need to see what the concept of the
soul can add to the way we understand ego in this book. I propose to see the soul
as *an opening*: an opening from the perception of reality as usually seen, to a sharper
and more immediate awareness of reality that is usually unavailable to us. As we were
saying earlier, we do not see the world and reality as it is, we see it as we are, clouded
by conditioning, self-deception and many other limitations that we have as human
beings. It is possible then that perception, if significantly and dramatically improved,
can create a temporary opening into a reality that we cannot know, Reality with a capital
R. It is possible that our inklings and anticipation of such an opening are associated
with the soul and manifested as a search for beauty, love, truth and goodness.

It appears that the first group in the list above have this opening regularly as the
result of meditation, prayer or other practices. It is also documented that very rare
individuals, who in some religions are called enlightened, appear to have this opening
permanently. There are cases when such an opening has occurred without any spiritual
activity but causing nevertheless a permanent transformation (Wren-Lewis 1988). On
the other hand, many authors of developmental theories suggest that to become this
type of person you have to be developed beyond the reformed ego (Cook-Greuter
1999; Wilber 2006).

If they are right, and at least the first group of the *ego with the soul* is a stage of development, what would have to change in the reformed ego to move to this later stage? At the reformed ego stage people are already amazing learners. They are consciously involved in anticipating and preventing blockages to organic changes and the functioning of the organism in congruence with presenting situations. The rider works really well for the whole organism. The only thing that is holding them back is confusion about the self. When this confusion is resolved and the self is seen for what it is – various stories put together by the narrator – then these stories stop taking up as much attention as they used to in the reformed ego. The narrator stops creating a wall between what it thinks the self is and the rest of the world. The rider stops its constant chatter, the mind becomes fresher, calmer, more immediate and the energy freed from it may create a temporary opening in this wall into Reality.

It appears that people in the first group, who have had such an opening often, or at least regularly, let go of desires and self-stories and begin to treat everything as impermanent. They become more loving and compassionate, and find greater equanimity. They begin to treat all environmental objects as if they were their own self. In this way the universal compassion that is described by the mystics is different from compassion or love that can be found at other stages. Here others are loved not because they love us or affirm us and support us but because they *are* us. This opening can bring to realization that 'there are no isolated entities – only continuously changing interconnectedness' (Wade 1996: 220).

It has been said that those rare people who are enlightened have a full and immediate perception of what is, a direct access to Reality. This rarity is not surprising if we consider Christ and Buddha as typical members of this group. All others may have a soul with a degree of opening into Reality. It is difficult to speculate what this Reality may be. Many different versions of it exist in spiritual scriptures, philosophy and even science. It includes the possibility that the nature of consciousness is field-like and common to all objects as well as human beings. It may also not be confined by the conventional categories of space and time (Forman 1999; Hayward 1999). The most typical vision is of interconnectedness of everything in the world as opposed to the illusion of separateness, as Einstein once beautifully described:

> A human being is a part of the whole called by us universe, a part limited in time and space. He experiences himself, his thoughts and feelings as something separated from the rest, a kind of optical delusion of his consciousness. This delusion is a kind of prison for us, restricting us to our personal desires and to affection for a few persons nearest us. Our task must be to free ourselves from this prison by widening our circle of compassion to embrace all living creatures and the whole of nature in its beauty.

When understood literally this process of freeing ourselves from this prison can sometimes mistakenly be understood as requiring the elimination of the ego, an idea particularly associated with New Age culture. It could also be a result of mystics' messages, a beautiful simplicity of which could be misread:

Why are you unhappy?
Because 99.9 per cent,
Of everything you think,
And of everything you do,
Is for yourself –
And there isn't one.

Wei Wu Wei

This idea persists in spite of the obvious paradox: 'If I want to get rid of my ego, who is the one who decides to do this? If I am to succeed in this task would it mean that I am strengthening my ego?' It has been argued by different authors that the self that is lost in mystic enlightenment is not the self essential to the practical carrying on of one's ordinary daily activities (Fingarette 1963: 307) or 'the only thing that wants to get rid of the ego is the ego' (Wilber 1999: 274). However, the theory developed here I think helps to clearly separate what is to be 'got rid of' and what is not even possible to conceive of as being eliminated. A person cannot function without an executive centre, so what we here call 'ego' will certainly be present in a mystic and in any unusual experiences that anyone might have. What seems to be disappearing is the frantic activity of the narrator and the false identity stories that it creates. So there is no problem with identification with the ego, it is only the exclusiveness of this identification that needs to be challenged if the client is interested in further development.

As we have already said, the people from the first group of 'ego with a soul' may not be the most typical coaching clients, but they still might choose to explore some of the themes characteristic for coaching the soul. The second group is a much wider one of those that have had a mystical experience – some degree of self-transcendence in which the sense of a separate self has disappeared. It may have shaken their worldview and they are seeking to integrate this experience in a new way. These clients could belong to any of the stages: unformed, formed or reformed ego, and so the challenge of understanding and accepting such an experience could differ significantly. Sometimes those who have had such an experience feel embarrassed to discuss it as they may find it so incompatible with the way others see them and/or they see themselves. In this case the developmental coach can be well placed to discuss these experiences as natural rather than weird.

The third group may be by far the largest in comparison to the other two among the coaching clientele, simply because it includes many of us who look for a meaningful explanation of what the world may be like and what life is all about. It could be a traditional religious route or it could be a quest with a high respect for science but without disregarding other important aspects of our lives. The longing and search for beauty, love or goodness may be an expression of this quest. My belief is that the third group is constantly growing and so it is quite likely that many coaching clients may find this dimension of life relevant to the coaching conversation. The problem with this group is that the underlying themes of coaching may clash: for example, some of them may require coaching towards a healthy ego and some, coaching the soul. It would be an interesting challenge for a developmental coach to address both.

Typical tasks and issues

Typical themes that may become apparent for all three groups of clients described above who may need coaching the soul are:

- realization of a conflict between a spiritual inclination and other internal needs and/or external demands;
- identifying their mission in life;
- confusion created by contradicting spiritual guidelines;
- trying to make sense of the unusual/mystical experience;
- explicit intention for spiritual development;
- dissatisfaction with progress in this development;
- disillusionment with their chosen spiritual path;
- coming to terms with the mortality of the organism;
- realization of the incompleteness of the work to which they have deeply committed themselves;
- overcoming spiritual illusions.

It is clear that there are already many spiritual practices in many parts of the world and in many cultures that address themes like these. I would say, however, that although a developmental coach may not have centuries of refined methods by highly experienced teachers behind her, she may have the advantage of a broader overview of these practices. This may help with seeing the potential illusions and pitfalls of these traditions if they appear to be too narrow. It is useful, for example, to see how spiritual practices might be different from organized religion and how one or the other may be answering the needs of clients from different stages. The coach may notice that the unformed ego, at least initially, is attracted to an organized religion because of the need for explicit guidance. However, practices such as Buddhism and particularly Zen, may appeal to the formed or reformed egos who are ready to be challenged about the existence of the self. Developmental coaches may identify the danger of what could be called 'translation versus transformation' (not the same as in Wilber 1999). Some clients may become highly articulate about particular values that they have developed or changes they desire, without necessarily committing themselves to any relevant action and actually changing.

There are some specific issues that many spiritual practices can stumble upon which would be useful for the coach to think about. One of them is the idea of a spiritual path. Practically all practices suggest the need for commitment to particular methods, such as meditation, that need to be followed precisely if one expects some progress in spiritual development. However, according to iconoclasts such as Krishnamurti this creates the biggest trap for the self – becoming.

'The movement of becoming, of the man who wants to become the Buddha or the manager, is the activity of the shallow. The shallow are ever afraid of what they are; but what they are is the truth. Truth is in the silent observation of what *is*, and it is truth that transforms what *is*' (Krishnamurti 1994: 205). He is warning that spiritual ambitions are the same as any other ambitions. They create ideals which distract and redirect the energy of the organism from current situations. They also create great excuses for not doing what the situation requires, being self-content just with being 'on the spiritual path'. Krishnamurti suggests that intention rather than result-orientation is a better way to approach 'soul work' and this intention should be to be out of the 'prison' of our current perceptions rather than to become 'highly spiritual'.

Similar to this is the issue of spiritual path versus being 'struck by lightning'. There is a view that doubts even the effectiveness of the spiritual path. A simple statistic shows that the number of enlightened individuals as a proportion of the great many people involved in spiritual practice even in countries that have strong traditions in this, is very low (Wilber 1999: 31). Krishnamurti (1991) and Wren-Lewis (1988) are among those who argue that what I call here 'the openings' have very little to do with practice. They happen unexpectedly and practice may even be an obstacle to them because of the preoccupation with time and the search for a 'true self'. The ultimate simplicity of the Zen tradition can also be interpreted in a similar way. ' "All this Zen stuff is nonsense', said the sceptic, "You are perfectly correct" responded the master, "but this is a teaching I normally reserve for only my most advanced students" ' (Freke 1997: 18). However, many others in this field, admitting the above argument, still believe that spiritual practice is a way that helps to 'thin the wall' in order for the opening to break through spontaneously. As someone said, 'enlightenment is an accident, but meditation helps to make you accident-prone'.

There are some interesting ideas of what is helpful for those who wish to become 'transpersonal learners'. Nearly all of them start from increasing self-awareness and self-knowledge, including the development of cognitive flexibility: being open to many different viewpoints and perspectives on the world and curiosity towards new information. Csikszentmihalyi (1993) claims that 'flow' experiences can escalate a development of this nature. He also thinks that we should seek out complexity in our daily choices to give development a better chance.

Several controversies exist in relation to the role of concepts such as 'mission', 'devotion' and 'sacrifice' as a route in 'soul work'. On the one hand working for something 'big' is important, because it may place an appropriate level of significance to the stories that narrators tends to create. It could serve as an antidote to self-importance and maybe self-pity: 'This is the true joy in life, the being used for a purpose recognised by yourself as a mighty one . . . the being a force of nature instead of a feverish selfish little clod of ailments and grievances complaining that the world will not devote itself to making you happy' (G.B. Shaw). On the other hand, paradoxically, associating oneself with a big and beautiful idea may also lead to self-inflation – the narrator does not give up easily. As an example of an antidote in this case I like a suggestion by Csikszentmihalyi to always act as if the future of the universe depended on what you do, while laughing at yourself for thinking that whatever you do makes any difference.

And finally, to make the developmental tasks of all three groups of the ego with the soul more concrete, we can say that:

- the first group is looking for a permanent opening to Reality;
- the second group is seeking to understand and integrate their opening into their worldview;

- and the third group is 'thinning the wall' by many different means to encourage an opening to happen.

Relevant approaches and interventions

It may look as if developmental coaches would be spoiled for choices in relation to coaching the soul with so many spiritual traditions working for centuries to provide methods and ideas for guidance. But coaches do not to attempt to manufacture the opening into Reality. They are there to help their clients to address their developmental themes. However, in their mutual effort they may find that as the mind/brain is freed from some conditioning and self-deceptions, the opening may become 'dis-inhibited' (Claxton 2002). Coaches can also use different strategies for working with the elephant and the narrator as part of their approach.

Improving the quality of perception

Improving perception is the most important task when coaching the soul. The obstacles to this still come from conditioning and from internal 'devices' such as self-deception. In terms of *conditioning* there is plenty to address when coaching the soul and the level of the conditioning that needs to be questioned goes much deeper. The influences come not just from parents or culture. We are also conditioned as human beings to see ourselves as separate from our environment. This stance is supported by the need to act as if we were separate. But this type of conditioning may hold us back in terms of opening into Reality because it suggests a very different picture of it. At least intellectually we can try to conceive that the boundaries between the self and the world are self established and therefore are movable. Exercises for expanding perspectives on the world are very useful for this purpose and even engaging with cognitive-developmental theories may stretch these perspectives, too.

The developmental coach can help the client to see how his perception is restricted by various factors including his own intentions. She can invite the client to experiment and to notice the difference when trying to shift from 'looking for' to 'looking at'. It is interesting that when the rider of the client loses some agendas, such as transforming the organism, it becomes a better organ of perception.

The self-deception of the ego with a soul can be quite sophisticated and the clients may feel disappointed when they catch themselves in this act. For example, the spiritual illusion of having arrived needs to be constantly watched for, particularly when the client invests too much in this kind of development.

> Walking the spiritual path properly is a very subtle process; it is not something to jump into naively. There are numerous sidetracks which lead to a distorted, ego-centred version of spirituality; we can deceive ourselves into thinking we are developing spiritually when instead we are strengthening our egocentricity through spiritual techniques. This fundamental distortion may be referred to as *spiritual materialism*.
>
> (Trungpa 1973: 3, original emphasis)

Another kind of spiritual illusion is a fixation on the mystical experience. The second group of clients may be particularly prone to it. This experience, whether spontaneous or as the result of prolonged concentration on an object, could be so deep and beautiful that the client may become entranced by it. In Buddhist traditions this would mean that you are now on a side track – you are just trying to cling to something that is pleasant and avoid what is not. This means that you have simply added another set of toys to your collection. They recommend not dwelling on it. This is the famous 'If you meet the Buddha on the road, kill him!' which means 'don't get caught in the experience, don't self-inflate yourself with it'. On the other hand, if the client tends to dismiss the experience or 'pathologizes' it, the coach needs to challenge this, too.

The best method of improving the quality of perception is to practise *mindfulness*. What we currently know of mindfulness practice, not necessarily attached to any spiritual tradition, suggests that this approach promises to be highly beneficial for individual development in line with all three mechanisms that we describe here. The main value of it is in improving perception. Mindfulness may look like a simple method: just noticing without commenting on what is happening in one's present experience, just seeing from moment to moment what the mind is up to. It is, however, not as simple as it sounds and needs serious practice. I recommend a useful text that can assist you in learning about this method: *Living the Mindful Life* by Charles Tart (1994).

In the terminology of the theory that I propose we can see that mindfulness is about keeping the attention of the rider on more immediate, less elaborated states, for example noticing the sensation in your hands when you do the washing up, watching and listening to the water running. If we do not share this sensation with the narrator, it does not hijack the attention into creating another story of the self washing the dishes. This allows useful associations between mini-selves to continue and it still inhibits any inappropriate physical response. Learning to do this is, according to Claxton, what the 'cultivation of mindfulness' is about and this is how he describes the potential benefits of this process:

> In this state of sharp awareness of experience at a low level of interpretation, three phenomenal effects occur. First the 'world' seems clearer, cleaner and more objective: less, to use Hermann Hesse's phrase, 'a cloudy mirror of our own desire'. Second, assumptions and projections which have previously been dissolved surreptitiously in perception now become visible in their own right. They operate, if they still continue to do so, 'downstream' of the moment of conscious perception, on the surface, rather than upstream, invisibly. And third, the mingling of cognitive currents that extended processing allows is freed of the narrowing concerns of self-reference: it is less firmly channelled by consideration of personal advantage and disadvantage, and 'creativity' becomes more playful and unbounded.
>
> (Claxton 2004: 221)

What is described here is mainly referring to the task of improving the quality of perception. However, in the task of working with the elephant, the cultivation of mindfulness may allow a fine-tuning in the work of the executive centre by a better relationship between the elephant and the rider.

Working with the elephant

> That is what Zen means by being detached – not being without emotion or feeling, but being one in whom feeling is not sticky or blocked, and through whom the experiences of the world pass like the reflections of birds flying over water.
>
> Allan Watts, *The Way of Zen*

Working with the elephant is not a straightforward activity in various spiritual practices. Some of them suggest treating the body as a temple, looking after it and listening to it. Some are so concentrated on the soul that the body is seen only as 'that garage that you park your soul in' and so is pretty much neglected. In developmental coaching it is the organism as a whole that is seen as a unit of change. Therefore, clients are encouraged to pay attention to the body and keep it fully relaxed and energized, sensitive and open to life.

We do not know much about the actual relationship between the rider, the elephant and ultimate Reality, so we cannot be critical or fully accepting of the precision with which the body is treated and exercised in different traditions. We can repeat though, after the yogis, that which is below cannot coerce what is above. Higher consciousness and opening to Reality cannot be caused by the manipulation of the rider or the elephant. A correct physical posture or moral behaviour seems to be of some help but do not determine or guarantee it. Therefore the attitude of the rider in this work is as important as it is humble. 'In the presence of something higher than itself, the mind needs to learn how to be quiet and to listen' (Ravindra 2004: 103).

In the light of this attitude the idea of *soft thinking* that I was promoting before is still important. It reinforces the main value of insight as a capacity of the mind to come to deep, intuitive answers to questions 'not through the busy application of conscious intelligence, but through patiently bearing with the predicament' (Claxton 1992: 116). This approach of bringing to the fore the wisdom of the whole organism rather than the cleverness of the rider is applied also in the Zen tradition of *koan* training. A Koan is a question or a little story that is unsolvable for an intelligent but 'unenlightened' mind. It is given to the disciple to concentrate on and to figure out the answer. This task forces him/her for years to drive a particular question more and more deeply into the mind, and in the process to exhaust conscious thinking completely. The reward, of course, is not the relief of finding the answer to the koan, but transformation of the mind in the process. We could say that the quality of perplexity that could accompany a genuine struggle with a problem in developmental coaching may be beneficial for similar reasons. The coach though, needs to restrain her natural drive for finding solutions as soon as possible but instead create an atmosphere for the client where *soft and mindful* thinking flourishes.

In relation to *communication with the emotional body* when coaching the soul, we need to clarify a typical illusion concerning the role of emotions in spiritual practices. It is a misunderstanding that emotional detachment is an ideal to work towards. The confusion might stem from the messages that warn about the dangers of attachments but the difference I think is best explained by Watts (1957):

> ... it is said that a Buddha is free from worldly attachment. It does not mean that he is a 'stone Buddha' with no feelings, no emotions, and no sensations of (anger or hunger?) or pain. It means that he does not block at anything. Thus it is typical of Zen that its style of action has the strongest feeling of commitment, of 'follow-through'. It enters into everything wholeheartedly and freely without having to keep an eye on itself. It does not confuse spirituality with thinking about God while one is peeling potatoes. Zen spirituality is just to peel the potatoes.
>
> (Alan Watts 1957: 171)

I have already advocated 'focusing' as a method (Gendlin 2003) for involving emotions and the elephant together in understanding yourself, your situations and finding answers to difficult issues. In the context of coaching the soul I want to reiterate that this method is profoundly linked with an idea of the book about the organism and its interconnectedness with the world. 'The living body is always going beyond what evolution, culture and language have already built. The body is always sketching and probing a few steps further. Your ongoing living makes new evolution and history happen – now' (Gendlin 2003: viii). Focusing is an invaluable tool for establishing communication between any levels of reality available to the client. It may not appeal to all developmental coaches as a method to use in the session, but I would not hesitate in advising an open-minded client to engage with this method on their own.

There are some unusual and perhaps artificial ways to create opening through the elephant. Some synchronized movements – in dance, religious ritual and military training are believed to set resonance patterns in the brain that make this mystical state more likely to happen. It has been documented that these movements are also known for creating harmony and cohesion within groups and cultivating altruistic motivation (McNeill 1995). It is interesting but I am not sure how this could be helpful for coaching.

Finally in this section I would like to revisit the topic of free will as interplay between the rider and the elephant. With some clients who are open to working with the soul, we can start questioning the issue gently and possibly explore the implications of a more reasonable view on it. It is possible to learn, some say (Blackmore 2005), to live without pretending that we have conscious free will, to give up on making choices or to see choice just as predictions of what the whole organism is about to do. Many others, however, even with full knowledge of this illusion, choose to live as if there is a self and there is free will, believing, probably, that in the long run their rider is still an active player in the organism.

> When I choose between definite alternatives set out in advance, my choice is probably partly the application of comparatively mechanistic problem-solving

techniques, and partly randomness. It is still my choice, in the sense that it arises from the whole of who I am, which has built up through the whole of my life, but it is not quite what I like to suppose when I talk about my 'free will'. On the other hand, when I creatively move into a new way of seeing things, a new framework of meaning, then I am changing the way my consciousness is selecting within the histories that I take part in. This lies outside the mechanistic dynamics of physics and goes to the core of the self. Ideas of value and responsibility flow from this source of creativity.

(Clarke 2004: 91)

For the developmental coach the field of values and responsibilities is where she engages with the client, helping him to deal with all the themes he faces. She may help him to see if his organism is like a leaf changing its direction by the many winds of influences. She may also help him to deal with his feelings about this. But at the end of the day coaching the soul might mean accepting what is and getting on with it, just like the way of a warrior in Castaneda's (1991) *Tales of Power:* 'A warrior takes his lot, whatever it may be and accepts it in ultimate humbleness. He accepts in humbleness what he is, not as grounds for regret, but as a living challenge.'

Working with multiplicity of self-models

> Angels can fly because they take themselves so lightly
>
> G.K. Chesterton, *Orthodoxy*

Multiplicity is not the most important topic when coaching the soul – it is the narrator itself that is targeted. Silencing the narrator is not easy, but may happen in some particular situations: in flow; under the influence of some drugs; at particular stages of meditation; when an opening into Reality is created. Cultivating mindfulness also enables the narrator to take a back seat in the moment of action, but does not prevent stories being created in between the actions. It is unlikely that silencing the narrator could become a full scale centre of attention in developmental coaching even at a stage of coaching the soul.

At the same time, a developmental coach may be able to help with eliminating some unsubstantiated fears that could be associated with silencing the narrator. People may think that without the narrator they may not be able to function, but it is the ego, which is never eliminated, that is responsible for this. Some may think that without self-models representing particular values of the individual, they may become antisocial or even criminal, but we are all social animals who have a natural instinct to care for others. When smaller mental space is devoted to the complex desires of the many self-models there is a better chance for kindness and consideration to come to the fore. There are fears, though, that are worth considering. For example, manufacturing a no-self state through the use of drugs may be damaging to mental health. When one is back from a 'spiritual holiday' to their 'normal reception' mundane reality may strike us as being more intolerable than before (Claxton 2004: 142).

There is, however, a self-model that could be useful for clients of the third group but whose ego is unformed. Claxton (2007) called this self-model a 'Benign Generalized Internalized Other'. In spite of the clumsy title the idea of it might be useful for an unformed ego which needs support and guidance and is not ready yet to generate it independently. When they experience an internal conflict or find themselves acting in contradiction to what they value, in order not to be overwhelmed with confusion or even self-hatred they could recall a self-model of another who will be accepting of them in spite of anything. From this position the dissonance can be tolerated and the client may become capable of action. This Benign Other can be modelled on the image of a known or imaginary person. Rowan (2010), for example, describes many ideas about these self-models which the coach can 'call for' in difficult moments.

In terms of the overall task of the identity centre, clients with a reformed ego may be interested in expanding their sense of who they are beyond the organism (Figure 14.1). It may sound strange and I am not aware of any methods to advance oneself in this direction, but we could start from noticing how we resist this process if it is designed to happen naturally, how we keep the skin as our boundary. For example, we can notice how we stop ourselves from really understanding another person, how we arrange our life with less and less connection to nature, how we shut out our senses when we hear of the world's troubles. At the same time we can notice how we can already expand these boundaries when we feel a real pain when a child is suffering, how we become full of joy through the deep connection with another person or when we care for nature not because it is a sign of a good citizen, but just because this is how we feel.

If Reality is as mystics describe it: the interconnectedness of everything that exists, then by noticing these boundaries we may be 'thinning the wall' and creating at the same time better conditions for the opening into this Reality to occur. And as the sense of self gets expanded it may include areas of the psyche that are less predictable but more mysterious and creative.

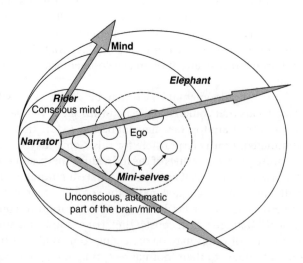

Figure 14.1 Going beyond the organism for establishing self-identity.

The role of the coach

> 'Did you make that song up?'
> 'Well, I sort of make it up', said Pooh. 'It isn't Brain . . . but it comes to me
> sometimes.'
> 'Ah', said Rabbit, who never let things come to him, but always fetched them.
> A.A. Milne, The House at Pooh Corner

It is probably unrealistic to see developmental coaching as soul-making. Our clients
come for coaching as equal partners for working on their themes. However, this process
may contribute to soul-making if the coach is there with her soul, too.

However, before being ambitious the coach needs to be careful. The task of development through engagement with the themes of coaching should come before the greater
task of seeing through the self. The coach should be particularly tentative when coaching the soul of the client whose ego is unformed. Spiritual work can be recommended,
but with full awareness that meditation, for example, 'is not a calm and steady process
of increasing relaxation, but a deep confrontation with oneself' (Blackmore 2003: 407).
It can make people less sure of themselves and those with psychopathologies may feel
worse as a result (Epstein and Lieff 1986; Delmonte 1987). Needless to say that even
with the best of intentions, a developmental coach should not lead the client to work
with the soul if it is not initiated by him. There is always a price to pay for any development even if it seems generally positive. Therefore, it is only the client himself who
needs to decide whether it is a fair price for what he wants to achieve.

In order to approach the specific themes in coaching the ego with the soul, the
developmental coach may consider:

- demonstrating an unreserved intention for understanding the spiritual concerns of the client and building a relationship conducive to coaching the soul;
- creating conditions in the session where intuition, effortlessness and trusting
  the process are prominent and enabling for both elephants;
- helping the client to identify his position towards the main contradictions of
  spiritual development and some spiritual illusions;
- exploring with clients the most appropriate ways of 'thinning the wall' in order
  for an opening to Reality to occur;
- helping clients with strong spiritual inclinations to also stay grounded and not
  to forget about dealing with the challenges of their current situation (Figure
  14.2);
- without 'robbing the client of his steering-wheel', challenging his attitude to
  the issues of free will, control and responsibility from the position of the soul;
- discussing with clients, if appropriate, their views on silencing the narrator
  while being true to the energy of each moment.

Although a great deal has been written on working with the soul not much has been
discussed on what is appropriate and useful in coaching. I can recommend, however,

Figure 14.2   Keeping the client grounded.

two chapters on this topic. One is by John Rowan (2010) who illustrates how the transpersonal approach to coaching can work. He also gives a good overview of the approach with a useful evaluation of it in comparison to other traditions. Another passionate proponent of this approach to coaching is John Whitmore (2008, interviewed by Kauffman and Bachkirova). He has written, together with Einzig, about what I call here 'coaching the soul', and has described practical ways which are mainly based on psychosynthesis (Whitmore and Einzig 2007). I would also like to direct those who wish to explore the literature beyond that of coaching, to any sources mentioned in this section but not given the attention that they deserve.

15 Conclusions about and for developmental coaches

Some cannot loosen their own chains yet can nonetheless liberate their friends.
Nietzsche, *Thus Spake Zarathustra*

I hope that by now it is reasonably clear what we mean here by developmental coaching. It starts with an assumption that the client acts as a whole organism which has a capacity to create multiple stories of the self. Developmental coaching, while keeping in mind the developmental significance of coaching themes, engages fully with them by improving the client's perception, mind-body communication and sense of identity. The coach who works developmentally acts as a companion to the client in bringing about organic changes that stem from the whole organism.

Is it possible for anyone to become a developmental coach? In principle, yes. Any coach who addresses the various developmental themes which are brought by the clients is already doing a developmental job. On the other hand, to be a developmental coach in the sense described here would require more than that. First of all, a developmental coach would address these themes with an understanding of the wider picture of what might be happening with a client. She might be less confused when she perceives insurmountable difficulties that some clients experience in some areas of their lives in spite of having great abilities in other areas. She will be able to find an individual approach to each client even when the presented themes are from different stages. Her approach would be systemic in terms of the applied methods, using the three main mechanisms of bringing about change: improving perception, dealing with the elephant and dealing with the multiplicity of self-models. She may be better able to recognize if the change that the client aims for is organic. These are only some of the capacities that could be characteristic for a developmental coach and from which the coaching process can significantly benefit. And, of course, all of them are possible to learn.

Does there have to be something special about a developmental coach as a person? Does she need, for example, to have experienced all the main themes that have been described here? It is easy to say no to the second question. However, if we ask if the coach needs to be of a certain ego-stage, the answer would not be as simple. Some developmental writers are quite explicit in their assertion that the coach's level of development should at least be the same or above the level of development of the client (Laske 2006a). I, however, argued elsewhere (Bachkirova 2010) that for some coaching genres such as skills coaching or performance coaching this requirement is unnecessary. A coach who is, for example, skilful in helping people to become better presenters does not need to be at a later developmental stage. She can do this job well and the result of it may well be developmental for a client. However, the coach could struggle in helping the client engage with the themes that may have a different meaning for her or may not be meaningful at all. For example, if a client experiences dissatisfaction with his job and/or a life situation in spite of high achievements – the themes of the reformed ego – the coach with a formed ego may take it as a need to look for an even higher challenge, while the coach with an unformed ego may not be able to understand this theme at all.

Is it possible to help someone without understanding their theme? Similarly, I have also been thinking about Nietzsche's aphorism at the beginning of these conclusions and was pondering how it could be possible to liberate others if you yourself are not free. I recalled an experience in my own life when such help was given and the process was beneficial. The explanation that I came to is in the quality of listening and a special atmosphere that it creates for the client to explore his own theme even when the coach cannot fully grasp it. This genuine presence of another who also has your best interest at heart can allow, I believe, the client to stay long enough with their issue, to silence critical self-models and to let the whole organism be creative. This kind of listening is not easy at any ego-stage, but any coach can aspire to listen like that.

The discrepancy in stages is also not a fixed predicament. Sometimes coaching starts with a reasonable match but gradually the complexity of themes may become overwhelming for the coach. Sometimes both of them will start changing and therefore be capable of addressing more and more complex themes. When supervising coaches I have heard so many times how surprised they become noticing the changing nature of the themes that new clients bring to them. I think it is a sign of the coach recognizing these themes as much as it is the self-selection of clients that choose to work with them. It is interesting though, that for some coaches the work with other 'earlier' themes is still engaging or fulfilling, but for other coaches it becomes less so.

What about your ego?

The coach may benefit from gauging her own stage of ego development as different from her level of experience as a coach. Everything that has been described in this respect for identifying the stage of the clients' developmental themes can also be useful and beneficial for a coach. I would like to add some aspects that could be specific only for coaches. See if you can recognize yourself in some of these descriptions.

If you think that your ego is unformed then, as a coach, you may tend to follow a concrete approach that gives you sufficient structure to rely on, with a solid kit of techniques and methods. You could well relate to clients with issues of confidence which could help in building rapport with them quickly and securely. It would be much easier for you to provide support rather than to challenge the client. You judge the quality of your work by how much the client felt understood and supported when working with you. You would probably choose a supervisor who works in the same tradition and it would be someone who can give significant support and share more coaching techniques, strategies and tips.

If you think that your ego is fully formed you may have identified, after careful consideration, the approach that works for you or you may have created your own approach to coaching and feel confident about using it. You can keep in mind many aspects of the client's situation and stay focused on the results and goals of the coaching process as agreed. Challenging is not a problem for you. You judge the quality of your work by the degree to which the client achieves his goals. You would probably choose a supervisor who is well respected in the field but can also appreciate your style and efficiency as a coach.

If you think that you are at a stage of reforming your ego you may be experimenting with working without specific coaching structures and tools but relying on your spontaneous and intuitive contributions to the process. You are interested in many different perspectives on the client's situation, including the interests of many stakeholders. You may feel restricted by the formality of some coaching contracts and disappointed with the slow development of the coaching field. You judge the quality of your work by your own criteria which are congruent with your philosophy of development and influencing people. You would probably choose a supervisor who can challenge you more than you already challenge yourself.

It is more difficult of course to be precise about coaches in all three groups of the ego with a soul. If they belong to any of the previous stages of ego development (Groups 2 and 3), the above descriptions may be slightly 'muddled up' by spiritual values and aspirations. And I am not going to imagine Christ or Buddha as a coach (Group 1). I can only speculate that it would be difficult and not advisable to copy their 'coaching style'.

Self-development of coaches

In all the coaches that I have met so far I admire their strong intention to understand not only their clients but themselves. They are dedicated to their own learning and development as human beings. I hope that this book will be as helpful for this purpose as for the actual developmental work with their clients. Here I will only add a few ideas according to our main mechanisms of change that would apply specifically to them as coaches.

In relation to *improving perception* we coaches need to be watchful about an extra conditioning that may come from our professional communities. It is inevitable that with all the good things done by various professional bodies and organizations also come expectations, rules, values and even a specific language that may shape what we as coaches perceive in our work and what we may find difficult to notice because of that.

We also need to be aware of self-deception in our work. Some people would say that in relation to coaching a degree of self-deception is regularly present and could even be beneficial. At the same time the consequences of self-deception could be costly for us and our clients. For example, if we see our client's situation through the filter of our own insecurities and other motives, our capacity to fulfil the coaching task of improving the client's perception will be limited. We may see patterns in the client's behaviour and stories where there are none and base our logic of interventions on these patterns, leading nowhere. By colluding with the client we may do a disservice to the organization's interests, which should also be taken into consideration. By deluding ourselves about the quality of our work we may fail to develop the coaching engagement appropriately or fail to refer a client on to another specialist when necessary.

These are not empty concerns as is being shown by emerging research. For example, Price (2009) found in his research that one of the most popular concepts that first came to coaches' minds when considering the boundary between coaching and therapy was the idea of coaching being present- or future-focused. At the same time only 37 per cent of those indicating this answer also believed that the process becoming past-orientated was a good reason to finish coaching. In my own research on self-deception in coaching very experienced coaching supervisors confirmed that it is an often-occurring phenomenon. They suggested potential explanations for it and some ways of addressing this in supervision. In fact, supervision is a good place where self-deception in coaching can be responsibly challenged.

In relation to working with their *elephant* coaches should remember that our regular behaviours in the coaching session are saturated with unconscious inferences. It is only when these inferences every so often turn out to be wrong that we become aware of them. If this makes you feel slightly nervous to see your coaching work as not being done with full awareness, think instead: wow, how clever the whole organism is if it can perform such complex work reasonably well and sometimes even exceptionally well. Interestingly, it is the desire to be a very good coach rather than concentrating on the client that could be a worse obstacle to a good coaching process. So coaches may benefit from learning and thinking about their coaching between the sessions, but also from trusting their elephant during the session, because the elephant has already absorbed their interim learning. In fact, various great qualities of a coach that play an important role during the coaching process can be explained in the light of this idea. For example, what is emphasized as the *presence* of the coach can be seen as harmony between the elephant and the rider or the rider being fully grounded in the elephant while they are coaching.

In relation to the *multiplicity of self-models* in the coach it would be great if coaches could be aware of these self-models and somewhat playful with them if necessary, during coaching. The identity of 'me as a coach' does not need to be restricted to one particular image. It can include a whole set of self-models with a full repertoire of creative behaviours that might be useful. We can assume the role of the dynamic coach with many different ideas and questions or a thoughtful coach who stands back and observes the client's situation and the coaching process in order to comment on it. We can be an emotionally charged coach or a reserved and analytical one. Do not let your own stories of the self restrict your options.

A concluding thought on this theory

> We should strive to make things as simple as possible – but not more so.
> A. Einstein

I am aware that the theory and the approach to coaching proposed in this book are not the easiest to learn and to apply in comparison to some others. They may probably require more time and effort to understand and feel comfortable in using them. But both human nature and the changes that we are striving to facilitate *are* complex. We cannot simplify all of these without paying a high price for such simplification. I hope that struggling to understand this particular version of complexity is worth the effort.

I offer this theory and an approach as one possible way of seeing coaching on the wider scale of the evolutionary process and at the same time as an intimate one-to-one interaction with a focus on a concrete theme important for a client. However, as any theory, this is only one particular map to a vast territory. I hope it makes sense to you as it does to me, but I am fully aware that it may be also just a story that appeals to my prejudice. I hope that this theory can be further developed by others who will be interested in questioning and researching it. We need more research in coaching and I am looking forward to new data that support or disprove any of the propositions in this book.

And finally . . .

People often want positive changes brought from outside for them to enjoy the results. But all of us, as we are, represent the world society or human system, as it is. There is no 'outside' for this system; we constitute it. Therefore, the changes to the state of the world that we need can only follow the change in us, individuals. As a person you, reader, are working on yourself: your sanity, honesty, passion for knowledge, responsibility to the environment and to people on a scale that is manageable for you. What may help a little bit is to drop your ambitions to be successful within the system that you disapprove of, because this is more likely to sustain the system as it is. But as a developmental coach you are incredibly lucky: you are working on this great agenda of psychological evolution by simply helping people to engage fully with their developmental themes.

Bibliography

Adams, G. and Fitch, S. (1982) Ego stage and identity status development: a cross sequential analysis, *Journal of Personality and Social Psychology*, 43: 574–83.

Aglioti, S., Goodale, M. and DeSouza J. (1995) Size contrast illusions deceive the eye but not the hand, *Current Biology*, 5: 679–85.

Ames, A. and Dissanayake, W. (eds) (1996) *Self and Deception: A Cross-Cultural Philosophical Enquiry.* Albany, NY: State University of New York Press.

Ansbacher, H. (1971) Alfred Adler and humanistic psychology, *Journal of Humanistic Psychology*, 11(1): 53–63.

Assagioli, R. (1993) *Psychosynthesis: A Manual of Principles and Techniques,* 3rd edn. London: Aquarian/Thorsons.

Baars, B. (1988) *A Cognitive Theory of Consciousness.* Cambridge: Cambridge University Press.

Bachkirova, T. (2001) Confidence versus self-worth in adult learning, in C. Rust (ed.) *Improving Student Learning. Proceedings of the 2000 8th International Symposium: Improving Student Learning Strategically.* Oxford: Oxford Brookes University, OCSLD, pp. 227–39.

Bachkirova, T. (2004) Dealing with issues of self-concept and self-improvement strategies in coaching and mentoring, *International Journal of Evidence Based Coaching and Mentoring*, 2(2): 29–40.

Bachkirova, T. (2010) The Cognitive-developmental approach to coaching, in E. Cox, T. Bachkirova and D. Clutterbuck (eds) *The Complete Handbook of Coaching.* London: Sage, pp. 132–45.

Bachkirova, T. and Cox, E. (2007a) A cognitive developmental approach for coach development, in S. Palmer and A. Whybrow (eds) *Handbook of Coaching Psychology: A Guide for Practitioners.* London: Routledge, pp. 325–50.

Bachkirova, T. and Cox, E. (2007b) Coaching with emotion in organizations: investigation of personal theories, *Leadership and Organization Development*, 7: 600–12.

Bachkirova, T. and Kauffman, C. (2009) The blind men and the elephant: using criteria of universality and uniqueness in evaluating our attempts to define coaching, *Coaching: An International Journal of Theory, Research and Practice*, 2(2):95–105.

Baldwin, J. (1897) *Social and Ethical Interpretations in Mental Development: A Study in Social Psychology.* New York: Macmillan.

Bandura, A. (1998) *Self-efficacy: The Exercise of Control.* New York: W.H. Freeman and Company.

Baumeister, R.F. (ed.) (1993) *Self-esteem: The Puzzle of Low Self-regard.* New York: Plenum Press.

Baumeister, R.F. (ed.) (1999) *The Self in Social Psychology.* Philadelphia, PA: Psychology Press.

Baumeister, R., Bratslavsky, E., Muraven, M. and Tice, D. (1999) Ego depletion: is the active self a limited resource?, in R. Baumeister (ed.) *The Self in Social Psychology*. Philadelphia: Psychology Press, pp. 317–36.

Baumeister, R., Cambell, J., Krueger, J. and Vohs, K. (2003) Does high sef-esteem cause better performance, interpersonal success, happiness, or healthier lifestyles? *Psychological Science in the Public Interest*, 4(1), May.

Beck, D. and Cowan, C. (1996) *Spiral Dynamics*. Oxford: Blackwell.

Berger, J. (2006) Adult development theory and executive coaching Practice, in D. Stober and A. Grant (eds) *Evidence Based Coaching Handbook: Putting Best Practices to Work for your Clients*. Chichester: John Wiley.

Berger, J. and Fitzgerald, C. (2002) Leadership and complexity of mind: the role of executive coaching, in C. Fitzgerald and J. Berger (eds) *Executive Coaching: Practices and Perspectives*. Palo Alto, CA: Davies-Black Publishing, pp. 27–58.

Berman, W. and Bradt, G. (2006) Executive coaching and consulting: 'Different Strokes for Different Folk', *Professional Psychology: Research and Practice*, 37(3): 244–53.

Berne, E. (1972) *What Do You Say After You Say Hello?* New York: Grove Press.

Bierce, A. (2007) *The Devil's Dictionary*. Digireads.com Books.

Blackmore, S. (2003) *Consciousness: An Introduction*. Abingdon: Hodder and Stoughton.

Blackmore, S. (2005) *Conversations on Consciousness*. Oxford: Oxford University Press.

Bluckert, P. (2010) The Gestalt approach to coaching, in E. Cox, T. Bachkirova and D. Clutterbuck (eds) *The Complete Handbook of Coaching*. London: Sage, pp. 80–93.

Brook, A. (1994) *Kant and the Mind*. Cambridge: Cambridge University Press.

Brookfield, S. (1995) *Critically Reflective Teacher*. San Francisco, CA: Jossey-Bass.

Brown, J.D., Collins, R.L. and Schmidt, G.W. (1988) Self-esteem and direct versus indirect forms of self-enhancement. *Journal of Personality and Social Psychology*, 55(3): 445–53.

Bruner, J. (2002) *Making Stories: Law, Literature, Life*. Cambridge, MA: Harvard University Press.

Buck, R. (1991) Motivation, emotion and cognition: a developmental-interactionist view, in K.T. Strongman (ed.) *International Review of Studies in Emotion*, Vol. 1, Chichester: John Wiley & Sons.

Burns, R.B. (1978) *The Self-concept: In Theory, Measurement, Development and Behaviour*. London: Longman.

Bursik, K. (1990) Adaptation to divorce and ego development in adult women, *Journal of Personality and Social Psychology*, 60: 300–6.

Campbell, J. (1986) Similarity and uniqueness: the effects of attribute type, relevance, and individual differences in self-esteem and depression, *Journal of Personality and Social Psychology*, 50: 282–94.

Campbell, J.D. and Lavallee, L.F. (1993) Who am I? The role of self-concept confusion in understanding the behaviour of people with low self-esteem, in R.F. Baumeister (ed.) *Self-esteem: The Puzzle of Low Self-regard*. New York: Plenum Press.

Carlozzi, A., Gaa, J. and Liberman, D. (1983) Empathy and ego development, *Journal of Consulting and Clinical Psychology*, 30: 113–16.

Carter, R. (2008) *Multiplicity: The New Science of Personality*. London: Little, Brown.

Castaneda, C. (1991) *Tales of Power*. New York: Washington Square Press.

Cavanagh, M. and Grant, A. (2010) The solution-focused approach to coaching, in E. Cox, T. Bachkirova and D. Clutterbuck (eds) *The Complete Handbook of Coaching*. London: Sage, pp. 54–67.

Chalmers, D. (1995a) Facing up to the problem of consciousness, *Journal of Consciousness Studies*, 2(3): 200–19.

Chalmers, D. (1995b) The puzzle of conscious experience, *Scientific American (December)*, 62–8.

Chalmers, D. (1996) *The Conscious Mind. In Search of a Fundamental Theory*. New York: Oxford University Press.

Churchland, P. and Churchland, P. (2005) The brain is a causal machine, in S. Blackmore (ed.) *Conversations on Consciousness*. Oxford. Oxford University Press, pp. 50–67.

Clarke, C. (2004) Quantum mechanics, consciousness and the self, in D. Lorimer (ed.) *Science, Consciousness and Ultimate Reality*. Exeter: Imprint Academic, pp. 65–92.

Claxton, G. (1981) *Wholly Human: Western and Eastern Visions of the Self and its Perfection*. London: Routledge and Kegan Paul.

Claxton, G. (1986) The light's on but there's nobody home: the psychology of no-self, in G. Claxton (ed.) *Beyond Therapy: The Impact of Eastern Religions on Psychological Theory and Practice*. London: Wisdom Publications, pp. 49–70.

Claxton, G. (1992) *The Heart of Buddhism: Practical Wisdom for an Agitated World*. London: Thorsons.

Claxton, G. (1994) *Noises from the Darkroom*. London: Aquarian.

Claxton, G. (1997) *Hare Brain Tortoise Mind: Why Intelligence Increases When You Think Less*. London: Fourth Estate.

Claxton, G. (1999) *Wise-Up: The Challenge of Lifelong Learning*. London: Bloomsbury.

Claxton, G. (2002) Moving the cursor of consciouness: cognitive science and human welfare, in F. Varela and J. Shear (eds) *The View From Within: First Person Approaches to the Study of Consciousness*. Thorverton: Imprint Academic, pp. 219–22.

Claxton, G. (2002) Mind Expanding: Scientific and Spiritual Foundation for the Schools we Need. www.guyclaxton.com/documents/New/Mind%20Expanding.pdf (accessed 13 Jan. 2010).

Claxton, G. (2004) Proximal spirituality: why the brains of angels are different from ours, in D. Lorimer (ed.) *Science, Consciousness & Ultimate Reality*. Exeter: Imprint Academic, pp. 129–44.

Claxton, G. (2005) *An Intelligent Look at Emotional Intelligence*. London: ATL.

Claxton, G. (2007) in the hall of mirrors: on the varieties of reflective experience. Presentation at the BPS/CEP Conference, Oxford, 14–16 September.

Claxton, G. and Lucas, B. (2007) *The Creative Thinking Plan: How to Generate Ideas and Solve Problems in your Work and Life*. London: BBC Books.

Clutterbuck, D. (2009) Personal communication.

Commons, M., Richards, F. and Kuhn, D. (1982) Systematic and metasystematic reasoning: a case for a level of reasoning beyond Piaget's formal operations, *Child Development*, 53: 1058–69.

Commons, M. (2007) Introduction to the model of hierarchical complexity, *Behavioral Developmental Bulletin*, 13: 1–6.

Cook-Greuter, S. (1999) Postautonomous ego development: its nature and measurement. Doctoral dissertation. Cambridge, MA: Harvard Graduate School of Education.

Cook-Greuter, S. (2004) Making the case for developmental perspective, *Industrial and Commercial Training*, 36: 275–81.

Coopersmith, S. (1967) *The Antecedents of Self-esteem*. San Francisco, CA: W.H. Freeman and Company.

Cox, E., Bachkirova, T. and Clutterbuck, D. (eds) (2010) *The Complete Handbook of Coaching*. London: Sage.

Cox, E. and Jackson, P. (2010) Developmental coaching, in E. Cox, T. Bachkirova and D. Clutterbuck (eds) *The Complete Handbook of Coaching*. London: Sage, 217–30.

Cox, G. (2006) *Sartre: A Guide to the Perplexed*. London: Continuum.

Cox, W. and Kindler, E. (1988) A motivational modle of alcohol use, *Journal of Abnormal Psychology*, 97: 168–80.

Csikszentmihalyi, M. (1975) *Beyond Boredom and Anxiety*. San Fransisco, CA: Jossey-Bass.

Csikszentmihalyi, M. (1993) *The Evolving Self: A Psychology for the Third Millennium*. New York: HarperPerennial.

Damasio, A. (2000) *The Feelings of What Happens: Body, Emotion and the Making of Consciousness*. London: Vintage.

Daniels, M. (2005) *Shadow, Self, Spirit: Essays in Transpersonal Psychology*. Exeter: Imprint Academic.

De Bono, E. (1969) *The Mechanisms of Mind*. London: Penguin Books.

De Bono, E. (1982) *De Bono Thinking Course*. London: BBC Publications.

De Chardin, P. T. (1959) *The Phenomenon of Man*. New York: Harper and Row.

Delmonte, M. (1987) Personality and meditation, in M. West (ed.) *The Psychology of Meditation*. Oxford: Clarendon Press, pp. 118–32.

Dennett, D. (1983) *Elbow Room: On The Varieties of Free Will Worth Wanting*. Oxford: Clarendon Press.

Dennett, D. (1991) *Consciousness Explained*. Boston and London: Little, Brown and Co.

Dennett, D. (2005) You have to give up your intuitions about consciousness, in S. Blackmore (ed.) *Conversation on Consciousness*. New York: Oxford University Press, pp. 78–91.

Drake, D. (2010) Narrative coaching, in E. Cox, T. Bachkirova and D. Clutterbuck (eds) *The Complete Handbook of Coaching*. London: Sage, pp. 120–31.

Drath, W. (1990) Managerial strengths and weaknesses as functions of the development of personal meaning, *Journal of Applied Behavioural Science*, 26(4): 483–99.

Druckman, D. and Bjork, R.A. (eds) *In the Mind's Eye: Enhancing Human Performance* (National Research Council Report). New York: National Academy of Sciences.

Dunning, D. (2006) Strangers to ourselves, *The Psychologist*, 19(10): 603.

Eccles, J. (1994) *How the Self Controls its Brain*. Berlin: Springer-Verlag.

Ellis, A. (1999) *How to Make Yourself Happy and Remarkably Less Disturbable*. Atascadero, CA: Impact Publishers.

Engler, J. (1986) Therapeutic aims in psychotherapy and meditation: developmental stages in the representation of self, in K. Wiber, J. Engler and D. Brown (eds) *Transformation of Consciousness. Conventional and Contemplative Perspectives on Development*. Boston: Shambhala, pp. 17–52.

Epstein, M. and Lieff, J. (1986) Psychiatric complications of meditation practice, in K. Wilber, J. Engler and D. Brown (eds) *Transformation of Consciousness: Conventional and Contemplative Perspectives on Development.* Boston: Shambhala, pp. 53–63.

Epstein, S. (1973) The self-concept revisited: or a theory of a theory, *American Psychologist,* 28: 404–16.

Farrell, B. (1996) Review of Bermudez et al. (1995), *Journal of Consciousness Studies,* 3(5–6): 517–19.

Fenwick, P. (1987) Meditation and the EEG, in M. West (ed.) *The Psychology of Meditation.* Oxford: Clarendon Press, pp. 104–17.

Fingarette, H. (1963) *The Self in Transformation: Psychoanalysis, Philosophy and the Life of the Spirit.* New York: Harper Torchbooks.

Fingarette, H. (2000) *Self-Deception.* London: University of California Press.

Forman, R. (1999) What does mysticism have to teach us about consciousness?, in S. Gallagher and J. Shear (eds.) *Models of the Self,* Thorverton: Imprint Academic, pp. 361–78.

Fowler, J.W. (1981) *Stages of Faith.* New York: Harper and Row.

Frankfurt, H. (1988) *The Importance of What We Care About: Philosophical Essays.* Cambridge: Cambridge University Press.

Frankl, V. (1966) Self-transcendence as a human phenomenon, *Journal of Humanistic Psychology,* 6(2): 97–106.

Freke, T. (1997) *Zen Wisdom: Daily Teachings From the Zen Masters.* New York: Sterling Publishing.

Freud, S. (1912/1958) Recommendations to physicians practising psychoanalysis, in J. Strachey (ed. and trans.) *The Standard Edition of the Complete Psychological Works of Sigmund Freud,* Vol. 12. London: Hogarth Press.

Friedman, M. (1976) Aiming at the self: the paradox of encounter and the human potential movement, *Journal of Humanistic Psychology,* 16(2):5–34.

Frijda, N.H. (2000) The psychologist point of view, in M. Lewis and J. M. Haviland-Jones (2000) (eds.) *Handbook of Emotions,* 2nd edn. London: The Guilford Press.

Fromm, E. (1956) *The Art of Loving.* New York: Bantam.

Gallagher, S. (2005) *How the Body Shapes the Mind.* Oxford: Oxford University Press.

Gallagher, S. and Shear, J. (1999) *Models of the Self.* Thorverton: Imprint Academic.

Gallagher, S. and Zahavi, D. (2008) *The Phenomenological Mind: An Introduction to Philosophy of Mind and Cognitive Science.* London: Routledge.

Gazzaniga, M. (1985) *The Social Brain.* New York: Basic Books.

Gazzaniga, M. (1992) *Nature's Mind.* London: Basic Books.

Gendlin, E. (1962) *Experiencing and the Creation of Meaning: A Philosophical and Psychological Approach to the Subjective.* Evanston, IL: Nothwestern University Press.

Gendlin, E. (1986) *Let your Body Interpret your Dreams.* Wilmette: Chiron Publications.

Gendlin, E. (1999) A new model, in F. Varela and J. Shear (eds) *The View From Within: First-person Approaches to the Study of Consciousness.* Thorverton: Imprint Academic, pp. 232–7.

Gendlin, E. (2003) *Focusing.* London: Rider.

Gergen, K. (1991) *The Saturated Self: Dilemmas of Identity in Contemporary Life.* New York: Basic Books.

Gibson, J. (1986) *The Ecological Approach to Visual Perception.* Hillsdale, NJ: Lawrence Erlbaum Associates.

Giles, J. (1997) *No Self To Be Found: The Search for Personal Identity.* Boston: University Press of America.

Gilligan, C. (1992) *Meeting at the Crossroads: Women's Psychology and Girls' Development.* Boston: Harvard University Press.

Goleman, D. (1995) *Emotional Intelligenc.* New York: Bantam Books.

Goleman, D. (1997) *Vital Lies, Simple Truths: The Psychology of Self-Deception.* London: Bloomsbury.

Grant, A. and Cavanagh, M. (2004) Towards a profession of coaching: sixty-five years of progress and challenges for the future, *International Journal of Evidence Based Coaching and Mentoring,* 2(1): 1–16.

Graves, C. (1970) Levels of existence: an open system theory of values, *Journal of Humanistic Psychology,* November.

Gray, E. and Watson, D. (2004) Emotion, mood and temperament, in R. Payne and C. Copper (eds) *Emotion at Work: Theory, Research and Application for Management.* Chichester: John Wiley.

Gregory, R. (1970) *The Intelligent Eye.* London: Weidenfeld and Nicholson.

Gregory, R. (1987) *The Oxford Companion to the Mind.* Oxford: Oxford University Press.

Gregory, R. (2005) Science is full of gaps, in S. Blackmore (ed.) *Conversations on Consciousness.* Oxford: Oxford University Press, pp. 104–14.

Gur, R. and Sackheim, H. (1979) Self-deception: a concept in search of a phenomenon, *Journal of Personality and Social Psychology,* 37: 147–69.

Gurdjieff, C. (1949) in P. Ouspensky, *In Search of the Miraculous.* Harcourt: Brace and World.

Haidt, J. (2006) *The Happiness Hypothesis.* London: Arrow Books.

Hamachek, D.E. (1978) *Encounters with the Self,* 2nd edn. New York: Holt, Rinehart and Winston.

Hamachek, D.E. (1987) *Encounters with the Self,* 3rd edn. New York: Holt, Rinehart and Winston.

Harre, R. and Gillett, G. (1994) *The Discursive Mind.* Thousand Oaks, CA: Sage.

Harter, S. (1999) *The Construction of the Self.* London: The Guilford Press.

Hawkins, P. and Smith, N. (2006) *Coaching, Mentoring and Organizational Consultancy: Supervision and Development.* Maidenhead: Open University Press.

Hawkins, P. and Smith, N. (2010) Transformational coaching, in E. Cox, T. Bachkirova and D. Clutterbuck (eds) *The Complete Handbook of Coaching.* London: Sage, pp. 231–44.

Hay, D. (1990) *Religious Experience Today: Studying the Facts.* London: Mowbray.

Hayward, J. (1999) A rDzogs-chen Buddhist Interpretation of the Sense of Self, in S. Gallagher and Shear J., (eds) *Models of the Self.* Thorverton: Imprint Academic, pp. 379–94.

Helmholtz, H.L.F. von (1925) *Treatise on Physiological Optics,* in J. P. C. Southall (trans.). New York: Optical Society of America.

Hesse, H. (1978) *My Belief: Essays on Life and Art (Concerning the soul).* Frogmore, St Alban's: Triad/Panther Books.

Higgins, E.T. (1987) Self-discrepancy: a theory relating self and affect, *Psychological Review* 94:319–40.

Hillman, J. (1983) *Healing Fiction.* Woodstock, CT: Spring.

Hindmarch, L. (2008) An exploration of the experience of self-doubt in the coaching context and the strategies adopted by coaches to overcome it, *International Journal of Evidence Based Coaching and Mentoring,* Special Issue 2: 1–13.

Holmes, D. (1981) Existence of classical projection and the stress-reducing function of attributive projection: a reply to Sherwood, *Psychological Bulletin*, 90: 460–6.

Hughes, C. and Flowers, V. (1978) *Value Systems Analysis: Theory and Management Application.* Dallas: Author.

Hume, D. (1739) *A Treatise of Human Nature,* L.A. Selby-Bigge (ed.) (Oxford: Clarendon Press, 1888, 1975).

Humphrey, N. (2000) One Self: a meditation on the unity of consciousness, *Social Research,* 67(4): 32–9.

Humphrey, N. (2002) James Arthur Memorial Lecture, American Museum of Natural History, New York, (1987). Reprinted in *The Mind Made Flesh.* Oxford University Press, pp. 65–85.

Husserl, E. (2001) *Logical Investigations I-II,* trans. J.N. Dindlay. London: Routledge.

Insckipp, F. (1987) *Counselling: The Trainer's Handbook.* National Extension College Trust Ltd.

Izard, C.E. (1993) Four systems of emotion activation *Psychological Review*, 100: 68–90.

James, W. (1890) *The Principles of Psychology* (2 volumes). London: MacMillan.

James, W. (1999) The Self, in R. Baumeister (ed.) *The Self in Social Psychology.* Philadelphia: Psychology Press, pp. 69–77.

Janis, I.L. (1972) *Victims of Groupthink.* Boston, MA: Houghton Mifflin Company.

Jopling, D. (2000) *Self-Knowledge and the Self.* London: Routledge.

Joseph, S. (2010) The Person-centred approach to coaching, in E. Cox, T. Bachkirova and D. Clutterbuck (eds) *The Complete Handbook of Coaching.* London: Sage, pp. 68–79.

Kasamatsu, A. and Hirai, T. (1969) An electroencephalographic study on the Zen Meditation (Zazen), *Psychologia*, 12: 205–25.

Kaufman, B. (1979) *Son-Rise.* Warner Books.

Kauffman, C. and Bachkirova, T. (2008) The evolution of coaching: an interview with Sir John Whitmore, *Coaching: An International Journal of Theory, Research and Practice*, 1(1): 11–15.

Kegan, R. (1982) *The Evolving Self: Problem and Process in Human Development.* London: Harvard University Press.

Kegan, R. (1994) *In Over Our Heads.* London: Harvard University Press.

Kegan, R. and Lahey, L. (2009) *Immunity to Change: How to Overcome it and Unlock the Potential in Yourself and Your Organization.* Boston, MA: Harvard Business Press.

Kierkegaard, S. (1959) *Either/Or,* vol. II, trans. W. Lowrie. New York: Anchor Books.

Kihlstrom, J. (1996) Perception without awareness of what is perceived, learning without awareness of what is learned, in M. Velmans (ed.) *The Science of Consciousness.* London: Routledge, pp. 23–46.

King, P.M. and Kitchener, K.S. (1994) *Developing Reflective Judgment: Understanding and Promoting Intellectual Growth and Critical Thinking in Adolescents and Adults.* San Francisco, CA: Jossey-Bass.

Kohlberg, L. (1969) *Stages in the Development of Moral Thought and Action.* New York: Holt, Reinhart and Winston.

Kopp, S. (1972) *If you Meet the Buddha on the Road, Kill Him: The Pilgrimage of Psychotherapy Patients.* New York: Bantam Books.

Krishnamurti, J. (1990) *Beginnings of Learning.* London: Arkana.

Krishnamurti, J. (1991) *Commentaries on Living, Third Series.* London: Victor Gollancz

Krishnamurti, J. (1994) *Commentaries on Living, First Series.* London: The Theosophical Publishing House.

Krishnamurti, J. (1996) *Questioning Krishnamurti.* London: Thorsons.

Krishnamurti, J. and Bohm, D. (1985) *The Ending of Time.* New York: HarperSanFrancisco.

Kunda, Z. (1990) The case for motivated reasoning, *Psychological Bulletin,* 108: 480–498.

Labouvie-Vief, G., Hakim-Larson, J., DeVoe, M. and Schoeberlin, S. (1989) Emotions and self-regulation: a life span view, *Human Development,* 32: 279–99.

Lahey, L., Souvaine, E., Kegan, R., Goodman, R. and Felix, S. (1988) *A Guide To The Subject-Object Interview: Its Administration And Interpretation.* Cambridge, MA: Harvard University, Graduate School of Education, Laboratory of Human Development.

Lalljee, M. (2002) The interpreting self: an experimentalist perspective, in R. Stevens (ed). *Understanding the Self.* London: Sage, pp. 89–146.

Lane, R., Quinlan, D., Schwartz, G., Walker, P. and Zeitlin, S. (1990) The Levels of Emotional Awareness Scale: a cognitive-developmental measure of emotion, *Journal of Personality Assessment,* 55: 124–34.

Laske, O. (2006a) From coach training to coach education, *International Journal of Evidence Based Coaching and Mentoring,* 4(1) Spring: 45–57.

Laske, O. (2006b) *Measuring hidden dimensions: the art and science of fully engaging adults.* Medford, MA: IDM Press.

Leary, M., Tambor, E., Terdal, S. and Downs, D. (1999) Self-esteem as an interpersonal monitor: the sociometer hypothesis, in R. Baumeister (ed.) *The Self in Social Psychology.* Hove: Psychology Press, pp. 87–104.

Lee, G. (2010) The psychodynamic approach to counselling, in E. Cox, T. Bachkirova and D. Clutterbuck (eds) *The Complete Handbook of Coaching.* London: Sage, pp. 23–36

Leonard-Cross, E. (2010) Developmental coaching: business benefit – fact or fad? An evaluative study to explore the impact of coaching in the workplace, *International Coaching Psychology Review,* 5(1): 36–47.

Lewicki, P. (1984) Self-schema and social information processing, *Journal of Personality and Social Psychology,* 47: 1177–90.

Lewicki, P. Hill, T. and Cyzyewska, M. (1992) Nonconscious acquisition of information, *American Psychologist,* 47: 796–801.

Lewis, B. (1996) Self-deception: a post modern reflection, *Journal of Theoretical and Philosophical Psychology,* 16(1): 49–66.

Libet, B. (1985) Unconscious cerebral initiative and the role of conscious will in voluntary action, *The Behavioral and Brain Sciences,* 8: 529–39.

Libet, B. (1999) Do we have free will? *Journal of Consciousness Studies,* 6(8–9): 47–57.

Lind, R. (2000) *The Seeking Self.* Michigan: Phanes Press.

Linville, P. (1987) Self complexity as a cognitive buffer against stress-related illness and depression, *Journal of Personality and Social Psychology,* 52: 663–76.

Loevinger, J. (1976) *Ego Development: Conceptions and Theories.* San Francisco, CA: Jossey-Bass.

Loevinger, J. (1987) *Paradigms of Personality.* New York: M.H. Freeman and Company.

Mack, A. and Rock, I. (1998) *Inattentional Blindness.* Cambridge, MA: MIT Press.

MacKay, D. (1987) Divided brains – divided minds?, in C. Blakemore and S. Greenfield (eds) *Mindwaves.* Oxford: Blackwell, pp. 5–16.

Mahrer, A. (1978) *Experiencing*. New York: Brunner/Mazel.

Manners, J. and Durkin, K. (2001) A critical review of the validity of ego development theory and its measurement, *Journal of Personality Assessment,* 77(3): 541–67.

Markus, H. (1999) Self-schemata and processing information about the self, in R. Baumeister (ed.) *The Self in Social Psychology*. Philadelphia: Psychology Press, pp. 123–38.

Martin, R. (1998) *Self-Concern: An Experiential Approach to What Matters in Survival*. Cambridge: Cambridge University Press.

Maslow, A. (1954) *Motivation and Personality*. New York: Harper.

May, R. (1967) *Psychology and the Human Dilemma*. Princeton: Van Nostrand.

May, R. (1969) *Love and Will*. London: Souvenir Press.

McCauley, C., Drath, W., Palus, P. and Baker, B. (2006) The use of constructive-developmental theory to advance the understanding of leadership, *The Leadership Quarterly*, 17: 634–53.

McGinn, C. (1999) *The Mysterious Flame: Conscious Minds in a Material World*. New York: Basic Books.

McNeill, W. (1995) *Keeping Together in Time: Dance and Drill in Human History*. Cambridge, MA: Harvard University Press.

Mele, A. (2001) *Self-Deception Unmasked*. Princeton and Oxford: Princeton University Press.

Metzinger, T. (2003) *Being No One*. Cambridge: MIT Press.

Midgley, M. (1984) *Wickedness: A Philosophical Essay*. London: Ark.

Milgram, S. (1963). Behavioral study of obedience, *Journal of Abnormal and Social Psychology*, 67: 371–8.

Miller, W. and C'de Baca, J. (2001) *Quantum Change*. New York: Guilford.

Milner, A. and Goodale, M. (1995) *The Visual Brain in Action*. Oxford: Oxford University Press.

Mruk, C.J. (2006) *Self-esteem Research, Theory and Practice: Toward a Positive Psychology of Self-esteem,* 3rd edn. New York: Springer Publishing Company.

Muraven, M., Tice, D. and Baumeister, R. (1998) Self-control as limited resource: regulatory depletion patterns, *Journal of Personality and Social Psychology*, 74: 774–87.

Murphy, E. (1965) *The Theory of Practical Reason*. Illinois: Open Court.

Nagel, T. (1986) *The View from Nowhere*. New York: Oxford University Press.

Neisser, U. (1980) The limits of cognition, in P. Jusczyk and R. Klein (eds) *The Nature of Thought*. New Jersey: Lawrence Erlbaum Associates, pp. 115–32.

Neisser, U. (1988) Five kinds of self-knowledge, *Philosophical Psychology*, 1(1): 35–59.

Newberg, A., D'Aquili, E. and Rause, V. (2001) *Why God Won't Go Away: Brain Science and the Biology of Belief.* New York: Ballantine.

Norman, D. (1968) Towards a theory of memory and attention, *Psychological Review*, 75: 522–36.

Nosek, B., Banaji, M. and Greenwald, A. (2002) Harvesting intergroup implicit attitudes and beliefs from a demonstration web site, *Group Dynamics*, 6: 101–15.

Nuernberger, P. (1996) *The Quest for Personal Power: Transforming Stress into Strength*. New York: A Perigee Book.

Oatley, K. and Jenkins, J. (1996) *Understanding Emotions*. Oxford: Blackwell.

O'Connor, E. (1971) *Our Many Selves*. New York: Harper and Row.

Osho (Bhagwan Shree Rajneesh) (2004) *When the Shoe Fits: Commentaries on the Stories of the Taoist Mystic Chuang Tzu*. London: Watkins Publishing.

Palmer, S. and Whybrow, A. (eds) (2007) *Handbook of Coaching Psychology*. London: Routledge.

Papineau, D. and Selina, H. (2006) *Introducing Consciousness*. Cambridge: Icon Books Ltd.

Parfit, D. (1987) Divided minds and the nature of persons, in C. Blakemore and S. Greenfield (eds) *Mindwaves*. Oxford: Blackwell, pp. 19–26.

Parnes, S. (1961) Effects of extended effort in creative problem solving, *Journal of Educational Psychology*, 52: 117–22.

Peltier, B. (2001) *The Psychology of Executive Coaching: Theory and Application*. New York: Brunner-Routledge.

Perls, F. (1969) *Gestalt Therapy Verbatim*. Lafayette: Real People Press.

Pert, C. (1997) *Molecules of Emotion: Why You Feel the Way You Feel*. New York: Simon and Schuster.

Perry, W.G. (1970) *Forms of Intellectual and Ethical Development in the College Years*. New York: Holt, Rinehart and Winston, Inc.

Peterson, C. (1988) Explanatory style as a risk factor for illness, *Cognitive Therapy and Research*, 12: 117–30.

Piaget, J. (1976) *The Psychology of Intelligence*. New Jersey: Littlefield, Adams & Co.

Pinker, S. (1997) *How the Mind Works*. New York: W.W. Norton.

Pinker, S. (2008) One on one with Steve Pinker, *The Psychologist*, 21(2): 184.

Plutchik, R. and Kellerman, H. (eds) (1980) *Emotion: Theory, Research and Experience*. San Diego: Academic Press.

Popper, K. and Eccles, C. (1977). *The Self and its Brain*. New York: Springer.

Price, J. (2009) The coaching/therapy boundary in organizational coaching, *Coaching: An International Journal of Theory, Research and Practice*, 2(2): 135–48.

Proust, M. (1981) *Swann's Way*. Vol. I of *Remembrance of Things Past*, trans. C. K. Scott Moncrieff and T. Kilmartin. London: Chatto & Windus, p. 5.

Rahula, W. (1959) *What the Buddha Taught*. London: Gordon Fraser.

Ramachandran, V. (2003) BBC Radio 4. Reith Lectures 2003 – The Emerging Brain. http://experiment.iitalia.com/librarysplit2/Bbc%20Radio%204%20-%20Reith%20Lectures%202003%20-20The%20Emerging%20Brain%20-%20Vilayanur%20S%20Ramachandran.pdf (accessed 16 November, 2010).

Ramachandran, V. and Blakeslee, S. (1998) *Phantoms in the Brain*. London: Fourth Estate.

Ramachandran, V. and Hirstein, W. (1999) Three laws of qualia: what neurology tells us about the biological functions of consciousness, qualia and the self, in S. Gallagher and J. Shear (eds) *Models of the Self*. Thorverton: Imprint Academic.

Ravindra, R. (2004) Yoga, physics and consciousness, in D. Lorimer (ed.) *Science, Consciousness & Ultimate Reality*. Exeter: Imprint Academic, pp. 93–108.

Redmore, C. (1983) Ego development in the college years: two longitudinal studies, *Journal of Youth and Adolescence*, 12: 301–06.

Rensink, R., O'Regan, J. and Clark, J. (1997) To see or not to see: the need for attention to perceive changes in scenes, *Psychological Science*, 8: 368–73.

Richard, J. R. (2000) *Human Nature After Darwin*. London: Routledge.

Rochat, P. (2001) *The Infant's World*. Cambridge, MA: Harvard University Press.

Rogers, C. (1961) *On Becoming a Person*. London: Constable.

Rokeach, M. (1950) The effect of perception time upon the rigidity and concreteness of thinking, *Journal of Experimental Psychology*, 40: 206–16.

Rooke, D. and Torbert, W. (2005) Seven transformations of leadership, *Harvard Business Review* 27(3): 66–76.

Rowan, J. (1976) *Ordinary Ecstasy: Humanistic Psychology in Action*. London: Routledge and Kogan Page Ltd.

Rowan J. (2009) *Subpersonalities – The People Inside Us*. London: Brunner-Routledge.

Rowan, J. (2010) The transpersonal approach to coaching, in E. Cox, T. Bachkirova and D. Clutterbuck (eds) *The Complete Handbook of Coaching*. London: Sage, pp. 146–57.

Rowan, J. and Jacobs, M. (2002) *The Therapist's Use of Self*. Maidenhead: Open University Press.

Rowan, R. (1986) *The Intuitive Manager*. Boston: Brown.

Sartre, J.-P. (1956) *Being and Nothingness*, trans. H.E. Barnes. New York: Philosophical Library.

Sartre, J.-P. (1997) *Existentialism and Human Emotions*. New Jersey: Citadel Press.

Sartre, J-P. (1999) *War Diaries: Notebooks from a Phoney War*, 1939–1940, trans. Q. Hoare. London: Verso.

Schooler, J. and Fiore, S. (1997) Consciousness and the limit of language: you can't always say what you think, or think what you say, in J. Cohen and J. Schooler (eds) *Scientific Approaches to Consciousnesses*. Mahwah, NJ: Erlbaum, pp. 241–60.

Schopenhauer, A. (2000) *Parerga and Paralipomena*, trans. E.F. Payne, 2 vols. Oxford: Clarendon Press.

Seligman. M. (1975) *Helplessness: On Depression, Development and Death*. San Francisco, CA: W.H. Freeman.

Sheldon, K., Ryan, R., Rawsthorne, L. and Ilardi, B. (1997) Trait self and true self: cross-role variation in the authenticity and subjective well-being, *Journal of Personality and Social Psychology* 73(6): 1380–93.

Shoemaker, S. (1968) Self-reference and self-awareness, *Journal of Philosophy*, LXV, 556–79.

Simons, D. (2000) Current approaches to change blindness, *Visual Cognition*, 7: 1–15.

Simons, D. and Chabris, C. (1999) Gorillas in our midst: sustained inattentional blindness for dynamic events, *Perception*, 28: 1059–74.

Singer, J. (1993) Experimental studies of ongoing conscious experience, in G. Bock and J. Marsh (eds) *Experimental and Theoretical Studies of Consciousness – Ciba Foundation Symposium 174*. Chichester: John Wiley.

Smail, D. (1984) *Illusion and Reality: The Meaning of Anxiety*. London: Dent & Sons Ltd.

Soon, C., Brass, M., Heinze, H. and Haynes, J. (2008) Unconscious determinants of free decisions in the human brain, *Nature Neuroscience*, 11(5): 543–5.

Spinelli, E. (2010) Existential coaching, in E. Cox, T. Bachkirova and D. Clutterbuck (eds) *The Complete Handbook of Coaching*. London: Sage, pp. 94–106.

Stevens, R. (2002) *Understanding the Self*. London: Sage.

Stober, D. and Grant, A. (eds) (2006) *Evidence Based Coaching Handbook: Putting Best Practices to Work for your Clients*. Chichester: John Wiley.

Stone, H. and Winkelman, S. (1985) *Embracing our Selves*. Marina del Rey, CA: Devorss and Co.

Strawson, G. (1997) The self, *Journal of Consciousness Studies*, 4(5–6): 405–28.

Strawson, G. (1999) The self and the SESMET, in S. Gallagher and J. Shear (eds) *Models of the Self*. Thorverton: Imprint Academic, pp. 483–519.

Strawson, G. (2009) *Selves*. Oxford: Clarendon Press.

Sullivan, C., Grant, M. and Grant, J. (1957) The development of interpersonal maturity: application to delinquency, *Psychiatry*, 20: 377–85.

Sullivan, E., McCullough, G. and Stager, M. (1970) A developmental study of the relationship between conceptual, ego, and moral development, *Child Development*, 41: 399–411.

Suls, J. and Wan, C. (1987) In search of the false-uniqueness phenomenon: fear and estimates of social consensus, *Journal of Personality and Social Psychology*, 52: 211–17.

Tart, C. (1994) *Living the Mindful Life: A Handbook of Living in the Present Moment*. Boston: Shambhala.

Taylor, C. (1991) *The Ethics of Authenticity*. Cambridge, MA: Harvard University Press.

Taylor, C. (1992) *Sources of the Self*. Cambridge, MA: Harvard University Press.

Toates, F. (2002) The embodied self: a biological perspective, in R. Stevens (ed.) *Understanding the Self*. London: Sage, pp. 35–88.

Torbert, W. (1991) *The Power of Balance*. Newbury Park, CA: Sage.

Torbert, W., Cook-Greuter, S., Fisher, D. et al. (2004) *Action Inquiry: The Secret of Timely and Transforming Leadership*. San Francisco, CA: Berret-Koehler Publishers.

Trungpa, C. (1973) *Cutting Through Spiritual Materialism*. Shambhala: Boulder.

van Deurzen-Smith, E. (2002) *Existential Counselling and Psychotherapy in Practice*, 2nd edn. London: Sage.

Vaugham, F. (2005) *Shadows of the Sacred: Seeing Through Spiritual Illusions*. Lincoln: iUniverse, Inc.

Velmans, M. (2000) *Understanding Consciousness*. London: Routledge.

Wade, J. (1996) *Changes of Mind : A Holonomic Theory of the Evolution of Consciousness*. Albany, NJ: University of New York Press.

Wampold, B. (2001) *The Great Psychotherapy Debate: Models, Methods, and Findings*. Mahwah, NJ: Lawrence Erlbaum Inc.

Watkins, H. (1993) Ego-state therapy: an overview, *American Journal of Clinical Hypnosis*, 35(4): 232–40.

Watkins, M. (1986) *Invisible Guests: The Development of Imaginal Dialogues*. Hillsdale, NJ: The Analytic Press.

Watts, A. (1957) *The Way of Zen*. London: Penguin Group.

Watts, A. (1972) *In my Own Way: An Autobiography 1915–1965*. Navato, CA: New World Library.

Wegner, D. (1989) *White Bears and Other Unwanted Thoughts*. New York: Vintage.

Wegner, D. (2002) *The Illusion of Conscious Will*. London: The MIT Press.

Wegner D. (2005) Don't think about a white bear, in S. Blackmore (ed.) (2005) *Conversation on Consciousness*. New York: Oxford University Press, pp. 245–57.

Wegner, D. and Wheatley, T. (1999) Apparent mental causation: sources of the experience of will, *American Psychologist*, 54: 480–92.

Weiner, B. (1992) *Human Motivation: Metaphors, Theories and Research*. Newbury Park: Sage.

Welman, P. and Bachkirova, T. (2010) Issues of power in coaching relationship, in S. Palmer, and A. McDowell, (eds) *The Coaching Relationship*. London: Routledge.

Wesson, K. and Boniwell, I. (2007) Flow theory – its application to coaching psychology, *International Coaching Psychology Review*, 2(1): 33–43.

Westenberg, P. and Gjerde, P. (1999) Ego development during the transition from adolescence to young adulthood: a 9-year longitudinal study, *Journal of Research in Personality*, 33: 233–52.

Whitherspoon, R. (2000) Starting smart: clarifying goals and roles, in M. Goldsmith, L. Lyons and A. Freas (eds) *Coaching for Leadership*. San Francisco, CA: Jossey- Bass, pp. 165–85.

Whitmore, J. and Einzig, H. (2007) Transpersonal coaching, in J. Passmore (ed.) *Excellence in Coaching*. London: Kogan Page.

Wilber, K. (1979) *No Boundary*. Boston: Shambhala.

Wilber, K. (1998) *The Essential Ken Wilber*. London: Shambhala.

Wilber, K. (1999) *One Taste: The Journals of Ken Wilber*. Boston: Shambhala.

Wilber, K. (2000) *Integral Psychology*. London: Shambala.

Wilber, K. (2006) *Integral Spirituality*. Boston and London: Integral Books.

Williams, H., Edgerton, N. and Palmer, S. (2010) Cognitive-behavioural coaching, in E. Cox, T. Bachkirova and D. Clutterbuck (eds) *The Complete Handbook of Coaching*. London: Sage, pp. 37–53.

Winson, J. (1985) *Brain and Psyche: The Biology of the Unconscious*. Garden City, NY: Anchor Press/Doubleday.

Wren-Lewis, J. (1988) The darkness of God: a personal report on consciousness transformation through an encounter with death, *Journal of Humanistic Psychology*, 28: 105–22.

Wyer, R. and Frey, D. (1983) The effects of feedback about self and others on the recall and judgments of feedback-relevant information, *Journal of Experimental Social Psychology*, 19: 540–59.

Yalom, I. (1980) *Existential Psychotherapy*. New York: Basic Books.

Zimbardo, P. (1991) *The Psychology of Attitude Change and Social Influence*. New York: McGraw-Hill.

Zuckerman, M. (1979) Attribution of success and failure revisited, or: the motivational bias is alive and well in attribution theory, *Journal of Personality*, 47: 245–87.

Index